# Long Distance Love
## Letters from a Pioneer Homestead

Editor Jodie Sewall

Long Distance Love 1855-1870
267 Letters from a Pioneer Homestead
ISBN 978-0-578-20862-6
All Rights Reserved
First printing 2009 Revised edition 2018
Printed in the United States of America

Long Distance Love
1855-1870

267 Letters from a Pioneer Homestead

## Contents

Acknowledgement ........................................................................................... 4
The House Had a Story to Tell ....................................................................... 5
Principal Characters ....................................................................................... 9
Florida – Seminole Indian War .................................................................... 14
Nebraska Territory ........................................................................................ 35
Newport Barracks, KY .................................................................................. 43
The Chicago & Glen Arbor Years ................................................................ 54
Epilogue ........................................................................................................ 178
Time Line ...................................................................................................... 179
Military Records .......................................................................................... 181
Genealogy Charts ......................................................................................... 191
Obituarys ...................................................................................................... 193
Pages from Family Bible ............................................................................. 195
Photo's and Memorabilia ............................................................................ 199
Glossary ........................................................................................................ 230
Index .............................................................................................................. 238

# Acknowledgement

I would like to thank Dave Taghon, president of the Empire Heritage Group for believing in me and allowing me to undertake this project. His interest in the project and his encouragement along the way were vital to the completion of this project.

The Empire Area Museum shared their large collection of letters and memorabilia with me which enabled me to read and transcribe each letter in its original state. The result is this book with all 267 letters from the Boizards. I would also like to thank Grace Johnson for the personal tour that she gave my family when we visited Glen Arbor in August 2006.

I am thankful for my family who persevered through the endless days of my *working on the book*. I *really* did eventually finish it, although I know there were many days when you doubted that I would.

I am grateful for my upbringing and for the love of family history that I learned from my parents, Jack and Michele Pattan.

I would also like to thank Edwin Fisher. His commitment to preserving local and family history spurred me on many times when the task seemed overwhelming and out of reach. Without his help and knowledge along the way we would never have seen a book printed that reunited both sets of Boizard letters.

Jodie Sewall

# Introduction

*Etta May Fisher Todd House in Glenn Arbor circa 1959*

# The House Had a Story to Tell

For over a hundred years, time had marched like an enemy against the old gray house as it languished forgotten in the hidden glen. It stood with aged dignity beneath the protective shadows of towering oak trees. Those ancient trees poised tall and straight, like age-old sentries guarding the house and protecting the memories of those who had once lived there.

The driveway to the aging house was just off the main street of the village of Glen Arbor, but as it gently wound its way through dense trees and underbrush, one instantly felt isolated from the hubbub of the present time and transported back to a simpler time when this house was younger, and its door swung open and shut with life.

For thirty-year-old Michele, this was the first glimpse of her great grandmother's house in over 15 years. Just the sight of the old gray house, brought color back to her faded memories of Great Grandma Todd, walking around her yard with her cane carefully tending to her flowers.

Throughout her childhood, Michele and her mother Jessie had picked up Great Grandma Todd and taken her to her annual visit to the Maple City Cemetery. Grandma Todd had always carefully and thoughtfully brought flowers to the graves of each of her loved ones. Each flower was tenderly placed on the graves as a tribute to the lives of those who had passed on before her.

For Michele, this visit to Great Grandma Todd's house was her tribute; her way of remembering and giving honor to her great grandmother. This would be Michele's final opportunity to visit the house that had belonged in her family for over 100 years and most recently to her great grandmother.

Michele's mom, Jessie, had urged this occasion, by encouraging Michele to "Stop by and see if there is anything left in the house that you would be special to you."

**Long Distance Love 1855-1870**

The house had sat vacant for sixteen years, and its dilapidated condition had, for safety reasons warranted its destruction. This demolition would take place within a week or two, so this visit would be the one and only opportunity to remember and to look around.

The thick layer of leaves on the porch bore testimony to the many seasons that had passed since anyone had come or gone from the house. As the key was turned in the rusty lock, the door heaved as if it had been holding its breath for this day. The musty odor from being closed was pungent and overwhelming.

The last activity in the house had been a sale of the contents of the house. The piles of stuff that were left had been deemed nonvaluable and abandoned. Michele, her husband Jack, and their five children began sorting through the piles of clothes and papers that were strewn about the rooms. The heavy dust which had accumulated over the years soon filled the air like a thick cloud.

Many 'treasures' were unearthed as they dug around: wooden marbles, hand sewn baby gowns, a hand-carved bed frame, a pencil box, a few tattered china dolls, a small cast-iron toy train, an iron toy car, hand carved canes and many other things. Some of the more unusual finds were bags of hair saved from hairbrushes, false teeth, a glass eye, a hardened old sandwich wrapped in paper, and a shoe box containing a dead parakeet.

Michele and her family searched through the piles from room to room. One thing kept drawing Michele's attention, the stacks of letters, cards, envelopes and tax papers strewn about as if they had been dumped out of bureau drawers. Curious as to what they might be, Michele picked up an old tin bucket and stuffed it full of the interesting looking papers, to look at when she got home.

Within a few hours, everyone in the family was coughing due to the dust cloud that filled the house. Out of necessity of health, the search ended, and the family left, knowing that any remaining treasures would remain hidden and lost forever with the imminent destruction of the old house.

After Michele, returned home, she began organizing and cleaning up all of the things they had collected from her Great Grandma Todd's house. She began to sort the papers and the letters and as she began to read them she was instantly drawn into the lives of relatives that she had never met before. Their devotion to one another and the struggles they endured with long absences from each other brought about a sincere appreciation for her amazing heritage.

The letters were like a hand-held time-machine allowing her to witness the emotions and life events that her ancestors had experienced one hundred years earlier. On occasion, she regretted not spending more time in the old house and collecting every scrap of paper that had littered the floor, but wishing for a different past wouldn't change the present, so she simply treasured the letters that she had and celebrated the family history they preserved.

# The Story Wasn't Over Yet

Word was out that the "Westcott" house, as it was known to the locals, was being torn down. Etta May Fisher Westcott Todd had died sixteen years earlier and her vacant house was in a serious state of disrepair. When Julia Dickinson & Jo Bolton learned that the house was being demolished, they made a trip over to the site and began an earnest search for anything that might have historical significance. They looked among the uneven floorboards and under the piles of plaster and lath that had fallen from the disintegrating walls. It wasn't long before their efforts were rewarded with exciting discoveries like old newspapers and magazines, and letters. They were most excited about the letters. Some of the names mentioned in the correspondence were names that were familiar in their town

**Introduction**

like Fisher and Westcott; but there were other names like Boizard and Dow that were unknown.

Gathering every letter, they could find, Julia and Jo were pleased to have collected over one hundred letters. After sorting the letters chronologically, they began reading them and soon found themselves enthralled with the lives of John Oliver Boizard and his wife Eleanor. This pioneer couple endured long periods of separation due to war, economics and health, and these letters were the evidence of their commitment to each other even when separated by many miles.

Julia Dickinson & Jo Bolton transcribed the letters and had them made into a book to preserve their rich local history and to allow other people to learn about life in the mid-1800's. In 1993, they published their book "The Boizard Letters, Letters from a Pioneer Homestead."[1]

## What an Amazing Discovery!

My mother, Michele Pattan, has been the custodian of our family 'treasure' ever since she discovered the Boizard letters in her Great Grandma Todd's house in 1974. As a child, I had been fascinated with the letters about the Civil War and my siblings and I always loved bringing specific letters to school to read aloud in our history class during units about the Civil War. We always felt so privileged to own such special pieces of history.

During the summer of 2005, I asked my mom if I could bring the letters to my home in New York State, to organize and transcribe them so that every member of my family could have a personal copy of our grandparent's letters. Of course, my mom said, yes, and that began what has turned into a decade long quest.

Shortly after I started organizing the letters, I casually decided to google search the name "Boizard." Much to my surprise and shock a book came up on E-bay entitled The Boizard Letters. There wasn't much information listed about the book in the item description, but I bought the book on the spot. I couldn't figure out how it could possibly be the same family, because I had the Boizard letters in my possession; but with the unusual name of "Boizard," I wondered how it could *not* be the same family? It was a complete mystery to me and I felt like a small child waiting for Christmas morning as I repeatedly checked the mailbox for days waiting for that book to arrive.

Finally! The book arrived, and I immediately sat down and thumbed through it and knew in an instant that it **was** the same family and that somehow the 'lost' letters, the ones my mom had left behind, were not 'lost' after all. It was astounding to discover that they had in fact been saved from destruction and eventually printed into a book. Calling my mother and telling her of my discovery was one of the highlights of my life. She was just as amazed and thrilled as I was.

My family certainly rejoiced in the discovery of the 'missing' letters and I know the Glen Arbor historians also celebrated finding the letters that had been 'missing' from their collection, but in fact, neither set of letters had ever actually been 'lost.' Each set was highly valued and treasured by their respective owners. This new book which contains all the letters could appropriately be called, 'The Boizard Letters - reunited.'

My personal connection to this project is vibrant and real and it is my earnest desire to preserve with integrity and accuracy each of the 267 letters that represent my grandparents' life.

---

[1] Dickinson & Bolton, *The Boizard Letters, Letters from a Pioneer Homestead,* Empire Heritage Group, 1993 page ix

**Long Distance Love 1855-1870**

Reading the letters that comprise this collection was both exciting and difficult. I loved the discovery of information that each letter brought but learning to decipher the writing styles of each writer took considerable effort. Oliver's letters are the easiest to read as his penmanship is beautiful and he generally uses punctuation. Eleanor however, did not write her own letters and in the early years she had several different writers, many of whom were barely literate themselves. When their daughter Marietta grew old enough to write, she took over the task of writing for her mother. The most difficult letters to decipher were those written to Marietta by her childhood friend named Emma Bridges.

It was my decision as the editor to transcribe all the letters as close to the original as possible. For the most part I have kept the misspelled words and the incorrect capitalization and punctuation, because I believe that is a true representation of the people and the times in which they lived.

If I thought that a misspelled word needed additional explanation or if I could not decipher a word, I added **brackets** with my suggestion in italics.

Because very few of these writers used punctuation, I added extra spacing in between sentences or where a new thought begins. This extra space is designed to keep the sentences from running together and it provides a 'break' for the eyes of the reader.

If a word or phrase is underlined or in parenthesis, it was written that way by the original writer.

There are many words, names and places mentioned that I was not familiar with, so I boldfaced those words and have included a definition or explanation in the glossary at the back of the book.

My greatest desire is that you will enjoy this amazing treasury of letters and come to love the people in the same way in which I have come to know and love them. They were ordinary people who stoutheartedly faced the challenge of settling a new land with very few resources because they believed that they could create a better life for themselves and in turn for their children. The book is full of people with great pioneering spirits who endured severe hardships to establish communities and those communities are their lasting gift to us.


Jodie Pattan Sewall
Great Great Great Great Granddaughter of Oliver and Eleanor Boizard and John and Harriet Fisher

# Principal Characters

This portion of the book is designed to put 'skin' on the people mentioned in the letters. I have gathered the personal information that we know about each person and created a short entry to introduce you to them with the hopes that when you 'meet' them in the letters, you will recognize each character as a real flesh and blood person, with sorrows and joys, struggles and accomplishments just like you and me.

**Eleanor Melvina McGill MaGill Boizard:** Eleanor Melvina McGill was born January 19, 1828, in Wheeling, WV. A scrap piece of paper within the collection of Boizard papers indicates that Eleanor's mother, Sarah McGill died in 1832. The note also mentions that her father's name was Charles McGill and that Eleanor went to live with a Quaker family in western PA.

On June 4, 1851 at the age of 23, Eleanor McGill married James MaGill. Their daughter, Marietta MaGill was born March 18, 1852. (This information is taken from the flyleaf of a Bible that belonged to Eleanor. You can see copies of this information on pages 224-225 in this book. Research to discover more about James MaGill is ongoing.) There is never another mention of James MaGill and it is presumed that he died prior to Eleanor's marriage to John Oliver Boizard, July 16, 1855.

The oldest letter in the collection is to Eleanor shortly after her marriage to Oliver in 1855. The letter addresses Eleanor as 'sister' and mentions that Eleanor's father is still living and that he is busy farming. The letter is signed E. A. Hudson. It is possible that this "E. Hudson" is the sister that Eleanor writes about on occasion and whom she often wishes to visit. Oliver makes mention of Eleanor and Marietta visiting "Aunt Lizzy." This could be a nickname for a sister named "Elizabeth."

Details gleaned from within the collection of letters reveal that Eleanor was not able to write her own letters, and that she solicited help from various people to take her dictation. Many of these 'writers' were barely literate themselves. As soon as Marietta was old enough to write, she became the primary writer for her mother. Census records from the late 1800's indicate that Eleanor did learn to read and write before she died. Eleanor lived to be 83 and died in Glen Arbor Michigan on March 29, 1911.

**John Oliver Boizard:** From military records, we know that "Oliver" was born in Philadelphia on September 20, 1811. He married Eleanor MaGill, when he was 44 years old. Oliver was fluent in French & English, and he had beautiful penmanship. At times, Oliver was fondly referred to as "Bus," sounding like a shortened version of his last name.

His first enlistment in the US Army was November 17, 1831. There is a detailed account of his service records in the back of this book, (pages 181-185) with some interesting correspondence about his lying about his age to enlist at the age of 20 instead of waiting until he was 21.

During 1856 and 1857 Oliver served with the 4th Artillery, Company "K," in the Seminole Indian Wars in Florida. It appears from the contents of his letters that initially Oliver may have been assigned field duties such as helping to build roads through the Florida swamp. In time it appears that he began to take on the responsibility of writing for some officers and later we learn that his primary assignment in the army is in the Quartermasters Department, filling out the muster rolls.

On November 17, 1859 Oliver was discharged from the army and he moved his family to a forty-acre piece of property that he purchased in the Glen Arbor area. Ten months later September 6, 1860, Oliver re-enlisted in the Army in Newport, KY and was stationed with his family at Newport Barracks, KY. Due to an Order from

**Long Distance Love 1855-1870**

Congress, service men could shorten their terms of service and Oliver served only 3.5 years of his five-year enlistment.

In 1864, Oliver moved with his family to Chicago where he worked as a civilian employee for Capt. Pomeroy in the Quartermaster's Department. Due to Eleanor's health problems she and Marietta moved back to Glen Arbor, purchased ten acres from John and Harriet Fisher and built a small log home. Oliver sent money and supplies to his wife and daughter in Michigan and they kept in contact through correspondence and occasional visits.

Oliver died in Chicago, in November of 1870, at the age of 59. The cause of his death is unknown, however, a military doctor responding to a letter from Marietta after Oliver's death used the word "paralysis." Marietta had written the doctor requesting help in securing a military compensation.

**Marietta MaGill Boizard:** Marietta was born March 18, 1852. She was not Oliver's biological daughter, but she was raised by him as if she were. She was affectionately known as "Ettie" throughout her life. Ettie's school attendance was sporadic but she was able to read and write. Once she became proficient enough, she became the primary 'writer' for her mother. *There are **many** times while taking dictation from her mother that Ettie slips into first person and writes directly to her father and then reverts to the dictation of her mother.*

Some fun and interesting letters in the collection are those written by Marietta to her boyfriend Charlie Fisher. They began their correspondence with each other when Marietta was just 14 years old. There is much to smile about as you listen to the drama of young flirtation. Sometimes she asks Charlie to destroy the letters so that no one else will ever read them, and here I am over a hundred years later printing them in a book for all to see! I hope she forgives me in eternity! In January 1870 just shy of her 18th birthday, Marietta married her long-time boyfriend and neighbor, Charles Andrew Fisher. She and Charlie had three children, John Edward, Etta May & Charles Frederick.

Marietta died in 1935 at the age of 83.

**Catherine Boizard:** *Possibly*, Oliver's mother. The 1860 census shows a record for a Catherine Boizard, in the city of Philadelphia. She was born approximately 1786. This date fits closely with Oliver's mom's age, which is mentioned in the letters. This Catherine Boizard was born in Ireland and could not read or write. She died April 25, 1871 at the age of 85. She is buried in Old Chester Cemetery, PA, Section M, Lot 147 grave 5. She is buried next to Elizabeth Boizard, probably her daughter, "Libby".

**Elizabeth Boizard:** Oliver's sister, affectionately called "Libby." There is a possible connection to cemetery record in Old Chester, it appears that Libby was never married and that she is buried next to her mom in lot 147, grave 4. Her date of death was October 7, 1871; she was 60 years old.

**Jacob Boizard:** Jacob was Oliver's oldest brother. Census records point to his birth as being in 1809 and that he resided in Philadelphia.

**Mary (Boizard):** Oliver's sister, Mary traveled to California in a covered wagon around 1856. She settled in the Sacramento area. Initially she and her husband ran a successful boarding house for California's former governor, John Bigler and his staff. Communications ceased coming from Mary in 1858 and the family surmised that she had probably died.

**Lewis Pierre Boizard:** Oliver's brother, Pierre was known as "Pete" and also by the nickname "Zarty," a word play of his last name. Pete was born in 1815. Pete was referred to as a day policeman and a shoemaker. He was married to Caroline (b. 1813) and they had a daughter named Caroline, nicknamed "Cally" (b.1849) and a son named Charles, referred to as "Charley" (b.1850). Charles Boizard grew up to be an accomplished early American artist.

**Principal Characters**

**Emma Bridges**: Emma Bridges was a childhood friend of Marietta Boizard. It appears that they met while their fathers were both stationed at Newport Barracks, KY during the years of 1860-1864. A sweet life-long friendship developed between the two girls and their parents as well.

Emma was married December 27, 1866, to Edwin A. Brown, a soldier in the army. They were stationed in several outposts in the Arizona Territory. In a family photo album there is a picture of a Mr. Brown with the following note, "married cousin Eleanor Boizard." Research is ongoing to see if there is an actual family relationship.

An 1880 census record lists an Edwin A. Brown (35 years old) married to Emma (27 years old), living near Fort Worth Texas, in Johnson County. Edwin is a farmer and Emma is 'keeping house.' They have four children: Charles E Brown, age 10, born 1870; Josh H. Brown, age 4, born 1876; and twins Fannie and Kate Brown born February of 1880. There is a high likelihood that this is the same family from our letters.

Unfortunately, the photograph of Edwin A. Brown in the family album has another note written on it "Killed by Indians on their way to California." It appears that this dear family were victims of the American Indian Wars which lasted until around 1890. Details about their deaths are not known, but this is certainly a very sad ending to this family, and especially the little girl that we come to know throughout the letters. In a November 22, 1868 letter, Emma tells Marietta that in three years when they have money they want to move to California to settle down for life. It seems likely that sometime after the 1880 census they did indeed begin their journey to California and met their terrible fate. Emma's dad, William Bridges died at Fort Walla Walla, Washington in November 1881. It is possible to construe the scenario that the Browns were moving west after that, possibly to be with her mother. Whatever the specific event or time, we do not yet know.

**William Bridges**: Military records show that William was born in Council Bluffs, Iowa. His first enlistment in the U.S. Army was in 1833 at the age of 11. He is listed as a musician. He remained a soldier through 12 enlistments. He died in Fort Walla Walla, Washington, on November 21, 1881. His cause of death was a strangulated hernia which he had surgery on but did not recover. He had been a soldier for 48 of his 59 years of life. He was buried in the Fort Walla Walla cemetery. He is buried in section 1; number 9.

Emma's mother's name was Eliza, and there appears to have been a very close friendship between her and Eleanor Boizard. Research is being conducted to determine if there is a family relationship between Eliza and Eleanor. It would be so rewarding to discover that Eliza is Eleanor's sister or step-sister, but that does not look likely at this point in the search.

There is detailed information about William Bridge's military service on pages 186-190.

**William & Evelena Brown**: Not much is known about this family. Mr. Brown's letters indicate that he was the Principal Musician with the 15th Infantry. He was stationed at Fort Adams, RI. He wrote to Oliver and he asked about Wm. Bridges. This leads to speculation that at one time, William Brown's regiment had also been stationed at Newport Barracks and then transferred to Fort Adams, RI. The Browns and the Boizards appear to have been good friends as there was talk about coming and visiting each other and their desire to move close so that they could be neighbors.

**John & Elizabeth Dorsey**: There is a detailed account of John and Elizabeth Dorsey's life in James Tozer's book, Glen Arbor Pioneers. This paragraph contains basic information, to introduce the Dorsey family. The Boizards first became acquainted with the Dorsey's, when the Boizards moved to the Glen Arbor area in 1859. When Eleanor and Marietta moved back to Glen Arbor in 1864, they ate a meal with the Dorsey's and then went to stay with the Fisher's. Elizabeth (Coggeshall) Dorsey is a niece of John E. Fisher. Many references are made about the Dorsey's in this collection of letters. They were true friends to the Boizard family.

**Long Distance Love 1855-1870**

**Kate Boizard Dow:** Kate was Oliver's sister. She was born December 2, 1830. She resided in the Philadelphia area and was married to C.C. (Christopher) Dow. They had one son, Phineas.

**Charles A. Fisher:** Charlie was the first son of John and Harriet Fisher. He was born in Fond du Lac, Wisconsin in 1849. The 1870 & 1880 census records list Charlie as a farmer. He was also involved as a commercial fisherman and in selling, pigeons, fish, apples and other products to companies in Chicago & Traverse City. Charlie's public service career included county surveyor, school board member, county supervisor and Justice of the Peace.[2] In January 1870, Charlie married Marietta Boizard. Charlie's obituary lists his death as 1909 at the age of 60.

**Harriet Maria McCarty Fisher:** Harriet McCarty was born on March 2, 1826, in West Martinsburg, Lewis County, New York. Her parents migrated to Wisconsin in 1841. Harriet McCarty married John E. Fisher, April 23, 1843. Harriet and John had two sons, Charles Andrew born August 29, 1849 and Francis born July 3, 1851. As a family they moved to Glen Arbor in 1854.[3]

In 1857, Harriet Fisher's brother, Charles C. McCarty also followed the Fisher's to Glen Arbor. He built an Inn in 1858 and a dock for ships in 1865. Harriet's sister, Sarah McCarty King and her family moved to Glen Arbor around 1867. Harriet died in 1914 at the age of 88.[4]

**John E. Fisher:** John E Fisher was born in Salem, NY in 1818. He enlisted in the army in 1838 and was in Co. F, Eighth Infantry. It is believed that it was during this time in the army that John Fisher became acquainted with John Oliver Boizard. In 1841, Fisher mustered out of the army in Brooke, Florida and John and Harriet moved to Fond Du Lac, Wisconsin. In 1854 the Fishers sold their Wisconsin property and moved to the Glen Arbor area in Michigan. John and Harriet acquired many land grants in the Glen Arbor area, and John became one of the 'founding fathers' of Glen Arbor. John built a sawmill and was also active in many areas of public service i.e. Justice of the Peace, Judge of Probate, County Clerk etc.[5]

John's enthusiasm for the beautiful land in Glen Arbor was influential in bringing many new settlers to the area.

John's sister Elizabeth, her husband Bishop Wilson Tucker and their three-year-old daughter Sarah moved to Glen Arbor in 1854 also. There are many references to the 'Tuckers' in the letters.

In 1855 the *US Saginaw*, chartered by George Ray, brought 14 settlers to Glen Arbor. Among those settlers would be another of John Fisher's sisters, Margaret Fisher Coggeshall. Margaret with her husband William, and their three daughters, Elizabeth Clark (Nov. 28, 1840), Margaret Mariah (Oct 18, 1846), and Sarah Jeanette (May 10, 1851) As the passengers were disembarking from the steamer, John Dorsey, one of the founding fathers of Glen Arbor, stated his intent to marry Elizabeth Coggeshall. He did marry her one-year later on September 18, 1856.[6]

John Fisher wrote several letters to Oliver during Oliver's service in the Civil War. John's letters read like speeches and are some of the most eloquent letters in the entire collection. He staunchly opposed slavery and was in strong favor of fighting to preserve the Union.

---

[2] Edwin Fisher, *Sawmills and Family Trees*, 2006 page 26
[3] James R. Tozer, *Glen Arbor Pioneers*, Glen Arbor, MI Leelanau Press, 2003 pages 32-33
[4] Edwin Fisher, *Sawmills and Family Trees*, 2006 pages 10-11, 25
[5] Edwin Fisher, *Sawmills and Family Trees*, 2006 page 26
[6] Robert Rader, Beautiful Glen Arbor Township (Traverse City, MI: Village Press 1983) page 21

**Principal Characters**

When Eleanor & Marietta moved back to Glen Arbor in 1864, they purchased 10 acres from John Fisher. This property adjoined the Fishers and that proximity played an important role in the eventual courtship and marriage of Marietta Boizard, to Charlie Fisher on January 19, 1870.

More information about John & Harriet Fisher and genealogy charts can be found in the highly recommended books. Glen Arbor Pioneers, by James R. Tozer, and Sawmills & Family Trees, by Edwin Fisher.

**Austin Newman**: From census records we know that Austin Newman was born in New York around 1836. He remained single at least through the 1900 census. Emma Bridges writes to Marietta in 1864 about an "Oscar Newman" who left Newport Barracks and left a picture of himself for Marietta. It is possible with Emma's poor spelling that this "Oscar" is actually Austin, or that they had nicknamed Austin, "Oscar." Austin Newman did serve in the army during the Civil War, and likely became friends with the Boizards at Newport Barracks. Austin shows up quite often in the Boizard's life. It appears like he was waiting for Marietta to grow up, so that he could court her. He would have been approximately 16 years older than Marietta.

**Aunt Tourison:** Catherine Boizard's only sister. When Aunt Tourison died in 1858 her daughters, Margaret and Elizabeth, withheld some important Canadian documents from Catherine Boizard. Mrs. Tourison was buried in St. Mary's Cemetery, Philadelphia, next to her husband.

My hope is that by the time you finish this book you will have come to recognize **all** these people with their pioneering spirits and their stalwart courage as **your own** 'relatives.'

Jodie

**Long Distance Love 1855-1870**

# Florida – Seminole Indian War
# 1855-1857

**Rev. John Henderson** married Eleanor Melvina McGill to James MaGill in Pittsburgh, PA on June 4, 1851. Marietta MaGill was born March 18, 1852. At the time of this publication, research has not yielded additional information on James MaGill. It is presumed that he died. Eleanor M. MaGill later married John Oliver Boizard on July 16, 1855.[7] Oliver was 44 years old when he married 27-year-old Eleanor.

How Eleanor and Oliver met and where they lived during their first year of marriage remains a mystery for now. There is a letter that refers to their living in or at least near Pittsburgh in 1855.

The first letters in this collection primarily introduce us to Eleanor and Oliver's family members. Comments are made about Eleanor and Oliver's recent marriage and the siblings desire to meet Eleanor. Names of family members and friends are frequently mentioned.

Oliver was a Sergeant Major with the 4th Artillery, in the U.S. Army at the time they were married. During the years of 1851-1856, the Regiment Headquarters for the 4th Artillery was in Fort Hamilton, New York. Its individual companies were distributed to Fort Lafayette, Fort Mifflin (PA), Fort Washington, Fort Hamilton and to some of the forts along the Great Lakes.[8]

Oliver makes a reference about having his mail forwarded to him in Florida from a Sergeant Bates**Error! Bookmark not defined.** in Brownsville. There is a Brownsville, PA which is near Pittsburgh and McClellandtown (the small town that Eleanor was raised in), but it does not appear to have had a military presence. There is also a Brownsville, TX which has Fort Brown nearby. This was an active fort with a military presence. I have not been able to determine if a company from the 4th Artillery occupied it around 1855.

In the fall of 1856 the 4th Artillery was sent to Florida, to engage the Seminole Indians and Eleanor accompanied Oliver to Florida.

In January of 1857, Oliver's Company K was sent on a mission to Fort McRae, on the eastern side of Lake Okeechobee. Eleanor remained at Fort Myers, and corresponded with Oliver for six months until she was able to join him at Fort McRae as a cook and laundress.

---

[7] This information is written in the flyleaf of Eleanor's little black Bible, which now belongs to Michele Pattan.
[8] The timeline of events for the 4th Artillery was gleaned from a website article http://www.usregulars.com/usartillery/4us_art.html

**Florida – Seminole Indian War 1855-1857**

From E.A. Hudson (Eleanor's adopted sister or brother), to Eleanor

New Salem<br>20 1855 August

Dear Sister

I received your letter on the 18th of this month and was glad to hear from you as it is the first we have heard from you for a long time   we having wrote three letters to you in the last year without receiving an answer   we are as well as usual this time   all your relations is well as far as we know   we would be very glad to see you but it is not likely we will come down to Pittsburgh   so you must come up and see us and bring your Sargent along as we would like very much to see him and hope that you will have all the happiness that mortals can enjoy   we have left **McClellandtown** and live near **New Salem** in the same house that we used to live in on Wobley's farm   your father lives on the same farm and has raised over 1 thousand bushels of oats and has a large crop of corn in which looks very promising   but I must close for the present   pleas answer this letter soon   yours as ever
E A Hudson


From Caroline Boizard, sister-in-law, to Oliver

Philadelphia<br>April 27 /56

Dear Major,

I was requested to answer your last letter, at the time we received it Kate was very sick and your mother was there attending on her, we do not wish you to think you are forgotten by not writing to you or acknowledging the amount sent to your Mother, it was received and gratefully to. for you know money never comes {?} with her, and always cheers her spirits when cast down. Mother is as well as usual and is much obliged to you for thinking of her in your absence, may none of us forget her while she is spared to us. we know not how long it will be. I was much surprised when I looked at the date of your last letter, I was not aware so much time had elapsed since you wrote, but "time and Tide wait for no man" Your brother Pete has been promoted to day Paliece {police} which is much better, he gets so tired when he gets home at night he is fit for nothing but goes to bed. I have been waiting for him to write but begin to think we will wait in vain. I hope you will be able to make this out, I am in a great hurry. Kate is much better, than when your letter came, Christopher, also and Phin, my mother & father and sisters are well as usual. we have not heard from Elizabeth lately but are in hopes she is well. Jakob has left the City and gone to Baltimore to see if he can get along any better   he is a teacher and willing to work but he could get nothing to do, he could get hardly enough to keep his teeth a going. Your Mother and all the Family send there best wishes to your wife and little Daughter and hope this will find them in better health than when you wrote last. we all like the likeness you sent very much. when will you send some more. I have wrote all that is nessary and more and hope you will answer this as soon as commencement. I believe you owe us one letter already, give us all the particulars of your family and office   we all feel interested in your wellfare you know you have allways been so punctual in answering our letters that we did not know what to think of your not writing to us, we did not know but what something was said in the last letter to offend you, we are glad to learn that you are promoted, I hope you will remain there for many years, do you think you will be able to come to P. this Summer with your little Family. tell us if you think there is any prospect of coming I would like to see you all very much indeed   the children often speak of you, and say they want to see Uncle Oliver

**Long Distance Love 1855-1870**

This from your affectionate friends and <u>Sister in law</u>,

<u>Caroline</u>

C.M. Boizard, No 18 Marian Street

*{Written on the bottom of Caroline's letter}*

<u>To John O. Boizard</u>

Sargt Major

Brother Olly,
I congratulate you on your good fortune of being promoted.  And I hope you will continue to aspire.  We have received a letter from Mary 2 or 3 weeks ago  She states they had a very hard time of it in crossing the Plains   they were attacked twice by the Indians and lost two wagons and four horses in the affair and narrowly escaped with their lives.  there was in company with them a man and his wife which were killed.  they left two small children the youngest five weeks old which Mary took in her arms and Doctor the other and escaped to the woods with them.  they finally arrived in Sacramento and set up Boarding house and had **Governer Bigler** and Lady and the upper ten boarding with them and was making out well.  but the lady they rented the house from thought they was doing so well she would try her fortune at it. consequently she ordered Doc. and Mary out   they now live about ten miles out in a valley private   with the expectation of visiting Phila. ere long.  No More at present  My love to your wife and family, Yours  Pierre Boizard


<u>From Kate Dow to brother Oliver</u>

Phila<br>Aug 29<sup>th</sup> /56

Brother Oly
Mom has been waiting for an answer to my leter   we thought you might be sick or left where you were   mom say she hopes you have not forgotten her as she has great need of your assistance you know the amount she rec'vs from Zarty is limited   she would like you to rite as soon as possible   she is not very well this summer the heat has been so great   how do you live this warm weather   how is Elenor and little girl   all the family is pretty well  Zarty and family are well   we received a leter from sister Mary a week ago she is well sends her love to you and say she hope <u>pa</u> words will come true that you will be the support of mom  old age as your young day you enjoyed to yourself with the care of mom   she say Oly be kind to mom and God will reward you tenfold   a dying fathers words must come to pass   these are your sister Mary words    she say how she would like to see you   she say she hope to see us all in two years the furthest   if she live    dear Oly rite soon and direct your letter to me   the last leter you sent mom was in feb or March and mom did not get it for a week after Zarty received it    send the answer to me and I will answer it immediately   rite soon   very soon   mom and all the family send their love to you  Phineas send his love to uncle Oly   Excuse this short letter as I am replying for mom  Brother Oly rite as soon as possible good by  from sister
Kate

**Florida – Seminole Indian War 1855-1857**

From Oliver to Eleanor

**Fort McRae**, Fla
January 28th 1857

My Dear Eleanor
Your few lines Came to hand this Evening, and did not come an hour to soon, as you and Etty had hardly for a moment been out of my thoughts. I thought you would suffer at night with the cold, and I hope that you will be as Comfortable as a tent will admit of. We are working constantly on this road across the Swamp and when it is completed it will be nothing but a foot path. What they intend to do after, it is hard to tell. The Paymaster came to **Fort Center** and paid off Company "D" but our company with the Exception of a few of us, was left at Fort Center Consequently we could not be paid off as our Rolls, were with the Company. I must manage Somehow or other to send you some money before 10 days as I know you must be in need of it. I am on Extra duty in the **Subsistence Deptmt**. And do the duties of the **Quarter Masters Deptmt.** Lt. Hudson is the Quarter Master, and Commissary and appears to be a good sort of fellow He wished me to wait upon him, and I thought I would not refuse, as it may pay.
And now Dear don't be uneasy for I will use my Endeavor to remit you a small sum of money as soon as possible. I hope the child is well kiss her for me and don't let her forget me. It is now midnight and the Musquitos are giving me **Jessee.** Don't forget to Enquire at the Post office for my letters from Philadelphia by way of **Brownsville**, if old Bates Ever Sends them to me and now Eleanor a long good night. Answer this as soon as you can
PS Tell Mrs Bowman her husband is on guard and is well and I suppose he will write to her this mail
and now once more Farewell
Your Husband
John O. Boizard


From Oliver to Eleanor

Fort McRae, Fla
February 1st 1857

Dear Wife

Friend Wood who is discharged will hand you 5 Doll's. (in gold) which I got from the Captain the sum is rather small but I thought there might be others wanting money, and Every body must have a chance of such favors. Don't be backward in letting me know what you require as I will contrive to get it for you. If you want Coffee or Sugar and cant get it out of the Commissary store let me know in your answer, and I will speak to Lieut. Hudson and either send it or the order. I am busy now making out my monthly papers for the Subsistence Dept'mt. My white shirts are all torn and rotten I have 2 Flannel shirts which will do me for the present. I wish I had 2 strong check shirts for the woods, and if I had taken your advice I should have them now. Dear Eleanor don't forget to go to the Post Office and see about my letters and have them forwarded to me. I cant tell you how soon you can join me but I hope very soon as the Company is 79 strong and there would be more work than you would like to do Keep up a strong constitution and don't be lonely, for He that's above soothes the Wanderer. Kiss the young one for me and receive my Blessings. Your Husband
Oliver

**Long Distance Love 1855-1870**

From Eleanor to Oliver (Dictated by Eleanor)

February 11th 1857

My Dear Husband
 i received your kind and welcome Letter and 5 Dollars with Wood on the 9th of this Month   with respect to Marietta i transfered the Kisses and you can do the same if you please to this letter   the money was verry usefull as i was near out   i bought you 2 shirts because they was nothing to buy to make them   i have sent you the likeness as we can not come ourselfs  Mrs Bereman as {*has*} left and living with Mrs Best   Mrs Paterson will leave soon   i would like for you to have me come up to you   the Black thread is for {*Cannada ?*}   the towel is yours   with respect to provisions we can not get extra rations   sugar and Coffee is not out but candles is scarce and there is none in the setters {*sutlers*} store   i have got Browns washing this Day and was surprised to know that he was here   i was at the letter office for to see but they was none come   you send word wether i shall rite to your Mother or not   Wood expects to Leave here tomorrow for New Orleans please rite by return Mail   God Bless you.
E.M.B.
Mrs Paterson and children are all well


From Oliver to Eleanor

Fort McRae, Fla.
February 15, 1857

My Dear Wife
Enclosed you will please find a 5 dollar gold piece   the mail had just come in and I seize this opportunity of answering your letter. The Company has gone on a Scout with Companies "E" and "H" 4th artillery and 2 companies of volunteers. They expect to be gone 20 days. I received a letter from Philadelphia from Mother, it came from Brownsville as I recognized Serg't Bates handwriting forwarding it, the other letter that the Post Master wrote about I have not received. Mother and all the family is well and send her love to you, and Etty. Kate says that Mother prays for us every day and says that <u>God</u> will bless us, Kate tells me that Elizabeth met with a heavy loss, she came up to shop for the winter and somebody Robbed her in the Market house. Some of her own money and a Bill of Mr. Little's. It will take a year for her to make it up. <u>Dearest Eleanor</u> you spoke of joining me   I had a talk with Capt. Roberts and he tells me that we will not occupy this place longer than 2 or 3 months as the rain will then commence, we will likely go over to the Atlantic Side to **Fort Jupiter**, or **Fort Lauderdale**, and very likely we may pass the summer at **Fort Myers**.  I have been more busy here than any other post.  For I had to issue to Seven Companies, Lt. Hudson has gone with the Company. Capt. Ireland is sick, Lieut Weed relieved Lt. Hudson as Commissary and Quartermaster. Lieut. Hudson paid me my Extra pay and gave me <u>Five</u> $5 dollars for taking care of his things.  I will be obliged to write hard all this month to close his papers and Lieutenant Weed's.  I have now Eleven dollars still in my possession and I wish you had it. I think some of the Sick from "K" Company is coming down to **Fort Myers**, and then I will be able to send you some more. You spoke of the likeness and the thread and towel. I suppose I shall get it in a few days.  Dear Ellen don't be uneasy we may meet again this Summer.  The End of the Month I will have 59 dolls Coming to me, and if I can collect what they owe you it will amount with my Extra pay, near 100 dollars, that looks like a start don't it.  I am afraid the likeness might get broke.  Give my Etty a big Grissley hug for me and Dear Ellen receive my Blessing. Your Husband,
Oliver
Please answer this letter as soon as possible as I am anxious also send me some letter stamps. J.O.B.

Florida – Seminole Indian War 1855-1857

My Dear Wife
                Enclosed you will please find a 5 dollar
gold piece, the mail has just come in and I seize
this opportunity of answering your letter. The Company
has gone on a Scout with Companies "E" and "H"
4th artillery and 2 companies of Volunteers. They
expect to be gone 20 days, I received a letter from
Philadelphia from Mother, it came from Brownsville
as I recognized Sergt. Bates hand writing, forwarding
it, the other letter that the Post Master wrote about I
have not received. Mother and all the family is well
and sends her love to you, and Elly, Kate says that
Mother prays for us every day and says that God
will bless us, Kate tells me that Elizabeth
met with a heavy loss, she came up to shop for the winter
and somebody robbed her in the Market house
some of her own money and a bill of Mr. Settles
It will take a year for her to make it up.
The g×t×a Dearest Eleanor you spoke of joining me, I
had a talk with Capt. Roberts and he tells me that we
will not occupy this place longer than 2 or 3 months as the
rain will then commence, we will likely go over to the
Atlantic side to Fort Jupiter, or Fort Lauderdale, and
very likely we may pass the Summer at Fort Myers,
I have been more busy here than any other post for I had
to issue to Seven Companies, Lt. Hudson has gone with
the Company Capt. Ireland is sick, Lieut Wead
relieved Lt. Hudson as Commissary & Quartermaster

**Long Distance Love 1855-1870**

From Eleanor to Oliver (Dictated by Eleanor)

**Fort** meres *{Myers}* Florada
February 26, 1857

My Dear Husband
 I received your welcom Letter two days ago   in said Letter I was glad to hear that you enjoy good health as this leaves Hety and I and feel thankfull to the Lord for preserving both you and us and I also got the 5 dollars you enclosed in it   my dear Husband  Brown of our cp *{company}* is dead on the 8th of said month and you better put in his wash bill as I wash hear *{here}* for him since he came back   I am having to make struggle hear *{here}* as well as I can   when ever I can get washing or sewing there is not much chance for there is too many woman hear *{here}* and all idle    but however I wish you would wright to your mother and send her some money if you can   for she will expect it and it may be that the winter is hard in the north   please go to the Sergent Dean for a bottle of pickels and a pare *{pair}* of drawers i sent to you   his wife was sending him a box   it would hold nothing more   Let me know if you stand in need of any over halls *{overalls}* and perhaps I might get some other chance to send them to you or any thing else   Hetty tells you kiss her likeness for her and send her word when can we both kiss you   no more at present but i bid you an affectionate fare well and ever   remain your loving and Affectionate wife untill death
Elinor Buszard

Lett sergent patterson know the 2nd artilary will be leaving hear *{here}* on the 20 of March and she wants to know if he will able to go home with the Company as it would save a good deal of money for him or if not Let him wright *{write}* and let Mrs patterson know if he would let herself and the children to go on before him.  Wright soon  good by




From Oliver to Eleanor

**Fort McRae**, Fla
March 4th 1857

Dear Eleanor,
Serg't Dean has just handed me a Bottle of Pickles, and a pair of drawers, which I needed very much. I do not Know whether you received 5 dollars Enclosed in a letter or not, which I Sent you, Since <u>Wood's</u> letter. I am very anxious about such matters. You will please find Enclosed in this <u>7 ½</u> dollars more, and be particular in acknowledging the receipt of it. I am well but I have So much to do at present, I have not had time to wash this week, and I got McLaughlin to wash me 5 or 6 pieces. I hope you are well also the girl. I have a new tin plate for her with the initials of her name on it. I sent you <u>Brown's</u> Bill   in case you do not get it I think I can get it at the next pay day. Dear <u>Eleanor</u> be not uneasy but Keep a good <u>heart</u>   I feel lonely Enough myself, and I miss the good cakes & coffee, we used to have. This is a poor place for fresh <u>Provisions</u>   we have had since we have been here about one day, Fresh Pork, and about <u>Venison</u>  Enough for one meal. We occasionally get Pickles & molasses, but I miss my Beef Soup very much. I suppose, you get enough to get along, slowly, for I suppose there is not much to do at **Fort Myers**, but try to get along as well as you can, and I will try to send you money at Every opportunity.  I will in about a <u>week</u> try to send you some Coffee, and <u>Etty's</u> tin plate in a little box, you will not forget to send me some letter stamps say about 6 or 8 if you can get them.  It is getting late and I will close my letter, Give my Etty a long kiss for me, and please receive my fondest wishes for your future <u>wellfare</u>.
Your Husband  Oliver

**Florida – Seminole Indian War 1855-1857**

From Eleanor to Oliver (Dictated by Eleanor)

**Fort Myers**
march 5th 1857

Dear husband
I received your letter and I was glad to hear - that you are well as this leaves Hetty and me   I am sending you a small box of notions and half of the tobacco is for patterson  half the cheese sugar  coffee   norman lost his knapsack coming from **fort denaud** and the parcel you give him   and candles is very scarce and I can't get one.  I would write more but I am in hurry  No more at present  but remains your loving wife
EMB


From Eleanor to Oliver (Dictated by Eleanor)

**Fort Myers**
march 8th 1857

Dear husband
I received your letter and the money and I was very glad to hear that you was well and I received your other letter and the money   you wished to know how I was getting along   I am doing very well and has plenty of work now and you need not be uneasy about me   you wanted to know how I am getting along in the tent   it does very well in dry weather but it is very disagreeable wet   I had a small box all ready packed to send you when donaldson was here but he did not like it   I sent that bill of Browns the day after I got the letter but is wasnt take until next day   there is not letter stamps to be had here but I have 2 that I will send you   I wish you would send me some candles if you can   there has been quite a massacre in fort keys *{Fort Keis}*  Friday 6th 15 killed and wounded    four taken prisoner one drummer and 3 fifers and we have one squaw and a child in the guard house
you wanted me to kiss Etty  I did so and she is growing a big girl and want to see her papa
No more at present
from your loving wife
E M B

tell patterson that his wife and children are well


From Oliver to Eleanor

**Fort McRae**, Fla
March 13th 1857

Dear Wife
I received your Box last night, which contained 3 Pairs overalls & one shirt (all Blue) and also some Tobacco, Coffee, sugar & cheese which I divided with Sergeant Patterson.  I also discover that there is 1 Box Lobsters, 2 pairs of Stockings, & 2 pairs Drawers, 1 Bottle of Tea which is really more than I can carry, should we be ordered off – However I can sell most of them.  I wish you would let me know if the shirt & pantaloons that was wrapped up in a newspaper (a Glasgow paper) is not for Sergt. Ford of "D" Comp'y the other two pair I suppose is mine   I found in my uncovering them a paper with Serg't Fords name on it, which I supposed was put in the box to let me know they

**Long Distance Love 1855-1870**

were his. You mentioned that you send me some notions but did not specify all the articles, which causes me to be doubtful whether they all belong to me or not. I wrote to my Mother the other day and told her how we were situated, also told her as soon as I could spare the money I would send her some. The Company is still on the Scout and Comp'y "D" has gone to Establish a Post near **Fort Jupiter** I have not heard of them since   Sergt. Dean desired me to write to his wife about his whereabouts and told me when he started that he would write to her, after he got settled. I sent you a small Box with Roach which contained some articles you may require. I am sorry that Norman lost them Candles as there are scarcely any here as "D" Comp'y took 2 Boxes with them.

I see by your letter that you are very busy, at present, that is better than doing nothing, I expect there is a great excitement about **Fort Myers**, about those men being killed  I hope the next news we get, that the Indians will get their dose  In answering this letter please tell me exactly what belongs to me and what belongs to Serg't Ford   I will let the overalls and shirt remain as they are, before I can make any use of them, until I receive your instructions. Dear Eleanor Please not send me any more untill I tell you  as my stock increases in Clothing and I will have too much to carry, in case we should be ordered off, we expect the Company here in about 7 or 8 days then there will be some further news.  The Musquitoes are awful, I put up the Bar but it don't do much good   Please answer this as soon as possible, and Believe me to be yours with sincerity.
Oliver



From Oliver to Eleanor

**Fort McRae**, Fla
March 24<sup>th</sup> 1857

My Dear Wife
This night the Boats have arrived from **Fort Center**, but they bring no news from **Fort Myers**, I have not news to communicate, with the exception of the Company returned, and they being paid off. I collected 28 dollars of your wash money, there are 4 men who still owes you, which is Roach (4 doll's) Poor Brown who is dead 4 doll's Meier 3 ½ dolls and Douglass 75 cents they say they will pay me at the first chance. Dieckman who is discharged will give you 15 dollars, for me and let me know whether you are in want of any more and I will send you some more with Leary who will leave us in a few days. You may if you please sell Deickman or Leary those 3 shirts of mine for $1.50 cents each, as I may not want them. I have written to my Mother and sent her 10 dollars, and I have 20 dollars in gold left for another remittance besides paying the Captain 10 doll's which I owed him and paying 2 doll's which I owed Lieut. Weed. There is now 7 months pay nearly due me, and I don't owe a cent to any body.  Since your letter dated March 8<sup>th</sup> we have had no news from **Fort Myers**. I sold one pair of them Overalls you sent me for 3 doll's. I wear the other pair. I still have one shirt and overalls which I suppose belongs to Serg't Ford which is near **Fort Jupiter**, but we have sent them nothing as we have no transportation.  Dear Eleanor I never was so home sick in my life. I know we cant stop here more than 2 months longer, but whether we will go down to **Fort Myers**, or **Fort Jupiter** I cant tell.  Try to Keep up a good heart   I hope you and my big girl Keep your healths, when you get this letter from Dieckman get him to answer it immediately, for this is a lonely place, especially if you don't give us any news, so I beg of you to write the same day you get it, and tell me all the particulars and how you get along. It is now one o'clock and yet I must not sleep until 2 more Boats arrive with Forage.   I am well enough in health, but I want to See you and Etty. You need not send me any more clothes as I have too much to carry now. I drank some of the tea and sold the rest, and the coffee and cheese, Pickles and Tobacco. I believe if I had a small portion of Tobacco I could sell it, but if you do get a chance to send me some up, let me know how much you pay for it. And now Dearest I will close this shortly, by wishing you a good night and pleasant dreams, give my girl a long kiss

**Florida – Seminole Indian War 1855-1857**

for me and receive my Blessing.  Don't forget to mention whether <u>Roach</u> gave you the little <u>Box</u> with the candles plate **& c**.  Once more good night
your Husband
Oliver


From Eleanor to Oliver (Dictated by Eleanor)

**Fort** Miris *{Myers}*
March 25th 1857

My Dear Husband
I received your welcome letter a few days ago and was glad to hear that you enjoy good health as this leaves Hety *{Ettie}* and I at present   thank god for it   we have great reason to bless the Lord for his kindness to us and so many dying and sick with diarear *{diarrhea}*   poor norman was buried today  I washed for him this last month   I want you to arrange that for me   I got the box from roach and all the things candles and coffy *{coffee}* and a plate for hety *{Ettie}*   it was as good as a play to be looking at her  she felt so glad when she hurd you sent is to self *{it yourself?}*  Mrs ford and I settled for the things she was sending to her Husband   I want you to dispose of them as well as you can or if you need any of them you may have them    also I paid her what they cost her   here miss patterson and the childrin is well also   I now conclude by sending you my best Love and ever remains your wife until death
Elinor obizard *{Boizard}*

wright soon  hety *{Ettie}* send you a ciss *{kiss}* for her papa


From Eleanor to Oliver (Dictated by Eleanor)

**Fort Myers**
the 30 March 1857

Dear Husband
I received your letter on the eighth from W. Dieckman with the amount of $15. and I am glad to hear that you are in good health. I am not in want of anything and in very good health.  the 2nd Art. is about to go from here and I will not have anything to do after they have left and therefore if you think that we will not meet together before next May I shall prepare to go North and it will be also better for Ette to go North for the purpose of going to school.  because she is not learning anything here   if you want me to send you anything let me know and I will send it to you   I am going to write to my sister and I will go and seek her if you let me go North  I am sending you three letter stamps  there being no other news
therefore I remain yours
E.M. Boizard.

*This note was written at the bottom of the letter, apparently William Dieckman was taking dictation from Eleanor and he added his own postscript.*

Between you and me   if you take my word from what I heard and see here  it would be better to send your Wife away from here because she will not *{more}* than she has already a bad name by being so close to Missus Patterson  I do not belief what I heard and I would take a solemn oath upon myself to be the truth   but as afore said   take her

**Long Distance Love 1855-1870**

away from here as soon as possible. It was her own wish to write this to you. Mss. Ptt. has a great deal of company with men but your Wife is innocent of everything.
Your Friend, William Dieckman


From Oliver to Eleanor

**Fort McRae** Fla
April 3rd 1857

My Dear Wife
Your letter dated the 25th of March, 1857, Came to hand last. I am glad that you and the girl enjoy good health. You mention Norman's Burial  Please let me know how long you washed for him, the number of days & c. And I will have it put on the Muster Rolls. Be particular as regards the number of days. I sent by Dieckman on the 25th of March 1857, 15 dollars which I hope you got. It takes about 10 days before any answer from your letters reaches me – Should you get any chance of Buying Tobacco send me up some. That is a reasonable quantity, say 10 pounds. Try to send the amount of Norman's Bill - before the last of this month.
Yours with Sincerity
Your husband
Oliver

Write soon and direct your letter's thus
John. O. Boizard
Compy "K" 4th Art.
**Fort McRae** Fla

N.B. I have no news of any importance   If you want any money tell me   J.O.B.   Tell me the Price you pay for the tobacco


From Eleanor to Oliver (Dictated by Eleanor)

**Fort Myers**
April 11th 1857

Dear husband
I received your letter on the tenth of this month and by it i am glad to hear you are in good helth as this leves me at present and the child   Dear husband this note will tell all about Norman   Mrs Dyer wants to know did Corporal weber got that boxes she sent up   Dear husband if Mrs Patterson is going North i will not go   i have got some tobacco at 50 cts per pound and as soon as i will get a chance i will send it up   Mrs Patterson is getting better   Dear husband if you make up your mind to send me North i would like you would come down to see me before i would go   there is good chance in May   if you would get a chance to send some money down   you may but i do not want money very bade {bad} Nor more at present from your Effectionate Wife and Daughter
E.M Boizard

**Florida – Seminole Indian War 1855-1857**

From Oliver to Eleanor

**Fort McRae** Fla
April 14th 1857

My Dearest Eleanor

I received a letter written by Dieckman which stated that you had received 15 doll's. and I was rejoiced to hear that you was in good health, and also that you are not in want of anything. I am indifferently well at present, and rather melancholy, at present, to think I cant be with you. Dieckmans letter gave me great uneasiness. I would to Heaven that we were together, and I think before the 1st June, we shall meet at **Fort Myers.** However write to your sister and try to hold on untill the 1st June 1857 and place your trust in Him that never deserts the honest and virtuous. It is now nearly 8 months, since we have been paid off, and as soon as I receive my Money, I will have it all for you and a sum besides, which will enable you to go to the north. I know the Child requires Schooling   We received a letter from Mrs Dean that Mrs. Patterson was dangerously ill   the letter was dated April 3rd and Patterson asked the Captain to go down, but the Capt. told him that there was a general order to let nobody go during the war. It seems strange that she got so suddenly ill. I have had a touch of the Fever but I am much better. I still attend to my duties. There is one thing which I fear of you going to the north alone, perhaps you cant get along without reasonable sum of money, but I hope you will be able to hold out another 2 months, which will give you the opportunity to get an answer from your sister after you write to her, and then by that time, we may be together. There is all probability that we will leave here in about a month, and it's the impression that we will go to **Fort Myers.** Dear Wife be not backward, in telling me whether you want money or not. I am devoting my whole time for your future welfare and trying to save Every Cent, so that I can have you go to your Sisters. I have not spend 1 Dollar foolishly since I left you. Poor Etty, how I would like to see her. We had a great Blow on Sunday and Monday and it is a blowing hard this day. I will be able with Saving up to the End of this month, my extra pay and my monthly pay for 8 months, it will amount to about 130 Dollars, and then Dear perhaps that will carry you through. This letter of Dieckman's has been 15 days Coming, and you may think how I feel in regard of you   Keep up a good heart and be persevering and things will turn out right yet. Enclosed you will please find 7 ½ Dollars, and I have 30 dollars, more at your disposal, if you wish it dear. If the 2nd Art'y. goes, why we may come down there ourselves. I know you must be greatly harassed, with Children, and waiting on other people from what I can understand., but be firm and resolute and may the Lord who is ever Kind to all never desert you.  I have just been looking at your likeness, it fills me with pain and pleasure, Poor Etty, looks so natural. But let me change this theme which grows sad. If you have not written to your Sister yet, get some trusty person to write to her and by the time you get an answer, maybe I will be with.  Kiss the girl for me and believe me to be your Husband in Sincerity
John Oliver Boizard

Recollect what old Sally told you about the slander of other people but don't mind them. J.O.B.
Capt. Ireland thinks you had better stay until about the month of June and then likely we will meet   yours J.O.B.

## Long Distance Love 1855-1870

From Kate (Boizard) Dow to brother Oliver

My love to Eleanor and child

Phila
April 14th

Brother Olly,
I received leter with ten dollers in and it came very actable *{acceptable}* we wher *{were}* glad to hear from you as we read of the indians   we felt as if you might be near them but I am glad to hear you have no orderly duties and that you are well and you have sutch a kind wife and so industerious   Oly be kind to her as a good wife is as precious as gold   I am pleased to hear that she sent you the word of God to cheer you up   trust in God and he will protect you throu your troubles.   Elisabeth was heare when your leter came and was glad to hear from you and send her love to you and wife and child   Dear Oly you want to know about Zarty   he is well and working at his trade   shoe making is very good now   it never was as good   Cally and children are well at present they have a nice house in Vane street between 9th street and washington and wallace   mom monthly dues has stopped since September last   Everything agreeable   Caley is as pleaset *{pleased or pleasant ?}* as a kitten since then but you Lib and myself has not stopped.   Fin dow sends *{there is a rip in the paper and there are some words missing.}*   you want to know about Jacob   he is as you left   getting a long for him *{?}* he is very well   hearty *{?}* a Buck   Dear Oly Tourinson are well sends their love to you all   Mom health is good except rumatism *{rheumatism}* she dont sew   her sight is so poor   she prefers to live alone as she likes her church so mutch   lent is over   mom sends her love to you and God bless you as a dutiful son   mom love to Elenor   Cris sends his love to you and says take care of yourself Old Boy   take care of the ingines *{injuns}* *{the next paragraph is badly soiled and only a few words can be distinguished. The words that can be read are as follows:* We have no news. . .   Federal street. . .between seventh and 8th street . . . No 700 . . . no 704 . . . south. . . has removed his shop . . . from house*}* I was very happy to leave but the walk was to long for Cris   Good By   God Bless you   rite soon and please let me know about *{Cris Mathew ?}* as *{?}* is so ancious *{anxious}* to hear   from your sister
Kate Dow
rite very soon


From Oliver to Eleanor

**Fort McRae**, Fla.
April 24th 1857

My Dear Wife
I received your Kind letter dated the 11th of April, and was rejoiced to hear that you was in good health, also my little Etty. I will give norman's account to the Captain and he will put it on the muster & Pay Roll, also Brown's   I wrote you a letter Since the one that Deickman conveyed to you with 15 dolls. in it, and on the 14th, I send you another letter with 7 ½ dollars in it, and I expect to get that answer next mail, I now send you (10) dollars more, in this letter saved up,  by Kennedy. The whole which I have sent you, is the 47 ½ Doll's. and I hope you have received it all. My Dear Wife, I am not in very good health at present. I have Every now and then that heavy feeling about the head, Something like the Fever. I have been taking **Quinine Pills**. I wrote to you about going to the north in a letter, and Dearest Eleanor  do not think of going away without Seeing me. If you only Knew the distress it gives me, you Certainly would give up the notion. I could not rest.  my happiness would be at an End, and then think of it a Lone Woman travelling without means in a Strange City or town without a Protector, Subject to the rude treatment, of every Ruffian, Oh, do give up the notion   I shall be able probably to see you about next June   The Company is on a scout for 20 days, they left here on the 18th of April, as for me coming down before the

**Florida – Seminole Indian War 1855-1857**

Compy. It is impossible, as **General Harney** has issued orders to give no leave of absence, to anybody, during the campaign. It is the general impression, this will be the last Scout, have patience until I see you, and the Lord will protect you. I console myself by reading in your little Bible, and looking at your likenesses. I expect you will hear that a letter from Philadelphia for me will be in the Post office, as soon as it comes, please forward it as soon as you can. No more at present, but remain yours with sincerity. Oliver

Mrs. E. M. Boizard  Laundress K Co. **Fort Myers**, Fla

Tell Mrs. Dwyer, that Corpl. Weber has received no box, nor did he write for any so he says.
Give Etty a hug, and don't let her forget me in her growing up so fast JOB

*The previous letter actually has the date of April 24, 1856 on it, but as it is an answer to the April 11, 1857 letter that Eleanor wrote to Oliver. I have placed it here, where it fits chronologically.*


From Eleanor to Oliver (Dictated by Eleanor)

**Fort Myers**
May 2nd 1857

My Dear Husband
I Received your letter yesterday morning and by it i am sorry to hear that you have the fever but i hope it will be nothing  me and the child are in good health at present   Dear O it was not my intention to go North until i see you and therefore do not be uneasy for i will not go  I hope the next letter i will get from you better news about the Company comming to **fort myers**  i have four boarders  they are giveing me four dollars a month and their rations each   three Clerks and the post butcher there all in the quartermaster employment  i thought it was easyer then to wash for i could not hall *{haul}* water Enough  it is so hard to get it here, i rote to my sister a week ago  I got letter from your mother and i opened it  but before opened i thought it was for me and i put another envelope on it and sent it up to you  i also Sent you box with the train Burdick went up in  Please tell Corporal Weber to send to **fort Center** for his Box  Mrs Duyer says it is there  Cornell got his discharge he is going to Tampa in the morning  he did not get a red cent of pay  Roche is still lame in left leg  But the doctor says he will send Jimmy Hasy up to the company again  My Dear O i have got fifty dollars yet and can give account for thirty, Burdick owes me twelve if he gets paid up there  i have received all the money you sent me that makes 47 ½ dollars correct
No more at Present  From your Effectionante Wife and Daughter
 E M Boizard


From Oliver to Eleanor

**Fort McRae**, Fla
May 5th 1857

My Dear Eleanor
The Box came to hand yesterday, and you don't Know how grateful I feel for you, for your Kindness, the tobacco I sold for 50 cents per plug, the cheese which was a little damaged, I got one dollar for it, part of the Ham I retained, the other I got 50 cents for it, the **Hickory Shirts** you send me I have sold them all.  I got $1.50 for the last one, I

27

# Long Distance Love 1855-1870

wear nothing but flannel as it suits my health better. The Tea will come good some Evening before I go to bed. The flannel shirt you send me was very acceptable however I have made a trade for 2 new ones, about one month ago, which leaves me 3 good ones and one old one. I also managed to trade for 2 pairs of good drawers, as the old ones are worn out. I was highly gratified to hear that you and my Cosey was in good health and that you had got somewhat out of the notion of going north before I see you. there is a rumour that the troops will be moved soon, where, I know not, but as our Company property is at **Fort Myers**, likely we shall come there if not you may be able to join me elsewhere, but I think you will not be long before you see me. Any other place but this and no doubt, but you could be with me. The fleas, Blowflies, an Musquitoes are Intolerable. I am well at present, as the dumb ague has left me. I relished those lobsters you send me with a Zest fit for an **Epicurean.** I am anxiously awaiting a letter from my Mother. You did not mention whether you wrote to your Sister or not. I am so glad that you are doing well. I am straining every nerve to get along, as I have something in view, if this war closes, however when we meet, I will tell you all, "and then we will smile" I send you since Dieckman gave you that letter, 2 letters one contained 7 ½ dolls, the other 10 dollars (17 ½ dolls in both) which I hope you have got. Burdick tells me he owes you 12 ½ dolls, which he says, he will pay me at the first pay day. I must close this letter as the Company has just returned from 20 days scout, and I will have plenty to do. So no more at present.
But remain yours with Sincerity.
Your husband "Oliver"

have patience dear, don't be uneasy, the child is 5 years old this month Kiss her for me, and try to learn her letters, and also Keep up her good behaviour, your's J.O.B.


From Eleanor to Oliver (Dictated by Eleanor)

**Fort Myers**
May 12th 1857

My Dear Husband
I Recived your letter on the 9th wich gives me great Plesure to hear that you are well of the dum egeu *{dumb ague}* as this leves me with a great head ached for the last week  Dear O we had a great Ball here and me and Mereatta was there  were *{where}* we enjoyed ourselvs very happy  let me Know if there is any talk of the company moving or comming to F Myers  there was none of the men in the hospital musterd *{mustered}* so i canot collect that Bill of Jimmy hasy  tell Corporal McCarthy there is none of them will get paid here as i here *{hear}* the Pay master has not come here yet  for to pay the last two months pay  Pendergast and Koler is here  they are going up as soon is the boat will come here from tampa  Mrs Patterson and the children are all well and in good helth *{health}*. Plese give this note to Corporal weber it is from Mrs Deen.  Mereatta is well and getting a very big girl  she is longing to see you No More at Present From your Effectionate *{affectionate}* Wife and Daughter
E M Boizard

**Florida – Seminole Indian War 1855-1857**

From Oliver to Eleanor

**Fort McRae,** Fla
May 13th 1857

My Dear Wife
The mail came here last Evening and I received three letters, one from Kate, the other two was from yourself. I have not heard any news about our going out of this place yet, but is was generally supposed that we would leave **Fort McRae** as it is very unpleasant here and not a fit place, for any body to live in much longer any how. I never was so troubled with fleas and other insects as I am here. I feel better than I was, but now and then I feel like the Ague. I am glad to hear that you are doing well, without washing so hard, it would be better for you not to work so hard, for the weather is getting so hot you will get sick. The news from Philadelphia is cheerfull enough. Since the mail arrived I hear the Indians is been giving the volunteers a brush and I fear that will prolong our stay in Florida  Try to Keep the girl in check and use all your energies to learn her to spell & c. Try to Keep up her behaviour and you will find it usefull some future day. Should the Paymaster come up here I will collect Brown's 4 dolls, Normans 75 cts, and Burdicks $12. It was thought by the officers of this Post, that we would be removed from this post, but what this mail has brought, I know not. Should there be any news that would be cheering to you I will let you Know at the Earliest Convenience  I received from **Fort Center** Some Bread and **Forage** in the Boat, which we cannot well do without, all other provisions we have plenty. You may Bless your stars that you are at **Fort Myers**. I believe you could not live here, particulary at night for the insects. I will close this letter as I have nothing of importance to Communicate to you further. And now My Dear Wife, give the Child a long Kiss for me, and Tell her I will buy her something nice when I see her. I hope you read Kate's Letter it would afford me great pleasure for you to read all the letters from Philada.  Farewell and God Bless You
Your husband
 Oliver


Invitation to Cotillion party

**Fort Myers**
May 14 '57

The honor of your presence is requested at a **Cotillion** party to be given this evening in the **Garrison.**

Very Respectfully
Jos. Miller   L. G. Murphey
Managers
To Mrs Boizard
Present

**Long Distance Love 1855-1870**

From Oliver to Eleanor

Please send me a Bottle of good Claret wine and pack it So it won't Break.  J.O.B

**Fort McRae** Fla
May 20th 1857

Dear Eleanor,
I received your letter with Corporal Weber's letter enclosed on the 19th of May'57 and was sorry to hear that you had a Bad Head Ache, I am well aware what you suffer while you have it. My Dear Wife I am not Exactly well yet, although I am doing duty. I took Medicine yesterday. I do not believe I can Keep my health here, we have about 20 men on the Doctor's list. As regards our moving, I really Cannot tell you when or where, we shall move, but as soon as I can get any word to that Effect, I will let you Know immediately. There is one sure thing that we can stop here not much longer than the month of May. Wherever we will go in all probability, you will join the Company. I am glad to hear that you and the girl Enjoyed yourselves at the Ball, as it was a nights recreation for you. Although it used to be a rather-unusual thing for Ball among Soldiers to be a genteel affair, as some fellows were sure to get drunk and Kick up a Row, or be insulting.

Dear Wife, by the time this letter reaches you I hope you will be in good health and still Sooner. I thought about you getting me a pair of Soldiers overalls, to have them ready. I don't care if you can get 2 pair reasonable, about no. 3's and also Boots about no. 8, I do not know that it is worth while to send me up any thing to Eat Except a little tea, as I Eat very little at present.  Dear Eleanor, do not work too hard, this approaching hot weather. Better make less money and not Kill your self for a few dollars. This is a bad Country for a man or woman to be sick in. Please Air my Uniform Coat the Captain's says we will all have to draw coats, after we get to Summer quarters. So get the pants and shoes if you can and lock them up until I see you. You might send me up a small can of Preserved Meat of some Kind. O'Connor, of our Company tells me a woman belonging to Company "F" 4th arty, was shot by a Musket going off accidentally. The ball lodged in her and it was not supposed she could live long. It took place as the Boat was starting from the Kissimmee where the woman was left.  Dear Wife try not to Expose yourself and keep good health. As this is the Season people get sick. The little money you earn strive to save it as it will come good to you. Should you have any money put aside that you would not like to use let me know in the answer to this letter. So I can send you some, as I am managing with my Extra pay to keep 30 or 35 dolls. ahead for your purposes and my Dear old Mother. There is a rumor about that we are ordered out of Florida soon. If so, and you really wish to go home with your daughter and the Almighty spares me, I then perhaps can send you direct from New Orleans or some other Port, and comfortable at that. This letter is not very well written, as I have just been washing 7 pieces of my clothing, which will save 1 Dollar any how. I do all my own washing and I hope when you see them, you can say I am a terrible washerman.  *{this letter has water marks on it, probably from his wet hand.}* Poor girl how I would like to see her, now she is growing up. Kiss her for me and tell her to be a good girl and her dada will buy her a nice carriage like them in Newport, KY for to take home to see her Aunt Lizzy, (that is if we all live) I have lost much flesh since the 1st April. During the months of January, February and March I made out to keep my health very well, since then I have failed greatly, well I have had a great care on my mind, the uneasiness about your being left alone and other cares, has certainly reduced to me in health and strength.  Dear Wife, I hope you read that letter from Kate. As they all feel friendly to you– Mother says God will Bless you for your gratitude in the 1st letter and now Eleanor be patient and I am pretty sure we shall meet in a short time, (Say in one month) Kiss my little girl and don't neglect at night her duty to the Almighty. As children about Camp learn every thing that is mischievous. And now Farewell.  Your Husband
"Oliver"

Write Immediately, Tell me in your answer if Packard gave you a small parcel or not.

**Florida – Seminole Indian War 1855-1857**

N.B. Your likeness looks as well as ever. Your Bible is taken care of – as for the <u>Souvenir</u> be not uneasy. J.O.B.


From Eleanor to Oliver (Dictated by Eleanor)

**Fort Myers**
may 30th 1857

Dear husband
I received your 2 letters and I was sorry to hear that you was not well and I have been very sick myself with the intemiton *{intermittent?}* fever and I had it two days and a night and never broke  I feel a little better for the fever has intinely *{instantly?}* left me and the doctor says I will soon get better  I will send you a box of things the first chance and the clothes that you want me to send you I cannot buy.  you wanted to know how much money I have  I have very little now for you must know what a large family I have to support  I do not know what patterson means he never writes to his wife  I hope dear husband that we will soon meet again  for that I am all most tired of my life Etty is well and getting so bold that I can do nothing with her.  I have nothing more particular to say
No more at present  from your loveing wife
E.M. Bayard



From Oliver to Eleanor

**Fort McRae**, Fla
June 1st, 1857

My <u>Dear Wife</u>,
I am improving in health, and hope you are also in Excellent health and <u>spirits</u>. Pendergast & Kohbe has come and he rather surprised me when he told me that you had not received my letter, but I suppose it was in the mail that they met at **Fort Denaud**. I do not Know what to say to you to Encourage you to <u>patience</u>, but there is no other way of getting along, but to wait. I have suffered both <u>mentally</u> and <u>bodily</u> on account of being apart from you, but what can I do. I hope the time will come soon, when we shall <u>meet</u>  I could send you down 40 dollars if you are in want of it, but I am afraid it might be lost. If you can hold on awhile longer, I may have an opportunity to send it, if it was Bills, there would be no difficulty, but as it is in <u>gold</u> it makes too big a bulk in a package or letter. It is the general impression that we will leave this place before long and all hands will be rejoiced at it, as this is certainly an awful place. Let me entreat you to have patience awhile longer and I hope all will be well. Pendergast tells me that you look better than Ever, well that's cheering news, "May your shadow never be less" but try to be contented, and do not work too hard this hot weather, and compose yourself, and He that's above will do the Rest. Pendergast tells me that <u>Etty</u> has grown 6 inches, <u>Bless my</u> **Cosey** may she ever prosper. he also tells me that it is supposed the Headquarters of the artilly. (4th) will be at **Fort Myers**, if so we may have a chance of being stationed there, anywhere but this place, if you and the child are present.  By the answer that I sent you, I wrote to you to send me some <u>wine</u> and something <u>fresh</u> like oysters or Lobsters - and some <u>tea</u>, and I suppose I will get it about the time you get this letter. I would write to my Mother if I had a good <u>Current Bank Bill</u> however there is time enough for that if reports are true about leaving here, and now <u>Dearest Eleanor</u> I have told you all I can think of at present, and hope this letter will find you cheerfull and the young one well, <u>look to her</u> particulary, as now is the time, if you have an opportunity to instruct her.  Please not forget about the overalls, and Boots, and a white <u>shirt</u> would not be amiss. Give my respects to Roach and all Enquiring friends, and tell me in your answer who writes your letters for you.
From your Sincere Husband    Oliver

**Long Distance Love 1855-1870**

Be not uneasy about the north, I am anxious that Etty should be schooled and she shall be if I am spared. Take Care of No. 1 and all will be right. yours. J.O.B.


From Oliver to Eleanor

**Fort McRae**, Fla
June 3rd 1857

My Dear Wife,
I received your letter yesterday Evening and the Paymaster also came up and paid the Company. I send you by the Paymaster (Lebuard) one hundred dollars ($100) in gold and may it arrive safely. It is directed to you in the care of Col. Waite and he will hand it to you. I was grieved to hear that you became sick so suddenly since Pendergast left **Fort Myers**, Fla. I have no encouraging news to give you. I believe by the last mail that we will remain here all summer and I am going to prevail on the Captain to have you sent up to me. Dear Wife it is rather hard for you to be the way you are and if I can get the Captain to consent for you to come up, the only difficulty will be in crossing the Lake. The rain has commenced and I am afraid it will be very disagreeable, however as we are situated now at present apart from each other, it is a life of anxiety and pain. I received your box, but I sold them all as I have recovered from my ill health, and when I am well, I can live on anything– Enclosed you will find 5 dolls, belonging to Romback of our Compy. He wants you to send him- wine, or something good to drink and Tobacco for the rest. When you send it up direct it to me. And go to the Setler {sutler} and see if you can get 10 dollar Bank Bill on some Bank of New Orleans, or Charleston S. C. Bill. Go to Col. Waite and you will get the money, (100) dolls in gold. Answer this immediately, after you receive the money, and Dear Wife take good care of it. Kiss the little one for me, and tell her be a good girl.
From your Husband
"Oliver"


From Eleanor to Oliver (Dictated by Eleanor)

**Fort Myers**
June 4th 1857

Dear Husband,
I Recevied your letter yesterday morning and by it i am glad to hear you are getting better as this leves me very wake {weak} at present   i still have to ly in bed   Dear husband what made me look so well when pendergast was here   the fever was comming on me then. I sent up Boxes wich {which} Contains too {two} bottles of wine  too {two} pounds of tea  one Boxes of lobsters  one boxes of roast beef   It cost me five dollars. Mrs Moonlight is doing my worke as Mrs patterson is Cooking for the band Master   don't say anything to patterson about it  Mereatta is well and in good helth   She is all the time asking when you will be home   Dear husband let us Know when the company is comming down   McSweeny and Broker come here too {two} days ago and three more of D Compy they says **Fort McRae** is an awful place   Dear husband you want Know who rites my letters   sometime Roche and sometimes Mrs Mcintosh  Roche sends his best respects to you.  Rite to me as soon as Possible and let me Know you are getting along   No More at Present
From your Sinceare Wife
M Boizard

**Florida – Seminole Indian War 1855-1857**

From Oliver to Eleanor

**Fort McRae**, Fla
June 1857

My Dear Wife,
I have been speaking to Captain Ireland about you coming to the Company, and he told me that you could come up on these conditions, that he will employ to cook for the officers Mess and Lieut. Hudson told me also, he would like you to wash for him, as he is obliged to send his clothes over the Lake to get washed, They will pay you well. It is a hard matter to get a cook among the men that Knows how to cook well, and Economise. Dear Wife I shall be so glad if your health is good Enough, to start after you get this letter. Enclosed you will find a note to the Quarter master, for your transportation to **Fort Center**, the Captain says you must make your load as light as possible on account of the transportation, be sure to bring all your cooking utensils along, as they are rather scarce here, if you can purchase a Gridiron do so and try to bring 2 Brooms up with you. I think if you have good weather you can come here in 4 days, the only difficulty will be in crossing the Lake, if the weather, should be bad, It has rained for 4 or 5 days consecutively here and this the rainy month, however we will have a place fixed for you by the time, you come up. You might buy yourself and Child shoes and such articles as you stand most in need of – and also try get an umbrella, for yourself it will be good in crossing the Lake, on account of the sun or rain. I hope the Child will not be scared in crossing the Lake. Sergt. Hall who has charge of the Boat, will see that you are as comfortable, as possible. Try to bring my 2 pairs of Cotton Pants if you have not bought the Soldier pants, and also 1 pair Bootees, No. 8 if you can. a few Hickory shirts and Blue Flannel shirts would sell well here, and about 15 lbs of Tobacco. if you can get the transportation, as regards the Provisions they will be furnished out of the Commissary so you wont require much of that, however Cook yourself a ham before you start (you Know best) you will with my help, be able to make some money here, and then we will have the satisfaction of being together. I have been thinking of this for the last 2 weeks, and as soon as I found there were no hope of leaving here, I made the application of getting you to Cook. Should you have anything that you cant bring along, get the quartermaster, to store it for you, and be careful to get somebody to mark all your things with your name on them. I hope you have received the money I sent you by the Paymaster. Dear Eleanor, take Care of it, as we will want if some future day. I know that you are not Extravagant, but every thing is high in the Country. I collected every cent that the men owes you. I got Browns 4 dolls, Normans 75 cts and nobody owes us any thing in the Company. Now I still have a few dollars left, Try to get me a good Bank Bill. Louisiana Money or some good Bill, that is not torn so I can send it to my mother. Tell the Postmaster, to forward your letter when it comes from your sister. take care of the child on your route up here, and May the Lord Bless you and Protect you. I like to forgot bring 2 or 4 lbs of nails some 8 penny and 4 pennys. take things Cooley and all will be right, bring your tent and Poles along. As soon as you can collect what is due you from the Men Why then try to get along as fast as you can. Get somebody to assist you, if Hahesy will pay you that money, for Corpl. McCarthy well and good. Goodby Eleanor for the present
your husband Oliver

Bring a fish line and a dozen large hooks. 6 Boxes of Matches also Don't forget Starch & Blue never Mind about Wash Tubs. Get me if you can 2 sail needles, & a ball Twine You might bring some under shirts, (good ones) Bring something food for yourself, Cordial, Wine & c. If you have my cleaning things, bring them up, a Brick and Brush & Blacking. I am afraid you cant think of all yours & c.
J.O.B.

**Long Distance Love 1855-1870**


From Capt. John H Meland, **Fort McRae** to Capt. W. S. Hancock, Fort Myers

**Fort McRae**, Fla
June 7th 1857

Captain:
The bearer of this, Mrs Boizard, a Laundress in Company "K" wishes to join her husband at this Post. Will you please furnish her with the opportunity to leave **Fort Myers** She wishes to leave some things behind, and will be very glad if you let her store them with the property of my Company.
very Respectfully
Your obdt. Servt..John H Meland
Capt. 4 Arty. For Capt. W. S. Hancock
A.Q.M. *{Army Quarter Master}***Fort Myers**, Fla


From Kate Dow to brother Oliver

Phila.
July 22 1857

Brother Oly,
I received moms letter with the check enclosed on the New Orleans Bank 24 dol 27 cents to be cashed at the broker dear Oly Mom is well and she very thankful for your present and she says when in danger of war the spirit of our father is hovering around you she hopes to live to see you a comfort to your wife and her and our fathers words are true as you are now the support with Lib and me of her Old Age Dear Olly, All we can do for mom is not much as she did for us when we could not for our self I am sorry to hear that Elenor is not well I am scarcely even well myself so I can sympathize with her I think it must be unpleasant where she is as the weather is warm enough let alone the insects of every kind dear Oly if you should go to Utah I hope you will be in no danger and should Elenor come by the way of Phila we shall be pleased to see her and Marietta I think she would be better at Pittsburgh where she is acquainted than where she is if you were to remain it would better for her to stay dear Olly we are all well at present except the great heat and you know how that Prostrates both Cris and I Phineas is well sends his love to Uncle Olly Zarty and family are well Tourisons are as usual Christopher saw John Dinnin Sunday he is well wish to be remembered to you Mr and Mrs Dow and girls Aunt Maggs Coss send her best respects to you Cip Priser and family and all your friends Dear Olly we have lost an old acquaintance Sarah Burn Sarah Evinson was her name I look around and all my friends pass from this world and who will be next Dear Oly, we have hurd no news from Mary Jacob and Libbe are well Jacob look well he is never sick has a constitution he take from mom to think the third day of August mom will be 71 Dear Oly Cris has gone in business for himself has invented a printing press and it is liked by all who see it and will sell very ready after he get a full start it is called the Star Printing press his place is on Charleston Street here is his card and press I thought it would please you so here it is Dear Olly I have no news at present mom sends her love to you and never forgets you in her prayers Libbe sends her love to you all the family Cris says take care of your self Old Cove Phineas Dow is quite Large by this time he is in North **Bonar** Grammar School. Good By from
Sister Kate.

## Nebraska Territory

In the fall of 1857 Oliver's regiment was moved to Fort Leavenworth, Kansas to help with the Indian trouble as well as the Mormon rebellion that was taking place. Eleanor was able to travel with Oliver to Fort Leavenworth.

Oliver's company was stationed at Fort Leavenworth, Kansas, for a year, but in August of 1858, Company K was sent to Fort Kearney in the Nebraska Territory. Eleanor received a letter of recommendation to travel with Oliver to Fort Kearney.

In the summer of 1859, Company K was moved to Fort Ridgely, Minnesota,[9] At that time, Eleanor remained behind at Fort Kearney.

Once Oliver's term of service expired in the fall of 1859, he moved with his family, for a brief time, to a forty-acre plot of land they purchased in Glen Arbor, MI.

---

[9] https://history.army.mil/books/R&H/R&H-4Art.htm

**Long Distance Love 1855-1870**

From Captain of 4 Artillery at Fort Leavenworth

**Fort Leavenworth** KS
May 12th 1858

I Certify that Mrs. Ellen Boizard is a Laundress of Company K 4th Artillery and is therefore Entitled to rations and Quarters.  Mrs. Boizard has drawn rations to include the 20th May 1858.
*{I cannot read the signature}*
Captain 4 Artillery
Commanding Co. K

Approved By order
Col Munroe   L. H Klouze  Adj 4th Arty.


From Kate Dow to brother Oliver

Phila
August 14

Brother Oly
I recieved your leter to Mom dated Augt 4 with a treasury note Enclosed for $20 dollars   Crisse had it cashed   Mom and family are all well   I am very glad you returned to take Eleanor and Marietta with you as it is very lonesome I suppose where she was   I hope you are all well and continue so   I felt very sad to hear you had left for Utah   but Oly there is a God every where to protect you   look to him and he will shield you from your foes   you know Oly thier is something in prayer to our heavenly father   look to him and he will deliver from all that is bad   you are the child of Mary*{ I believe this is a reference to their Catholic faith}*   A prayer poor mom prays three times a day for us all but you and Mary she has spechel *{special}* prayers for you both being absent from us   all the family Enjoy pretty good health mom was 72 third of August she is smart of her age   her sight is very bad and she cant walk so smart as she did   she has a good constitution   Aunt Tourinson fails so mutch you would not know her   She wont last long we all thought she was gone last Thursday   Mr and Mrs Dow and famly are all well   Martha and Sarah send their Respects to you and Eleanor   Zarty is well and Calley and children all well   Calley a large girl and Charly he is the same very roguish   they are very fine looking children   Phin Dow you would not know him he has grown   he is five foot and stout in proportion   he often speaks of you   Phin has bin *{been}* drawing some fruit for Marietta   he has an idea of drawing   the large pears are for Aunt Elenor   give my love to Elenor and kiss Marietta for me   rite soon and as often as you can   by the by I almost forgot   Brother Jacob he is well and looks well and doing as well as can be expected for the hard times   times are hard these few days   and sister Elizabeth you would be surprised to see her   she is well but so thin she is as thin as Calley   she has bin *{been}* very sick but is well at present   she sends her love to you and Elenor and Except *{accept}* both a share of mine   Oly I believe I have told you all   Mrs Copps sends her respects to you and wife   I will leave a space for Criss I believe   good by may the Lord Bless you all
from your Sister
Kate

Phinehas sends his love to you and Aunt Eleanor and kiss Marietta for him.

**Nebraska Territory 1858-1859**

*From Chris Dow to Oliver written on the bottom of Kate's letter.*

My Best Wishes a pleasant time to you and Family.  Good Luck attend you & bring you Safe home in good health.
Your brother
C. C. Dow
write soon



From Kate Dow to brother Oliver

Phila<br>Dec 19 1858

Dear Brother Oly
I have not yet recieved an answer to my last leter   I hope you are all well   Dear Oly how did you like the papers i sent you   we are all well at present but mom   Grief is the cause of her illness   Dear Brother Oly we have lost our only Aunt   she died on the second day of December my Birthday at 6 oclock in the morning   she was concious *{conscious}* of her leaving this world of sorrow and perfectly resigned to go   she asked for us all   she said she would like to see you and Mary before she died   it was a sad sight around her dieing Bed   she was surrounded by many Friends for she had been a mother to any person she knew   she had a very large Funeral   it was attended with 45 carages *{carriages}*   she was taken to the church prayed for and Buried in her lot at St. Mary Cemetery.  Where Uncle Tourison and Cate Garson lays   poor Mack he will go next he is very ill   I believe he has the **dropsey** on the Brain that desease *{disease}* is seldom cuerd *{cured}* if ever   Dear Oly rite as soon as you receive this leter for we all feel ancious *{anxious}* about you   I enclose you Aunt Tourison death in this letter   the famly are all well and send their love to you and Wife   Stephen Tourison asked partickulary *{particularly}* after your health and Famly Also William and wish me to remember them to you in my letter to you   <u>Libe</u> *{Libby}* was up and sends her love to you and Ellenor and Marieta   Mr Lytle will not last long   he grows very feeble   My dear old Friend Mrs Priser Died a month since and I have lost severl *{several}* of my most worthy Friend by <u>Death</u>   this has bin *{been}* a sad year to <u>me</u>   Dear Brother Oly   we have had no news from Mary   I feel sad when I think of her   she usualy *{usually}* rote one a month and it has bin three long years since we have had a word from her   I hope she is living but we all doubt it   but we must not grieve as we must all pass away one by one from this Earth
Dear Oly I beleiv *{believe}* I have told you all that will interest at present   we all send our love to you and famly and mom in particular   Dear old <u>soul</u>   Every day she grows near to us all for we don't know how soon her time may come   she take Aunt death very mutch to heart but seems rather more reconciled   <u>Cris</u> send his love to you and <u>Elenor</u> and the little <u>Pet</u>   <u>Phin</u> Dow you would not know him he grows so fast   I think he will be as tall as <u>his</u> uncle Oly   he is five foot now   that is a large boy for 13 years   is he not   and as good natuerd *{natured}* as a <u>kitten</u>
Mr and Mrs Dow and famly send thier love to you all   Mrs Copps is stoping with me a short time sends her respect to you an famly   and all your friends   A Mrs Dean called sevel *{several}* times to hear from <u>you</u>   she dresses in Black   she say she is an interested Friend of yours   she came from Leavenworth City send her love to you all   <u>is</u> she a Worthy person Oly   Good by Dear Brother Oly   Absent But not forgoten
From your sister
Kate Dow

Dear Oly We all wish you a Mery Christmas and a Happy New Year and May the Blessing from Our Heavenly Father rest upon you and family   I forgot to say Zarty and Brother Jacob are well and Cally and Children   Dear Oly since Aunt Tourison Death I Feel rather bewildered or forgetful

**Long Distance Love 1855-1870**

From Kate Dow to her brother Oliver

Phila.<br>March 27, 1859

Brother Oly,
I recieved your letter of Feb 26th and would have answered before this but there has been bother about the Canada papers that was in Aunt Tourison hands for many years and being as Aunt Tourison is no more   of Course they belong to mom and mom asked for them to keep them as long as she lived and Margareth and Elizabeth refused to give them to mom and insist on keeping them  it has bothered mom considerable   she is the only heir that should hold them   so we have been so full of business that I wanted to rite but could not   they are so obstinate they will not give them up with out going to law about them and we don't want to do that   they want to throw of {off? out?} mom claim   it has annoyed us all very mutch   they think they will realize a fortune thier family alone   I hope they will grow fat on hope for the present   Dear Oly  I am sorry to hear you are so unfortunate in money matters   Cris has lost considerable this winter   we must take the bitter with the sweet   there are a series of Misfortune seems to follow us all but as Chris says it is all for the best   I think the best is now sometimes   there is no use crying after the past we must all hope the future will be better.   Dear Oly, I have nothing new to tell you.   Only I saw John Dinnin last week and told me to tell you he would like to see you once more.   <u>Poor Bus</u>   All the family are well at present and hope you and Elenor and Marietta are well  no news from sister Mary   Libb and Zarty and all the family sends their love to you  the children grow fine   Cally sings like a nightingale   she takes after Aunt May Parkhurst, she looks like   Charly is a singer also   they will make smart children I hope   I was up at Cip Prisers  they all send their respects to you  they all seem like sisters to me and use me sutch    they are all soul people they love little and love long   Dow folk are all well   send their respects to you and family   McNeal is the same he suffers mutch   McLytle grows very feeble   he will leave us shortly for a better world I hope     Mom told me to say to you she won't give up the ship yet   at nite she grows feeble but generally healthy she keep up through every thing considerable  Cris will send you some few paper for to read   I forgot Brother Jake  he is well  old fashion as ever  Li Dow sends his love to you all   he laughed when I told him about Etta   Give my love to Elenor and give Etta a kiss for each of us   Good by rite soon   absent but not forgotten
From your sister
Kate Dow


From Oliver to Eleanor

Fort Ridgeley, Minnesota<br>July 12th 1859

My Dear Eleanor
We arrived her 2 days ago, after a march of 40 days from **Fort Kearny**. We left Sioux City on the 20th of June and Since that time we have Scarcely been dry 24 hours at a time, it happened to be a very rainy Season and that accounts for So much water in the **Sloughs** and Creeks. This Post is a very pretty location and compact. It is Situated on the St Peters River and during this high stage of water the Steam Boats come up here. I hope the River will Keep high until the Middle of September and then I hope I Shall be able to get a furlough for 2 months and I also hope you will be able to Start from **Fort Kearny** at the Same time. I write a letter this afternoon to Mother, as Soon as I finish this, and when we get paid off,  I shall write about the Recording of the deed. My Dear Wife you cant conceive how lonesome I am without you and Etty and **Pinky**, although we have been very busy, since we came her, Cleaning quarters & c.  Company "L" of 2nd arty. is Stationed here at present   the Battery Company and

# Nebraska Territory 1858-1859

the 2 Companies of the 2nd Infy are out trying to make some agreement with the Sioux Indians. I suppose as Soon as the Infantry Companies come in they will march for **Fort Kearny.** There are about 15 women at the Post but most of them will go away with the 2 Compy's of the 2nd Infy. Mrs Fitzgerald and Hoffman are well and Send their love to you, they were heartily tired of the march   everybody dislikes Major Pemberton on the road, he always took us out of the way. Dear Eleanor I hope you have Kept in good health and also my little Etty, poor little thing. I never have a moment's leisure, but I think of her. She is a fine girl and I truly miss her   Tell her to be a good girl and Dada will never forget her. I was just thinking whether you was in the old house yet or not, or whether they had put you in a tent. I hope the Summers heat and your washing will not effect your head, well try Dear and Keep up a good heart, and the Lord will not forsake you. By a General order all the Citizens of the Post are discharged and Soldiers are detailed to work in their places. I am at present doing duty in the Company. Well I don't care much about it for in 2 months I will try to get a furlough. The Recruits for this Post under Lt. Dana have not arrived nor any of our women yet. I believe they went up the Missouri River to **Fort Randall**, and I expect they will have to march across the Country the Same as we did – What dirty clothes I had   I washed them myself, and I found them hard to get clean as they were very much stained with the Swamp mud. I have seen nobody here that I know, and in fact I don't much care about forming new acquaintances, all I think of now is getting off, and joining you and the Girl. Well my Dear Wife I have nothing more to state to you at present, but hope that you and Etty may Keep in good health and Spirits and not be too lonesome   Give my best Respects to the Hospt. Steward and all the Enquiring friends, and also let me Know in your answer how the Sick man is coming on, and whether you still prepare his meals. My best wishes to Serg't Paxson   and Dear Wife and Daughter receive my fervent wishes for your future welfare.
Your Husband
John O. Boizard

Mrs. E.M.Boizard
Laundress of Co. "K" 4th Arty **Fort Kearny**, NT


From Oliver to Eleanor

**Fort Ridgely**, Min.
July 24th 1859

My Dear Wife
Your letter dated the 7th July came to hand 3 hours since, and I hasten to answer it, as the mail leaves tomorrow morning. I received your first letter (Murrays) and it Somewhat Surprised me to hear that he was in the vicinity of Leavenworth. Mrs Fox and Stoneham have arrived. Mrs Fox is quartered in the Capt's quarters and Mrs Stoneham in the tents. Mrs Fox's boy looks big and healthy. I have mounted 2 or 3 guards since I came here but at present I am not quite well having been on the Sick Report for the last 4 days, with a Cold, however awhile I am writing this, I am much better. The Doctor has Kept me in the Hospital, in a day or two I expect to be for duty. I have written you a letter Since I arrived here about the 12th of July. Mrs Fox tells me that she did not see Cleebe or his Wife, but States that Mrs Dwyer has bought Cleebe out, and Mrs Dwyer States that our things are Safe. I hope such is the fact. The 2 Companies of the 2nd Infy and the Battery "E" of the 3rd Art'y. is still out. I found 2 letters Enclosed in your Envelope from Philadelphia and was quite gratified to hear that Mother received 20 Dollars I gave to Capt. Roberts. The other was from My Sister Elizabeth an answer concerning Fury. You Should always read the letters Coming from Philada. to me, if you have not done it. They all Send their love to you and Etty – I am Sorry my Big Dudu has had a Sore head. It is wonder it was not noticed before. I used to See her frequently rubbing her head.

**Long Distance Love 1855-1870**

My Dear Eleanor you tell me that you have plenty of work. I hope you will not overdo yourself, for Health is precious. I have been in very good health Since I left you, until about 8 days ago and Since that time I have Coughed Considerable in the night but now I think in 2 or 3 days I shall be all right   Last mail I Send off the deed to Traverse Michigan for to have it recorded and to pay the first years Tax - I Suppose I will get an answer before I am ready to leave for Leavenworth. The Paymaster has been Expected to come on every Boat, if he does come Shortly, he will pay us off for May and June and then if I can collect what the men owe you, It will pay my expenses. (if the Capt. lets me go) to Leavenworth. This river Saint Peters or Minnesota is falling fast, and by the month of September, Boats will not be able to Come up to **Fort Ridgely** – Consequently, I shall have to desend a great portion of the way by Land, to Saint Paul. The women are all well and Send their respects. Mrs Fitzgerald wishes to be remembered to Mrs Murphy.   Dear Eleanor the time truly hangs heavily. It Sems *{seems}* like a year. Chris, tells me times are dull in Philada. And they hope to See us next November in Philada. But I think their wishes will not be gratified. My Dear Wife, I must Close as I have no more news of any importance. Give my best wishes to the Hospt. Steward and all Enquiring friends, and tell Etty She ought to mind her book and not forget her Spelling or Reading, give her my Embrace, and receive my blessings for your never failing Kindness –
Your  Husband
Oliver

Mrs E.M. Boizard
Laundress of Compy. "K"
4th Arty  Fort Kearny, NT

**Nebraska Territory 1858-1859**

From US Army Paymaster to Oliver

Paymaster's Office  
Detroit, Mich  
November 30<sup>th</sup> 1859

John O Boizard
Late Private 4<sup>th</sup> Regt U.S. Arty

Sir

I enclose for your signature duplicate final statements, upon signing and returning which to this office a draft for the below amount will be transmitted to you. The following is a correct statement of your acc.

| | |
|---|---:|
| Pay from June 30. '59 to Nov. 17.'59   4 mos. 16 d @ $10 per mo. | $45.33 |
| Ret. Do. | $60.00 |
| Due for traveling from Pittsburgh Penn__Fort Ridgely Minn. 1100 m. @ 20 m per day | $20.16 |
| Subsistence for 55 days (as above travelling acc. @ 23c per ration | $12.65 |
| Amt. Due you for clothing | $68.30 |
| Total – | $206.44 |
| Deduct for Asylum 59c    – 59 | |
| | $205.85 |
| Deduct for Ordnance Stores –    .40 | |
| | $205.45 |

Yours Very Respectfully  
(Signed) Sackfield Maclin  
Paymaster US Army

Your furlough & discharge will be returned to you with Draft –

**Long Distance Love 1855-1870**

Research at the Traverse City office of land records revealed that John Oliver Boizard purchased a 40-acre plot of land in 1859. I could not find a plat map of Glen Arbor from that time period, but with the help of Dave Taghon at the Empire Museum, and this 1881 plat map we were able to locate the 40-acre plot of land that the Boizards purchased in 1859. It is marked as a light colored square in the middle of this picture with an arrow. (S/E quarter of the N/W of Sec. 15 in township numbered 28)

It is interesting to note on this 1881 map, that the Fishers owned the land just north of the 40-acre plot owned by the Boizards. It is probable that the Boizards were neighbors with the Fishers in 1859 as well as in 1864 when Eleanor and Marietta purchased a 10-acre plot from him. That 10-acre plot is noted with an arrow on the right side of the picture. It was on the smaller 10-acre piece of land that Eleanor and Marietta built a cabin in 1864.

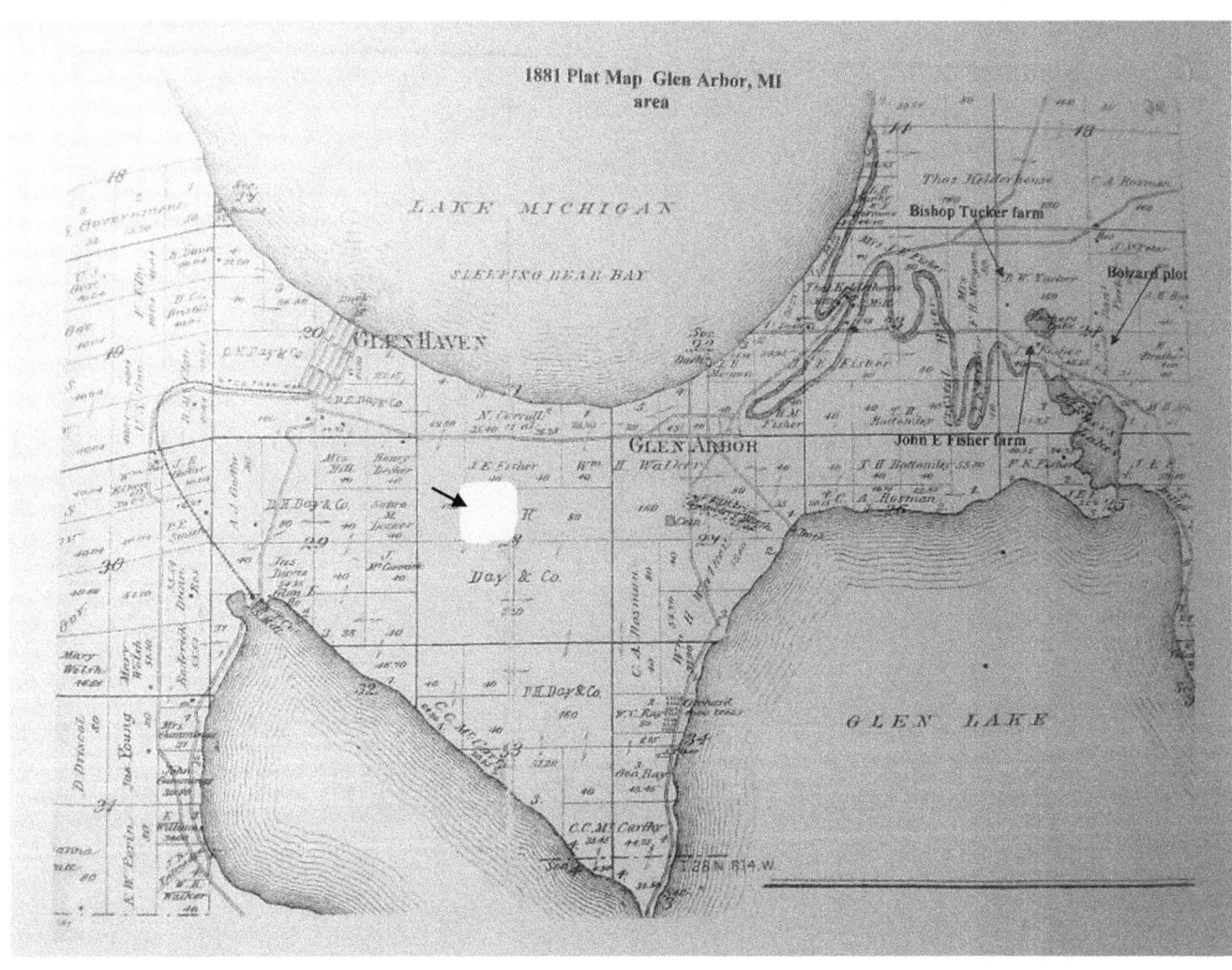

# Newport Barracks, KY
1861-1864

Oliver was discharged from the army in November 1859. Their plan was to move to the forty-acres they purchased in Glen Arbor. It appears like they lived there for ten months. They developed a close friendship with John and Harriet Fisher and other early settlers in Glen Arbor.

On September 6, 1860 Oliver re-enlisted in the army at Newport Barracks, Kentucky. Eleanor and Marietta were able to join him there. The American Civil War began in April of 1861.

Oliver was a clerk, providing general support, probably in the Quartermaster Department.

Oliver & Eleanor were together from 1860-1863 and the only correspondence that we have during those years are letters to the Boizards from the Fishers in Glen Arbor, and from a military family, William and Evelena Brown. The Browns were friends who had been transferred from Newport Barracks to Fort Adams, RI.

The letters written by the Fishers to the Boizards are perhaps the most eloquent of all the letters in the collection. John Fisher was a true patriot and he was a staunch believer in the Union cause. His letters read like passionate speeches against slavery and for the preservation of this great nation.

Oliver was discharged on February 3, 1864. He served only 3 ½ years of his five year enlistment. The Boizards moved to Chicago upon Oliver's discharge.

**Long Distance Love 1855-1870**

From J.E. Fisher to John O. Boizard

Glen Arbor<br>Dec 21<sup>st</sup> 1861

Friend Boziard

The last mail brought your letter, I have not received a letter in a long time which done me as much good as yours.  I had often wondered where you were and what you were doing, now your letter tells me you are in the right place ready and armed to do battle for the old <u>Flag</u> and the existence of our nation. May you deal heavy blows and may the God of battles nerve your right arm; is the prayer of your Friend.  History gives us no parallel to this rebellion and never did rebels deserve the halter more than the rebels of the Seceded States.  I am very thankful I now know where you are as you will be kind enough to keep me posted in relation to matters and things pertaining to the war in your vicinity.

   Now for matters here, Mr. Goffart lives up west of Town about two miles, near Mr. McCarteys.  He has **preempted** forty acres, they are well  two of their children go to school.  Mr & Mrs McCarty are well  they with us were pleased to hear from you   they wish me to present their compliments.  Mr. Dorseys, Tuckers, Rays, in fact all the old neighbors were glad to hear from you.  they send their respects to you and to Mrs. Boizard.  There has been some changes in affairs and business since you was here.  The N T line of Propellers have called here regularly all summer, on an average of one a day for the season.  it has made good times  every body is busy.  there has been a large immigration here this past season.  Families are now living near your old place   Some are settled three or four miles back from the Lake.  I am keeping the Saw Mill busy.  next summer more are coming to Settle  we have had a good School for the past year, and this fall a preacher moved into town and preaches to the sinners, weekly or <u>weakly</u>.  So you see we are coming up.  As I told you we would.  I am writing this letter lying on my back afflicted as was poor Job of old; sore boils from the soles of my feet so up along.

   You did not mention to what Regiment you belonged, please do so in your next, also the names of your Com. Officer and Adjutant so if you move I can get a letter to you   And Dear Friend know this that the Prayers, heartfelt earnest prayers, of every lover of his country are continually offered to Heaven for your preservation and the success of your arm.  Mrs. Fisher wanted to write some in this letter to Mrs. Boizard but I have filled it up.  we both and our Boys send our Love and Friendship to you both   write me old Friend.
Yours Truly,
J. E. Fisher

I shall write again next mail.


From John E. Fisher to Oliver

Glen Arbor<br>Jan 2<sup>nd</sup> '62

Friend Boizard
I sent you a letter last Mail and now I am going to have Uncle Sam carry you another and by the way I love that same old Uncle Sam.  my earliest recollections of reading was how he whipped his Dad (Old England) and told him to his face that he was of age and intended to Set up Housekeeping on his own account and that how he grew, prospered and multiplied till the nations of the World call him the Great Modele Republic  and with our own eyes we have Seen him fostering care for and protecting his children far more than any other National Parent in the whole world – Then with what regret, grief and anger it is to us to See a portion of his Family attempt to take his life, virtually to enact the Savage custom to draw and quarter him.  How often it is that the History of Families, we have often Seen the favored Son or Daughter in a family the very one that gives the Parent the most trouble   So with our

Nation the government has paid more of its means, given more of its appointments, more of its patronage in fact that portion of the Nation now in Rebellion has itself administered the government for four fifths of the time since we commenced our national existence. So they had but to help themselves to all they wanted and they did.

Now Friend Boizard when I think over all these things and many more connected with the history of our government my blood boils with anger while a deep, deep grief burdens my mind to think that so large a portion of our People Should be so ungrateful as to attempt to destroy tear down and annihilate so good a government.

And now Friend B I have preached this little sermon it will do for this letter I shall write you next mail. you recollect our mails come and go but once in two weeks, so it will take a month maybe more to Send a letter & get an answer. Write at your earliest opportunity – give my best regards to Mrs Boizard and your little Daughter and for your-self I feel a deep and earnest Solicitude that the God of Battles will preserve you and those with you till this Rebellion is crushed, and History Shall engrave your names on its brightest page and millions, aye, millions on millions shall point to that page, and Say, there are the names of the Preservers of the Great Republic.
Yours truly J.E. Fisher

J.O. Boizard Sergt. Mj.


From John E. & Harriet M. Fisher to Oliver

Glen Arbor
Jan 31st 62

Friends Mr & Mrs Boizard
This weeks mail brought us a letter from you for which accept our earnest thanks. Mr Fisher was quite sick when he answered your first letter and has been ailing, since. some of the time obliged to keep to his room. and our Lounge can testify, to his companionship. (You know what disease he suffered when you was here.) so he has appointed me his Secretary, Pro Tem. We have had beautiful weather thus far, snow now about eighteen inches in the woods, not as deep near the shore. no ice as yet on Lake Michigan. Glen Lake is covered with ice. Business is quite lively in fact the road past our House is quite a thorough fare Horse and Ox teams passing daily with cord wood & c. Mr Oliver has **Preempted** and moved on to a piece of Land near the new Dock (Mr Fisher spoke of it in a former letter) which is about four miles north of here there is quite a settlement in there. I believe they are well. Mrs Oliver had a little Daughter about a year ago. The people of your acquaintance here are well, except Mrs Dorsey and the bright eyes of her little three day old Boy will I think affect her recovery.

We had two hired men cutting and drawing saw logs the mill is not running and probably will not, untill warmer weather you have I think ere this received our second letter in which I told all the news, and as our place does not improve much in Winter I have but little to write this time. News reaches us that England is ripe for a broil with us that Canada is arming and that we are on the Eve of a terrible struggle, will it be that the God of Freedom will forsake us – I think not, while her sons and Daughters, aye her Daughters too are willing to do Battle for Right. Mr Fisher had concluded our news Paper news was very imperfect, we would be very, greatfull for all information it is agreable for you to give us, in fact the neighbors as well as ourselves Hail a letter from Mr Boizard as a god send in the way of news for that we all know is reliable. The Boys attend school, they also attended a Dance last Evening, they think they are almost men, they are very anxious we should let them attend a Dancing school that is to commence next week. we have not decided yet. they send their love to Etty. Mons. Goffarts is greatfull for your kind remembrance of them. Mr & Mrs McCarty send their best regards to you both – Now Mr & Mrs Boizard at your earliest convenience we shall be most happy to receive an answer,
yours with lasting Friendship
J. E. & H. M. Fisher

**Long Distance Love 1855-1870**

<u>To Oliver</u>

Treasury Department,
Second Auditor's Office
Sept 8<sup>th</sup> 1862

To: S Burbank
Lt. Col. 13<sup>th</sup> Inft. Comm.
at **Newport Barracks** KY

Sir:

The application in the cases of, Sundry Laundress enclosed inqs form of Aug 20<sup>th</sup> as per statement List Subjoined, has been received. It appears to be correct, and will be audited as soon as reached its turn, and the result communicated to you.
Very respectfully,
Your obedient servant,
Ezra B. French, Auditor

| | |
|---|---|
| Claim of E.M Boizard – against John Kendrick - Boch 8<sup>th</sup> Reg. US Infty– | $3.25 |
| Margaret Ostermayer– Sundry Soldier same Co – | $10.10 |
| Priscilla Michaels – — — — — | 7.50 |
| Hanny Tagier – Rudolf Howard " " | 4– |
| Augusta Hammerle Sundry Soldier " " | 17.10 |
| | |
| Carolina Greible – " " " " | 8.75 |
| Mary Leary – " " " " | 17.75 |
| Selina W. Holt " " " " | 7.25 |
| Mary Swady Charles Butt " " | 3– |
| Johanna Pfarromiller Sundry Soldier " " | 35.20 |
| Katharine Lang " " " " | 10.50 |
| – Buehl " " " " | 21.75 |

**Newport Barracks, Kentucky 1860-1864**

From William Brown to Oliver Boizard

Fort Adams RI
June 1st 1863

Dear Oley,
I take the pleasure to write you a few lines to inform you that we are all well and we hope that these few may find and your family enjoying the same blessing. You must excuse me for not writing before but I was waiting to hear wether we would be ordered out or not. We had orders to leave about two weeks ago, but they was countermand  we have Col. Sheperd for our Col now   things goes on better than they did before  Col. Sanderson is order out but where to we don't know.
My wife says she is glad to hear that Mrs. Boyzard is better. She says she expects her sickness while full in to her arms  it is about time you do something for your self  we have no news but plenty of hard work  we wash for 40 men and 3 officers   we have about 20 men on recruiting service but no recruits coming in yet   Neley and Saly sends their Love to Mary Etta and wishes to see her   my Wife sends her love to you all and so do I   give our respects to all inquiring friends  and we hope to hear from you soon   no More at present.
From your Effecinate Friend,
William Brown
Principal Musician 15th infy


From Harriet M. Fisher to Oliver & Eleanor

Glen Arbor
July 6th 63

Dear Friends Mr. & Mrs. Boizard
We received your ever welcome letter a few mails since pardon us for not sooner answering it we are very sorry to hear of Mrs Boizards ill health   I really think the climate of Glen Arbor would restore her and I should very much like her for a neighbor again   you would be really surprised to see how our country has improved since you left. there is no government Land in our Town   all has been taken and mostly by actual settlers. crops are looking very well.  we are living up on our farm   moved here last fall, as our sawyer lives at the mill  it makes quite a long walk for Mr Fisher morning & evening and his health is not very good, but our fruit trees and things were being destroyed and needed the care of the owner so we moved on to the farm
My Brother C C McCarty is keeping a Hotell in Town, has built a little way from the Glen Lake road but a short distance from the Dock, has considerable custom   there are so many Land lookers and families moving in. there were forty couples at the Fourth of July Ball held at his house. All of your acquaintances here are well and very much pleased to hear from you. we have a weekly mail. – Our peach trees are loaded with peaches   we shall probably have six or Eight bushels.  Mr. Barret will probably have 25 or 30 bushels of apples on his farm  he has been offered 1000 dollars for his place.  quite a number have enlisted from here 13, I think so you see Glen Arbor has contributed her share towards putting down this rebellion and what a terible war it is. So many lives lost   I wish it would end but not untill the South are whiped. *{whipped}* I have no patience with them or those that sympathise with them   it really seems to me, as though our Generals have been too afraid of hurting somebody, while the South were fighting to kill, we have been afraid of hurting our Brethren, but I think they ought to be delt *{dealt}* with like enemies for they are, and of the worst kind. I always considered family fights the very worst, and what is this, but a family fight, if I was a man I would see what I could do. I see by the papers Gen. Mead has taken Gen. Hookers place, what is the trouble with the Gen's. that they are so often changed.  are they not competent, or are they considered not trusty  or is it politics as some charge. I hope the right man will be found and soon to.   what is your

opinion about England & France taking sides against us. I think they would be glad to see us divided but I hardly think they will come out openly in favor of the South unless she frees her slaves, as both those foreign powers boast of being enemies to Slavery, but if they come we will be enough for them, crippled as we are. for if necessary a woman can carry a gun and use it too, so I think we might raise quite an army. now don't laugh at the idea for I am seriously in earnest   Charly say if the war lasts untill he is old enough he shall go –

July 24th You see by the first part of my letter it is sometime since I commenced it   the truth is I have so little time for anything but work   I have eight & nine in my family and a girl only thirteen to help me   I am from necessity compelled to work and that pretty industriously too

Well Miss Etta I intended my boys should answer your nice little letter but they are both at work so I will   I think you are improving nicely in writing. Charly & Franky I presume you remember, they do you, and if you was here would like to take you to the Parties with them. they both attended a dance on the fourth of July and each took a little girl. they had a nice time, Charly is nearly as tall as I am   do you grow as fast as that. I am sorry your ma is unwell, you must be very kind to her   when she leaves you as my mother did me this winter, we shall think of every naughty thing we ever did with sorrow   your ma may think best to come here   we should all be very glad to have you. I hope you will write agin soon. we often speak of you   do not think you are forgotten by us because we do not oftener write   I will tell you how Mr Fisher works and then you can see for yourself   to begin with his health is not very good   he gets up at four in the morning, goes down to the Mill before breakfast to oversee affairs sometimes comes back to his breakfast but oftener I send it to him   generally is not at home untill dark   then he is very tired Sundays. I say 'now do write to Mr Boizard'  'I will'   he says 'as soon as my head feels clear, but I must lie down and rest first I am so tired and I have writing I must do'   he is the Judge of Probate for this Co. & Town Supervisor besides Justice of the Peace and School Trustee so you see his hands are full, but I am in hopes he wont take any of those offices again   then he will have more time to write to our friends.   but do write often and I will answer your letters

My father is living with us   Father & Mother came here last fall, and it pleased the ruling power to take my mother from us. she died the thirteenth of last April, after a long and painfull sickness. Father is 75 years of age and very much broken down.

We are having such grand victories now we hope the war may soon close   they are trying to raise two more Regts. in the northern part of Mich. A Mr Brooks speaks in town Saturday Evening. war of course is the subject and to raise volunteers the object of the meeting. if ladies are allowed to, I shall attend. I hope you will write soon   our best love and wishes to your ma and accept the very best wishes for yourself

from your sincere Friends

J. E. & Harriet M Fisher


the boys do not go to school this summer, they will next winter, they have to work for their Father   we have so much to do   I think I will send this letter by a boat it will reach you sooner   give my very best love to your ma and accept the very best wishes for yourself from your friend

Harriet M.Fisher


To Miss Etta Boizard

**Newport Barracks, Kentucky 1860-1864**

From John E. Fisher to Oliver Boizard

*There is no date on this letter but from the events mentioned in this letter it can be assumed that this letter was written in the late summer/fall of 1863*

Friend Boizard

Since I wrote you last the Union Cause has made a great progress, the taking of Vicksburg and the tightening of the **Anaconda folds** of the Union power, gives promise that treason is about soon to find that ditch of which the man Stealers and women whippers of **Secessia** have told so much   if down in the depths of the lowest hell there is still a lower hell then possibly those who have tried to destroy this only free government may there find a punishment Suitable to their crime.  to think of the Hundreds of thousands of lives lost and the untold suffering endured, the Widows and orphans made – causes us to curse the instigators of this rebellion.  at the same time we are thankful that their crime has developed such a noble class of defenders of Freedom.  Freedom to All.  ALL not a part of the people.  it is a truth well known to all who have observed that where Slavery exists at all,  it to a certain degree enslaves the whole, it demoralizes the whole, but thank God the people of this land are  beginning to see the value of full and unrestricted freedom and though the lesson is costing dear, very dear, yet I presume we could not have learned at any other School.   J.E. Fisher

**Long Distance Love 1855-1870**

Bill from the US Post Office to Sgt. Boizard

Post Office Newport KY
October 8th 1863

U.S. Barracks
To Newport Post office

For Postage during the months July, August, September '63     $8.13

Sgt. Boizard
Dear Sir– Above you will find the Barracks Postal account for the past Quarter. He cannot take the time as heretofore to copy the names of parties getting letters. They are in the office and subjection to your inspection.
Respectfully,
Mr. Andrews
P.M. {Postmaster} Thursday Morning Oct 8/63

*Added to the bottom of this letter in J. Oliver Boizard's handwriting is the following note*:

Paid $8.15 on the 9th of October '63


From Didier A Fermet to Oliver

Corinth
October 17, 1863

My dear friend Boizard,
I would tell you that a lot of things have happened since we left each other. Luck has not been on our side in our music since we left. In leaving {?} caught a rheumatism in his legs and has not been able to play since we left Newport. Sergeant Pertz is pretty sick as well. I thought we would be coming back to Newport, going by Wisburg {Vicksburg?} we got the musician George of Iver in the beat. After staying a while at Wisburg {Vicksburg} we left for Memphis where we stayed 8 days and then left for Corinth but bad luck had it that we had a battle for four hours. We lost a good amount of men but were victorious. We got a musician prisoner, his name is Frederick, and the two horns captured by the enemy. We must leave tomorrow and maybe within a few days we will have a big battle. I have nothing else new to say, since you must know more than me. Sorry if I didn't write sooner because I myself was very sick but thank God I am fine now. Excuse me for writing with a pencil but it is not easy to write in the camp. I will be happy to hear your news and what is new in Newport. I wish to return as soon as possible. I am anxious to hear your response. Write in English, I can read it perfectly. Give my compliments to the young ladies of the Barracks. I extend to you the hand of friendship and hope to see you soon.
Didier A Fermet
Musician of the 13th U.S.

*{This letter was written in French and translated for me by Josh Filler.}*

**Newport Barracks, Kentucky 1860-1864**

From Mrs. Brown to Eleanor & Ettie

Fort Adams RI
Oct 21st 1863

Dear Friend,
I received your kind letter and was glad to hear that you and your mother and Father was well and I hope this will find you all in good health as they leaves us at present. I thought you all had forgotten us. Tell Oley if he would forget his bottle as easy as he does his old friends it would be a good thing for him. Elen says she is sorry that your doll was wounded but she has had a dozen killed since she seen you. Harry is a big boy and talk and run all over the Fort and the baby, is as fat as a pig. We have no news here only plenty of hard work. Tell Oley, that Brown is going to reenlist for 5 years more. Give our respects to Bridges and all inquiring friends. We May be down about Christmas. No more at present but remains your Efficinate friend till death
write soon
Evelena Brown

*There is a lot of extra paper at the end of this letter and written on those empty lines in very 'young' writing is the following note, probably written by Marietta as she practiced her writing skills. Marietta would have been 11 years old at this time.*

Dear Mother
I am writing you a note   how are you I am well and I hope that you are the same   I had to write a letter for school and i did so   but no dictated it for me.   To E.M Boizard   Newport KY


From John E. Fisher to Oliver

Glen Arbor
Nov 5th /63

Dear Friend Boisard
you are thinking I am not useing you well in not ans'g your letters but if I do not write it is not because I do not think of you, no, we often think of you and your Family and wish it was in our power to See and have one good familiar chat with you all.  I have to work as hard as my poor Strength will bear. when I come into the House I am so tired I have not the energy to write. my health is improving I am better this fall than I have been for the past two years, and am quite free from pain.
I was talking with Mr Goffart about your wanting a few acres and he said he would Spare you ten or twelve acres, at gov't price.  He owns and lives about two & a half miles west of town and is doing well. his land is good, it is the nearest place that I could find where you could buy a piece of good land cheap, if you should like to have Mrs. Boizard come here I will See that She has some place to go into. there is also about 44 of government land adjoining the piece you can get of Goffart but it is marsh and is only good for grass, yet I would advise you to buy it if you buy of Goffart. if you Should not want the whole of the 44 acres I would be glad to join you and buy half of it. the country has filled up verry fast the past Season. it is verry different from what it was when you was here  it is much more like an old country. Mr Dorseys - McCartys, Rays, and all of your acquaintance here are well. Mrs Fisher and the Boys join me in Sending our best respects to yourself Mrs Boizard and Etta and believe us always your friends and well wishers.
 J.E. Fisher

**Long Distance Love 1855-1870**


From William Brown to Oliver

Fort Adams RI<br>Jany 17<sup>th</sup> 64

Dear Oly

I now take the pleasuer to write you a few lines to informe you that we are all well and I hope that this few lines will find you and your family enjoying the same   I wrote to you the 20<sup>th</sup> Dec to let you know that we could not come to see you by Chrismas on acount of the weather being so cold but you may look for us when the weather gets warm   tell MarryEtta that we wont forget her shells   please tell Mrs Smith that we have wrote two letters to her and has received no answer to ether *{either}* of them   I hope you had a merry chrismas at Newport   we had a big diner *{dinner}* hour and plenty of Egg Nog and Lauger *{**Lager**}* Beer   tell Marry Etta that we named the baby Malisa it was a favarit name of the grandmothers   she is four months old and she weighs 16 lbs and can sit alone   tell Marry Etta that when my Wife can go to town She may look for her chrismas gift   Nely and Saly sends their Love to you all and Shoney is the bigest rowdy in the crowd   Dear Oly please to do me the favor to ask Col. Sanderson if he knows any thing about the wash Bills that was against Elev of the 2<sup>nd</sup> Bat.   they was put in hands to Colect and *{he}* Colected the Sutters *{**sutlers**}* Bills and let the wash Bill lay   I understand that they are laying at the auditor office and I think that it is his place to see to it   that is about all I have to say   give our respects to all enquiring friends and the same for yourself   Write Soon   I remain yours for ever
Wm Brown
Pr Musian 15<sup>th</sup> Infy.


From Wm Brown & Evelena Brown to Eleanor & Marietta

Fort Adams RI<br>Jan 22<sup>nd</sup> 1864

Dear Friends
We received your kind and welcom letter and we was glad to hear that you was all in good health as this leaves us at present only my Wife has a **felon** on her hand and she aint able to do mutch Dear Friends I am very sorry you was so lonesom on Christmas   but I hope you had a happy New Year   my Wife would like very well to be with you

when you write again please let us know what kind of place it is for a Baker or any sort of work and if there is a place near yours   we will buy it so we can be nabors *{neighbors}*   Santa Claus com to see the children Christmas and New Years both Neley and Saley wants to see MarryEtta   the next time I write I will send you our potagraphs. *{photographs}*   when you write to your Father Please send him our best respects and the same to you all we have no news worth writing   I hope to hear from you soon   we remains yours forever.
Wm Brown
Evelena Brown

**Newport Barracks, Kentucky 1860-1864**

<u>From Didier A Fermet to Oliver</u>

Huntsville, AL<br>February 28, 1864

My dear friend,

Excuse me if I am slow to write but I am so greatly busy that I could not answer your letter. I am in good health and desire that this letter find you the same way. I cannot tell you anything about the war but you can rather hear about me. We cannot see anything from where we are, the town is very pretty but there is no pleasure. The women behave extravagantly and don't like soldiers like us but this is not worth Newport. I have heard that we are returning to Newport and if we return I will tell you what intentions are. At this moment I am working so that when I get to Newport I will choose myself a little wife and get married, make a home for myself and a family and make some money. I think it is the best way to secure a job for myself. Please inform me if I really have to do five years of military service or only three. You know I enlisted for five years and some of the officers are saying that an order of congress in Washington announced that those enlisted for 5 years only have to do 3. Please inform yourself because I would wish to be able to cut two years off but I need to at least be sure. Mr. Clark compliments you and your family. All our musicians are well and compliment you as well. Our Sargent William Besse passes his complements as well as his wife's. Give a friend's handshake to the young ladies that I know and tell them I wait impatiently to get back to Newport and choose which one I want to marry. If you can embrace them for me. I have nothing else to say. I shake your hand friendly,

Didier A Fermet  Musician of the 15th

Excuse my writing but I am tired and I have a heavy hand.

*{This letter was written in French and was translated for me by Josh Filler.}*

**Long Distance Love 1855-1870**

## The Chicago & Glen Arbor Years
## February 1864 - November 1870

Oliver received a discharge from the U.S. Army on February 3, 1864. This was a year and seven months earlier than his original enlistment period. An order from Congress allowed men who had enlisted for five years to be discharged after serving three years if they desired. It appears that Oliver took advantage of that opportunity.

Upon leaving the Army, Oliver moved with his family to Chicago, Illinois and was able to find employment as a clerk with the US Mustering and Disbursing Office. Oliver was a civilian employee at this job. He was responsible to provide his own housing. Within a few months of arriving in Chicago, Eleanor & Marietta took a boat and moved to Glen Arbor. Eleanor had recurring headaches and bouts with a poor heart and those health conditions may have contributed to their decision to move to Glen Arbor and leave Oliver behind in Chicago.

From 1864 until 1870, when Oliver died, the Boizards communicated mostly by letters. There were occasional visits to Glen Arbor by Oliver; and during the winter of 1867-68, Eleanor and Marietta moved to Chicago to be with him.

During the period of 1864-1870 we are introduced to William and Eliza Bridges and their daughter Emma. After the Boizards moved from Newport Barracks, the friendship between these families continued through correspondence. Marietta and Emma formed an especially close and sweet friendship as young girls and they remained friends through the years.

In 1866, Emma Bridges married Edwin Brown, a soldier in the Army. There are several photographs of Emma and Edwin in a family photo album and one of the pictures has a handwritten note on it that says, "Married cousin of Eleanor." Research into the possibility of Eleanor being related to Emma and the Bridges family is being conducted, but to date, a family connection has not been discovered. Unfortunately, one of the pictures also has the notation that Emma and Edwin were killed by Indians on their way to California. Edwin and Emma appear in the 1880 Federal Census, living near Fort Worth, Texas. So, their deaths would have occurred sometime after 1880.

Austin Newman is another person that we are introduced to during these Glen Arbor years. Austin served in the Civil war and it appears like this friendship was also made while stationed at **Newport Barracks**. He was a single man and visited the Boizard family frequently. He seemed to have an interest in Marietta; he was sixteen years older than her.

Marietta was 14 years old, when she and Charlie Fisher began to take a special interest in each other and started corresponding. During the winter of 1867-1868, when Marietta and her mother moved to Chicago to be with Oliver there were many letters exchanged between Marietta and Charlie. They were married on January 19, 1870; Marietta was 17 and Charlie was 21.

The last letter received from Oliver was November 7, 1870. He died later that month. It is believed that he died in Chicago.

# Chicago and Glen Arbor 1864-1870

From E.J. Bridges to Eleanor

Newport KY
March 11, 1864

Dear friends,
we received your letter today we were all glad to hear from you that you arrived safe there   we are all well at the present   we got your photograph and i give them Mrs. Johnson and Mrs. Jones.  there has been some changes here   a order came to send some men away   in the order they named the men, oscar, harry, with several others too numerous to mention   we were very sorry to hear that you had a cold and hope that you will get over it soon   poor picket is gone at last   he died last night at 1 o clock   Mrs Alberty moved into your house without ever cleaning   she just swept out and put down her carpet.   you did not tell us where to write so i did not no {know} what to do about senden you your money   it has been payday here and all the men that owed you paid my father, but one   and he was not paid off   Jack doran and Mcloney were transferred to their old regiment the fourth artilery.   sergent devere took them there   Mr Johnson took the others   Emma is sleeping with Mrs. Johnson every night   it was reported around that Mr. Boizard was in newport.   hanigar said he seen him up at rits and spoke to him   no more at present but rite soon, yours truly,
 E. J. Bridges


From Emma Bridges to Marietta

Dear Etta,
lets have a little chat   sarah Maryan Jiny tomy is all well but we missed you from amonst us   we were all lonesome on sunday   i went to church with Sarah    mother went to sleep on the chair   Mrs devere came up in the afternoon a little while   oscar newman give me something for you   i would not send it this time for fear you would not be there to get it   he went down to the boat and got yours and paid a quarter for it and got 6 of his own   he gave me one and gave me one for you the day he was a going away   he had  great times running in and out giving us all little things   he gave jiny, a bucet *{bucket or bouquet}* and a box of butons *{buttons}* and a botel *{bottle}*   he gave Maryan a box of butons *{buttons}*   he gave me a pertfoalia *{portfolio}* full of writing paper   tomy said for me to write about him a running a way and cetching *{catching}* whiping *{whipping}* poor oscar   tommy is teling me what to say in my leter   i must stop now as it is time for me to quit   it is 9 oclock and i must go down to Mrs. Johnsons   no more at present   answer my leter as soon as you get this   yours forever
 E. Bridges


From Wm. Bridges to Oliver

Newport, KY
March 24th 1864

Dear Friend
I lift my pen to drop you a few lines.   hoping and trusting thay may find your self and famley enjoying the verry best of health by the blessing of god our heavenley father--
Bus -- I had a verry hard spell of it.   for about ten days -- all hopes of men were given up and dispared of -- I trust to god it may never be my lot to pass through such an ordeal again.   I supose you guess what was the matter   I have

**Long Distance Love 1855-1870**

onley bin *{been}* out ove *{of}* the Hosptel 3 days and am not well yet -- I succeeded in collecting $2.75 cts of your bill which you will pleas find enclosed  one man received no pay -- now for sum *{some}* nuse *{news}*  the Depo *{depot}* is broken up & the P.P. & Band ordered to **Governors Island** we leave on Sunday week the 3$^{rd}$ of April. Eliza goes a long sum *{some}* two of the other famleys   Gallagher was discharged & enlisted again   farewell to Newport Ky. and old senss *{sins}* -- My *{?}* tens *{?}* due sume *{some or soon?}* to come forth and pay up
Wm Bridges


Etties Letter of the 20$^{th}$ was received   Eliza happy to hear that Mrs Boizard had recovered from her cold   the hole *{whole}* famley was hapy to hear that you were all well as this leaves them that these few lines may find you in the continuation of the same favored blessing   glad to hear that you had gained employment we have bin *{been}* successful in selling off our furnature   Tommy is a bad boy he wont keep still while I write but sends his love to Ettie & Mrs Ard--  I dont know ov *{of}* any thing more to say at this time   more next time   we all join send our love and best wishes to you all   wish you were her *{here}* to go a long   answer this soon in order that we may hear from you before we leave   I remain yours for ever  Wm Bridges


From Emma Bridges to Marietta

March 1864

dear Eta,

i take the pleasure to write you a few lines to let you know that i am well and  hope that you are the same   when oscar newman went away he left his photograph for me to send to you   you will find it enclosed in here and he bought one of yours and paid a quarter for it   he said for you to write to him   i cannot give you that until he writes   sarah does not know that we heard from you this time   for we had to get supper and we sat down to answer   i am sory that you are not here to go with us   my cousin is spending the night with us   Jiny was up there two nights   i was not up there yet   we are a going take diner with my aunt on sunday and then we are all a going down to Mrs. Johnson on friday evening and stay till sunday evening and then we will start for the depot   this is all at present write before we leave.  yours forever  emma bridges.


From Eleanor and Marietta to Oliver (Written by Marietta)

Glen Arbor, Michigan
Tuesday May the 10$^{th}$ 1864

Dear Papa

I take the pleasure to let you know that we are well and hope that you are the same   we did not get here until Saturday morning we laid at milwakee all day   the boat run about two hours and then laid up the rest of the night at a wood yard.  we were very sea sick.  we ate breakfast and dinner at Dorseys and then we went to Fishers and staid there until Monday morning   we live in the house at the mill.  we don't know wether it will be two or three dollars a month for rent   it cost us three dollars for to get our things into the house.  we have been hard at work cleaning house.  they was glad to see us.  potatoes is a dollar a bushel.  when you get my shoes made   get them with pegs in because the sand cuts the sewed ones.  we think that the place has improved much since we was here before   we don't see anybody here but has strange faces   we have not seen of the old neighbors yet.  will you send us the

ledger the last number was eleven and the next one is twelve  you might send us the daily paper as the war news is acceptable  Fisher got the paper you sent him  no more at present as it just now struck 10 oclock and we are sleepy and tired  We Remain Yours Truly
Eleanor M Boizard
Marietta Boizard


From Oliver to Eleanor

Chicago<br>May 18<sup>th</sup>, 1864

My Dear Wife,
Your welcomed letter came to hand this morning with the Detroit Post Mark on it. It has been 7 days on the road. I felt somewhat uneasy about you, I though you might be sick. I send this by the Propeller "**City of New York**" and also Etty's shoes. They cost $2.75. I send you also a music box, which I received from the Post Office. No letter came with it. I suppose it came from Austin Newman. I bought at Auction 2 packages of Soap, I send you one, with the shoes. I am very busy in making out Muster Rolls, the Capt. Has employed one more clerk. (5 in all). I am boarding at Pfeiffer's. I sleep by myself, there are 2 others sleeps in the same room. About the beginning of next month I will try to send you some Mackrel.  There has been terrible Fightings between the Two Armies, and I suppose they will fight terribly at the taking of the Rebel Capitol (Richmond)  You state that Potatoes are $1.00 per bushel, I hope you will content yourself and keep your health. After you get fixed let me know how you get along and the price of articles such as you use about the house. Also let me know how you can secure yourself a homestead. Tell Fisher I will send him the news of the Big fights. I suppose by this time you have seen many of the neighbors and you might answer this letter on the first propeller. Well Ellen, I will close for it is time to go to work. Give my best respects to Mrs. Fisher, Dorsey and all enquiring friends, not forgetting Mr Goffart & family. Truly yours, your husband,
"Oliver"

Tell me how the house looks after its fixed and about the stove. JO

Kiss "Moll the Madd" for me, She is 12 years old today
I found your pictures in my stockings, best I have seen.
(Note) Write soon. How is Dick   J.O.B



From Eleanor & Marietta to Oliver (Written by Marietta)

Glen Arbor, Michigan<br>Saturday 21, 1864

Dear Papa,
We received your letter and was glad to hear that you was well as this leaves us the same.  I got my shoes and they was most to small me but I can just wear them  we got the papers and was glad to get the ledger as we have nothing much to read here  you wished to know how the house looked  it looks very well but it looks empty  momma says you had better send her a table and an oil cloth instead of fish  a good one for the things that we got from that man is a coming apart  momma wants you to send in some barley and wheat as a substitute of coffee and some teller

## Long Distance Love 1855-1870

stamps   also a small jar of lard   we was up to Goffarts and he has a fine place he has about six acres cleared   Alix is here and is married to that Irish woman the one he used to go and see and he has two children and he also has a place on the homestead bill   but mama spoke to Mr. Fisher and he said that you would have to come and see about it yourself   you would have to go the land office yourself and that you would have to pay about 14 or 15 Dollars and it would be about 5 or 6 miles away   mama thinks that we had better buy a few acres of land   be as saving as you can because if mama has the money to pay for it right down she thinks that she might get it cheaper   we had not much time to look about yet   you wished to know how much the things are here   flour is nine dollars a barrel and tea is $2.00 and $2.50 a pound and it is not as good as that we brought   and for the worst brown sugar they ask twenty two cents a pound   eggs is twenty five cents a dozen   pork is 15 cents a pound   there is no school here there is no teacher here   they are looking for one   there is not hardly a boat but that they bring more settlers   Mr. Fisher says that when you have any papers   for you not to tear them up for to send them by the boat   Mama says for you to send them to us   Goffart's sends their love to you   we can get fresh white fish here for 10 cents a piece when you write send the things in care of Mr Dorsey for he is always there   the stove is as big as ever only it wants a length and an elbow   we can do without it until you come up   no more at present but remaining yours   truly yours forever Oh we forgot Dickey he sings as loud as ever   he was on a visit for a week to Mrs. Fishers.

Mrs. Eleanor M Boizard (mama says do not laugh at her name) *{Eleanor had signed her own name in a very childish script.}*

Miss Etty Boizard.

*{There were three columns of figures on the back side of the letter.}*

| Table  | 8.00 | 15.75 old w   | 74.25 |
|---|---|---|---|
| Glue   | 0.25 | 2.50 coat     | 37.25 |
| Lard   | 2.00 | 2.00 (?)      | 37.00 |
| Box    | 0.25 | 14.00 board   |       |
| **Pomatum** | 1.00 | 2.00 washing |       |
| Wheat  | 0.50 | 36.25         |       |
| Oil cloth | 1.50 | 1.00 stamps |       |
| Freight | 2.00 | 37.25        |       |
|        | 15.75 |              |       |

From Eleanor Boizard to the Land Office

Glen Arbor Michigan<br>Monday 23<sup>rd</sup> 1864

Dear Sir

I take the pleasure to ask you to let me have the southeastern part of north east quarter from sexion 30 township 29 arrange 14 does it belong to the government yet   can I have it on a homestead bill   my husband is not *{here}* for he is a clerk in Captain Pomeroys office in Chicago   be so kind as to tell me by letter   Eleanor M Boizard

*{Written on the bottom of the letter}*
A married woman cannot enter land under the Homestead Act.
Yours, Morgan Bates   Register

**Chicago and Glen Arbor 1864-1870**

From Eleanor & Marietta to Oliver (Written by Marietta)

Glen Arbor, Michigan<br>Tuesday, May the 24<sup>th</sup> 1864

Dear Papa
We are well and hope that you are the same   mama was speaking to Mr. Fisher and he can spare 10 acres of land and there is two acres almost cleared   mama was to look at it this morning   there is water about thirty rods from where the house would be built and he would ask one hundred dollars   it is east of Mr. Fisher's farm house about one half mile and there is a wagon road cut through to the clearing.  if you can send forty dollars to mama then she can have it to pay right down for it them.   mama can have 10 dollars for to pay the rent and other expenses   you need not send the table this time as we would rather do without it just now and pay for the land now   I will tell you about what Mr. Goffart says    I don't think that is worth while but I will tell you what he has to say as Mons. Goffart can't sell before the terms of four years   he has a log house just the frame of logs   he will let us lease it for twelve dollars and he will rent us 10 acres of land for 4 years   he will ask one dollar and a half when we would clear it per acre and at the end of 4 years he will sell it to us for 8 dollars an acre   now you see that Mr. Fishers offer is the best one   Monsieur Goffart wants you to send him some things to make medicine for a sick woman  one quarter of a pound **camphor germ**   one pint of the **spirits of hartshorn**   quarter of a pound of **bitter aloes**   one pint of alcohol   when you get them send a receipt of how much they are and then he will pay me   did you ever answer Bridges & Joneses letters   no more at present But remaining yours true
Mrs. Eleanor M Boizard
Miss M.E. Boizard

Dicky is well and he sings like he was a going to deafen a body signed by Richard the 1<sup>st</sup>

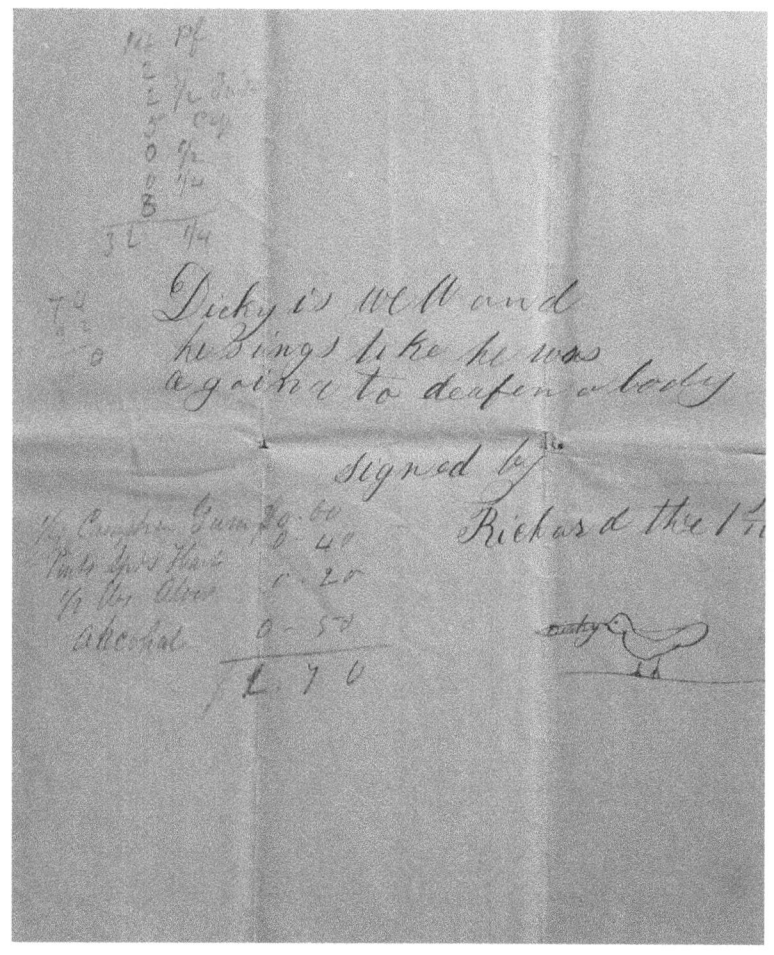

**Long Distance Love 1855-1870**

*There are some figures written on the page, probably from Oliver as he calculated the cost of the provisions they requested. There are additional figures on the back of the letter that seem to be his budget.*

| | | | |
|---|---|---|---|
| 1/4 camphor gum | $0.60 | Pffeifer | $15.00 |
| Pints Spts Hart | 0.40 | Tailor | 2.50 |
| ½ lbs Aloes | 0.20 | Purdee | 2.00 |
| Alcohol | 0.50 | Capt. | 5.00 |
| | $ 2.70 | Mach st | 0.50 |
| | | Mitchell | 0.25 |
| | | Table | 8.00 |
| | | Lard | 2.00 |
| | | Lamp | 1.50 |
| | | Wheat | 0.50 |
| | | Sundries | 1.00 |
| | | **Pomatum** | 1.50 |
| | | | $ 37.50 |
| | | Goffart | 1.75 |
| | | | $ 39.50 |
| | | Washing | 1.00 |
| | | | 40.50  74.25 |

40.50
33.75

74.25
39.50
34.75

**Chicago and Glen Arbor 1864-1870**

From Oliver to Eleanor & Marietta

Chicago, Illinois
June 3, 1864

Dear Wife,
I send you by the "**Propeller Granite State**" your table and oilcloth. Cost $8.50. also a jar of lard, a bag of wheat and $30.00 enclosed in the letter. You Speak of buying 10 acres of land from Fisher, well it is a good idea, but you should not pay for it at once, Say you might pay $60.00 down and let him wait for the balance 40 doll., which I will pay in 4 months, 10 dollars per month, because if you pay all the money you have, in case I Should get out of employment you have nothing to subsist on. Keep the $30.00 which I Send you until you can get another remittance. You will require Some provisions Shortly, and I Suppose it will take $100 to put a house on the 10 acres, and at the present prices it will take at least 100 dolls. for your winter stores. Things are still getting higher, my expenses have been high this month, I paid for my board and have to pay $1 per dozen for washing and I bought 2 linen coats, I got them cheap. I paid $2.50 for fixing my overcoat, and a number of other little expenses. I also Send you Goffarts medicine which amount he must pay you when he gets them. You will please find the bill with them. I hope that you will remain contented in good health, also my big Dudu. I am busy now in making out muster rolls for the 100 days now. After that is done, there will be a Slack of business. I would try to do more for you, but is it rather hard to be without money all the month. Next month I Suppose you will require some provisions, you will tell me what you want and I will Send them to you. Try to keep Etty in her Studies, don't neglect her. Tell me in your next letter whether Fisher has any lumber to build a house for you and tell me if the land is good. I suppose the timber is not very good. Act for yourself for the best and I hope all will be well. I still board at Pfeiffer's. He talks about raising the price of board. How did your pickled Beef turn out, and tell me how your coffee and Sugar holds out. If I can keep employment this Summer, well enough, if not I must go elsewhere. I will try to come up and see you about October, if nothing happens. How do you spend your time, do you not get lonesome. I wrote to Bridges but have got no answer. I felt no desire to write to Jones, well I will close this letter hoping you will receive the articles safe and the money. Give my complement to Mr. Fisher and Lady and all enquiring friends. Kiss Etty for Me. Tell her to take more care in her writing. Truly yours
Your Husband
"Oliver"
Patrick send his compliments to you. J.O.B.


From Eleanor and Marietta to Oliver (Written by Marietta)

Glen Arbor
Michigan
9th 1864

Dear Papa
I take pleasure to let you know that we received your welcome letter and was glad to hear that you was well   we got the table and the oilcloth and the jar of lard   there was no wheat put ashore   did you mark the wheat as they wont be accountable for things that is not marked   mama is sorry about it for she wanted it as a substitute of coffee   we got the money and Goffarts medicines and we got the Hair oil and it is very nice   our meat kept very well   you asked about coffee and sugar we dont use much of it but as to the coffee it goes the fastest   mama paid Mr Fisher for two months rent   4 dollars for May and June   you wished to know about the 10 acres of land   the timber is good   it is

# Long Distance Love 1855-1870

principley beech and maple   mama thinks we could not do better   there is two acres of it cleared   you wished to know whether Mr. Fisher had any lumber  yes he has plenty of it   mama thinks that it would be cheaper to put a log shanty on it   she was speaking to Mr. Fisher about one and he will see what it will cost to put one on it and we will tell you some other time and we will have to get on it by fall for Mr. Fisher might get another miller and he might want the house   mama feels better than she has been these two summers   you wished to know if we was lonesome we are some times   I wish that you would send us the ledger every week as we have nothing at all to read   the last number was 12 there is 4 back number   you will find money inclosed in it for it and some books and the name of them on a slip of paper   I go to school and I think that the teacher is a good and educated one   she explains things to us children   when you write tell us what str. your office is on and what number of the haus {*house*} and where you board as we forgot the number   Mr. McCarty went to chicago and we could not tell him where to find you   and maybe Mr. Fisher will be out this summer   tell us what butter is per pound   we will tell you in the next letter whether we want any provisions   mama could have got some boarders but the provisions will cost more than it would come to as they don't pay much for board here   if there is any money left get a copy book No. seven there will be fifty cents for the ledger and two dollars for books   no more at present but remaining yours.  yours Forever
Signed by Eleanor M. Boizard
Signed by Marietta Boizard
Postscript   Don't be downhearted it is nine o'clock.


From Oliver to Eleanor & Marietta

Chicago<br>June 13<sup>th</sup> '64

My Dear Wife
I have received no acknowledgment I Sent you $30 by the Cap't of the "**Granite State**" along with the Table, 1 Jar of Lard, also a Bottle of **Pomatum** among the articles for Goffart, if you have not Send me a letter Stating that you received the money you should immediately apprise me of it, for Such things Should be promptly to.  I Saw Mr. McCarty and was highly gratified to think I was so lucky to meet him, he gave me pleasant news of you, you will answer this direct on the 1st propeller and let me Know what articles of Provisions, you are in want of I will also send you Some money about the 1st of July for your 4th of July Anniversary.  I Send you 2 papers and also 2 for Mr Fisher   I am well and hope that you and Etty are well.  I was dreaming rather an unpleasant one about you.  I suppose you will require some Tea   I forgot your Wheat but I think the Best Coffee is the original. Tell Mr Fisher I went twice to hear **Leo Miller** lecture on Truth & Philosophy.  I like him well.  I Send him a copy of one of the papers of that denomination. Give my best wishes to all Enquiring friends and let me know whether you received the money or not and how you liked your Table and oilcloth, the **Pomatum** I suppose has been applied to your head allready.  Let me Know how Goffart likes his medicines for "Sick Women" a hard dose I should think and whether he paid you for it.  I have no more to Say,
Yours truly Your Husband
"Oliver"

Mr. MrCarty told me he saw the Table & carried it to the Store but did not Know whether your received the letter or not.

**Chicago and Glen Arbor 1864-1870**

From Oliver to Eleanor & Marietta

Chicago Ill
June 15th 1864

My Dear Wife
Your letter dated the 9th just came to hand this Morning, and I hasten to answer it. I Send a letter by the Prop. **Cleaveland** Scolding to you for not acknowledging that letter with the money & c. However I went to the post office and found the letter. I Send you with this letter Ettys Books and 4 Copies of the Ledger, which will Keep you in reading Some time. Mr.Dakin has gone East to get married and Capt. & his Wife are going East also for a Short time. we have been very busy, we have 5 Clerks in the office now - besides the Captain. I will Send you $30 dolls. at the End of this month, also what provisions, you may need. I Suppose you might buy the Land from Mr. Fisher  I Suppose he will take $60 down and rest in 3 or 4 months, try to get a good house if you can on it for the Winter, it will require a tight house on account of the cold.
There is news that Gen. Sturgess of our party has been defeated in Mississippi. I am sorry for it. No More at Present  Do you think the Table is worth $6.00 and the Oil Cloth $2.50   The Lard cost 3.20
Yours & c.
Oliver


From Eleanor and Marietta to Oliver (Written by Marietta)

Glen Arbor Mich.
June 17, 1864

Dear Father,
We received your kind letter and also the papers and was glad to hear that you are well and we was sorry that you didn't get our letter as we wrote right away   we put it in the post office and we told them to put it on the boat and Mr. Ray might not have done it  he might have sent it by mail  we got the money $30  the table and the rest of the things  we put $2.50 in the other letter for the papers and some books  **McNallys Geography** and **Sanders new series spelling book  Clarks Grammar** and a number 7 copy book and the numbers of the ledgers is 13.14.15.17 and so on until you send them, because we got the 16 no.  please send them as it is lonesome here and we have nothing to read   Mr. Fisher is having the logs cut for our shanty as he might sell the mill and they might want this house  Mr. Fisher might come to Chicago the latter part of July   you might send us some tea and butter as butter is 40 cents a pound here  we aint quite out as we might have a bee and then we will need them things and also a smoked shoulder or ham and when you send the things you might send some rhubarb always for Mrs. Dorsey to eat as she has the sore mouth and she can't get it here   we have some lectures here twice a week   Mr. Gofferts son lives on the corner of Huron and Pattin, northeast side or southwest  it is in the same place that they used to live in  no more at present.
But remaining yours truly yours
Mrs. Eleanor M. Boizard
Marietta Boizard


P.S. We have not seen Mr. McCarty since he came in.

**Long Distance Love 1855-1870**

From Eleanor and Marietta to Oliver (Written by Marietta)

Glen Arbor<br>June 26<sup>th</sup> Michigan

Dear Papa,

We received your letter and was glad to hear that you was well   we are well but mamma has the headache today   it is the first time she has had it since she came in.  we got the books and would like to know the price of them as the teacher wants to know the price.  they have commenced of our house   mamma was up there and she says that they have to get the log together and then we will have to have a **bee**   Mr. Fisher wrote on a piece of paper what things that we need and you will find it in the letter   you said that you would send us $30 at the end of the month   get the things and send us what you can   we got the ledgers and the last number is 16 no more at present. But remaining yours, Yours truly
Eleanor M. Boizard
Miss Marietta Boizard.

*A small piece of paper was found with the following supplies written on it:* get Sash for five Windows, 12 lights in each. also one Box glass 8 by 10. See that the glass to sash correspond as to size. get lock & cheap trimmings for door. and 40 lbs 10 penny Nails


From Oliver to Eleanor

Chicago Illinois<br>July 3, 1864.

My Dear Wife,

I send you by the Propeller **"Cleveland"** 20 lbs. Butter, 2 lbs Tea, Sash for 5 Windows, putty, also 3 hams, and 40 lbs nails & lock & c. I find the things are So very high, that I cannot Send you any money (of any amount) this time. Consequently I will defer it for this month (June). Hams are 18 cts. Butter 35 cts. Flour $11. by the Hundred Barrels, Tea $2 per lbs (good). I hope you will Still retain your health, and Keep up Cheerfully. I will try to reach you about October next. You Stated that Mr. Fisher proposed coming down about the end of July, tell him to come to no. 70 Washington St. near Washington St. Etty wants to know the price of the Books, as far as I recollect the Geography was $1.25, the Grammar 90 cts, and the spelling Book 50 cts.   You did not inform me whether you purchased the land or not, but I suppose you have. Let me know how you Stand in circumstances and also the progressing of your 'Shanty.' Will you Shingle it or not. Etty Says in her letter about your headache and that can't be helped. I hope that you will keep your health. Tomorrow being the (4<sup>th</sup>) we will not work. We are very busy at Present, there are now 6 Clerks in the office, and I presume that there will be Employment for the Summer. It is astonishing how every thing is raised. I think hereafter it would be better to Send you Monthly a Barrel of Flour, for it is hard to tell what prices May come to. I presume your coffee is going fast, also your Sugar. Let me prevail on you to take Care of Etty. See that She attends to her **cyphering** and let her take more pains in her writing. Let me Know as Soon as you have your "**bee**" but don't Entertain <u>Boarders</u> you will find that you will be loser at the present prices. Try to get along, if you find that you are pressed for Money, let me Know I can get it from the Captain. On the receipt of this please acknowledge it on the first Propeller, No more at Present,
your husband
"Oliver"
Kiss Etty for me.   N.B.  My Compliments to Mrs. Dorsey & Husband and Fisher & Lady J.O.B.

**Chicago and Glen Arbor 1864-1870**

From Eleanor & Marietta To Oliver (Written by Marietta)

Glen Arbor, Michigan
July 6th, 1864

Dear Father
We are well and I hope that you are the same We received the things   the window sash and 2 lbs of Tea and a jar of butter and 3 hams   a box of glass and a box of nails and no letter no papers. the last was number 16   mama thinks that we can afford 6 cents a week for her a paper   no more at present   but we will tell you more in another letter as we wrote a few lines to let you know that we did not get any letter.
We remain Yours Truly yours
Marietta Boizard


From Oliver To Eleanor& Marietta

Chicago, IL
July 14, '64

Dear Ellen,
Mr. Goffart just came in this morning and he told me he had put a letter in the office for me.  I went up and took it out.  I was quite surprised to hear that you got no letter with the articles I sent you.  Those articles should have been shipped on the "**Cleveland**" I went there saw them weighed, marked myself and paid $1.50 for the Freight.  The boat Started in the night and next-morning I went down to See if she had gone, and there I found the agent had neglected Sending them he had got asleep, however it caused Some delay.  The hams cost 20 cts per lb. $7.00, the tea $4, the butter and jar $7.00.  The sash cost $5. The glass $5.25.  The nails 4.00.  The Lock & c. 1.25, the putty 80 cts. ($34.30) in all.  He told me the logs were put up and boards were being hauled down  I am quite glad to hear that they are getting along So well,  You have not told Me whether you have bought the land or not, Mr. Goffart Said he thought you had.  Let me know all about it how you Stand, and whether you owe much or not and what it will Cost.  I send you 5 Copies embracing no's. 17 & 21 of the ledger.  You must not think hard because I did not Send you the Ledgers, I also forgot the rhubarb for Mrs. Dorsey.  I have So much on my mind, I can attend to all the small matters, I look principally to the high price of Provisions, at Present Flour $12  a barrell, pork $45 barrell and in fact a pair of Common Shoes Cost $4.00.  Pfeiffer has raised his board to $4.50 cts. Washing $ 1. per dozen.  I hope Etty is well and attends to her Schooling, don't neglect her in regard to her religious duties -- Does She grow much.  I have a Small locket for her in my chest and when Mr. Fisher comes down, I will Send it to her.  Tell me whether you will Shingle the house or not.  I suppose they can't make it a tight room without them Mr. Goffarts Son looks Bad he has had the **Typhoid fever**, I don't mean Felix, he looks Strong.  Mr. Goffart told me he had no meat for 2 weeks.  Is that So.  Please answer this at your earliest opportunity no more at present
Truly yours
 your Husband, "Oliver"

*The actual date written on this letter is **June** 14 '64.  However in the sequence of the letters, I believe that Oliver mis-wrote the month, I believe it should have been July and I have amended the date and placed the letter here where it seems to place chronologically.*

**Long Distance Love 1855-1870**

From Eleanor & Marietta to Oliver (Written by Marietta)

Glen Arbor<br>Michigan<br>July 18th, 1864

Dear Papa,
We received your welcome letter and papers also and we was glad to hear that you was well  we was glad to get a letter as it is almost a month since we got a letter   you wished to know whether we got the land   Mama thought that she told you   now we will tell you all about it    Mama has paid Mr. Fisher $80 on it and she owes 20 on it yet   She would like you to send her $25 next month if you can so that she could pay Mr. Fisher and get the deed and then she can have $5 left  Now I will tell you about the house it is 12 by 24 and Mr. Fisher says that it will cost $75   Mr Fisher pays the men and we are pay him    It would have been done but Mr. Fisher cant get men to get to work on it when he comes down you and him can arrange it about the house as mama is anxious to get the land paid for now  i will tell you what we want   some flour  we are not out yet but we wont have enough to last the month out and next we want some shugar {sugar} and also some wheat or barley as Mama does not want to buy any Coffee until we get out of debt   that is all until you come in yourself   you say you have a locket for me and I thank you for it  Mama says that I am getting big and I am getting fat    I go to school everyday and the teacher says i am learning fast   Mama is knitting you a pair of socks.  you spoke about Goffart not having meat for two weeks   Mama says that she cant see how that can be  he has had since we come in  two barrels of flour and some meat besides and she got some flour down town the day that he went away   there is plenty of flour down town  but Mr. McCarty had none as his dock is not done   it was last week $14 downtown and Mr. Dorsey says that it has come down since then   Mr. Fisher has sold his mill   he is about closeing the bargin {bargain} and we dont know what moment might they may want the house as they are talking about keeping **bachelors hall** until fall you will find the monthly report of school. no more at preasent  But remaining truly yours forever,
Mrs. Eleanor M. Boizard
Miss Marietta Boizard

Post Script  Come Home as soon as you can.  Dickey is well and sings as loud as ever.  Signed by King Richard the Third.

You ought to know Mr. Goffart better than that, because you know he is always growling


From Oliver to Eleanor & Marietta

Chicago Ills<br>Augt 2nd 1864

My Dear Wife
Enclosed you will find $25- I also Send you 1 Bll. Flour $13 and 10 pounds of Sugar at 25 c'ts per lb. The Flour cost $13 and Some Wheat. I could not think of Sending you 1 Bll. Of Corn Meal you would soon get tired of it having no Flour. I also Send you by the Propeller "**Young America**" 4 pieces of Pipe (new) and elbow which costs 3 Dollars. You Say Mr Fisher will be down tell him to come No. 70 Washington St. near Dearborn Street he cant miss the office. I almost had made my mind up to come and See you for 10 days, but as Mr Harris is going East to See his mother, it would not do for both to go at one time and so I did not ask the Captain. Try to Keep cheerfull I am very lonely and I must come up next month to See you. In fact my clothes wants overhauling "Button Come off" and I want some rest. the weather has been intensely hot and these **Dutch Stews**, and **Slush** takes away

appetite. I dont feel none of the Best. Tell Fisher the Rebels are making another raid into Pennsylvania. I have nothing more to add of any interest  Has Goffart got home  he returned from the country without finding any work but left his son there, he came to the office and complained of being Sick and wished me to let him have money to go home on. I told {*him*} it was pretty hard for me to loan money as it took every cent I could earn to get along. however I had made up my mind to let him have $5 Dolls. but the Capt. went East that Same day and I did not get it for him, however he did not Come back to the office, and I did not Know whether he was taken worse or not or whether he went to Glen Arbor or to his son's house. Tell Etty to be a good girl, and let her not forget her <u>Maker</u> you will find her <u>great monthly Report</u> with the money. No. of Days without whispering "15" rather extraordinary feat - an awful task for her.--

And now **de olddest of de wimmins** Good Bye.

Your Husband

Oliver


Answer this at your first chance  Gen'l Grant has mined & Blown up a Rebel Fort at Petersburg, VA  Loss Great

N.B. Kiss Etty for me, and tell her to take Care of Dick

Please send my Black Thin Coat down by Mr Fisher  J.O.B.

I Send you 2 Ledgers No. 22 & 23



From Eleanor & Marietta to Oliver (Written by Marietta)

Glen Arbor Mich<br>August 2<sup>nd</sup> 1864

Dear Father

we are all well and i hope that you are the same  Mr Fisher will go out on the **Maine** and we will send this by him they are working at the house and as soon as they are done we are a going to move in it. dont wait untill Mr Fisher comes back but send the provisions before because we will be out of flour  mama told you what to send in former letters dont forget wheat and you may get dicky some seed  ask for seed mixt for a canary.  dont forget mamas papers the last number was 21 no more at preasent but write soon  remaining yours  truly yours

Mrs Eleanor M Boizard

Miss Marietta Boizard



From Eleanor & Marietta to Oliver

Glen Arbor Mich<br>August 7 1864

Dear Papa

We received your welcome letter and was sorry to hear that you are not very well  we got $25 in the letter  Mr Fisher started the same night  the same night that we got the letter he went on the **maine** and so we could not send your coat to you  perhaps you can come in with Mr Fisher  we got a barrel of flour  a sack of meal and package wheat and some sugar and the stove pipe and the papers and was glad to get them  when you come in you can have

**Long Distance Love 1855-1870**

as many fresh fish as you can eat at 10ts a peice   mama hops *{hopes}* that we will be in our house before you come   we are on our second ham and it is not very good   it is very strong   we use more butter than meat   that butter was very good   mama is very glad that you did not give Goffart any money   them shoes that you sent in mama had to get them mended and pay a dollar and i will have to have a pair before winter   no 2 and high in the in step and high around the ankle   them others would have been to small for to wear with woolen stockings   mama had to pay $1.80 for 3 pairs of misses hose or stockings   when you come in dont forget dicks seed   he sings as loud as ever and eats as much   here is my 2$^{nd}$ monthly report   mama has two hens now F *{Fisher?}* gave them to her and I have kitten so you see we have a large family   now if we had a little piggy   we will have one when we get in our own house   no more at present   but remaining yours
Mrs Eleanor M Boizard
Miss Marietta Boizard


From J.E. Fisher to Oliver

Denney PO Ill<br>Aug. 12$^{th}$ /64

Friend Bozard
I became so overpowered by the heat in the city that I was compelled to leave, though I should have been glad to have stayed longer. I left on the Evening train on the Burlington & Quincy Road on the evening of the 10$^{th}$   I went to your office to tell you but you had gone   I am now safe and sound with my friends all right. Enclosed I send a letter I wish you would forward to Glen Arbor by the first Boat   if I send it by mail it will not get there in time
Your Friend
J.E. Fisher


From Marietta to Teacher

Glen Arbor Mich<br>August 23 1864

Dear Teacher
I take the pleasure to let you know that I am well and I hope that you are the same. We are moved in to our new house and we like to live here. The water is so nice and cool it is just like ice water. I expect my father home the first of the month I will be glad to see him   he said that he would bring me a present when he came in. We were thinking of going a black berrying this week if it dont rain I went to get my tooth pulled but Mr Walters had taken his instruments home and I will have to put it off untill I come to school next week. I wish that you would come back next summer and teach school for I like you better than any teacher I ever went to   I dont expect that I will go to school much this winter because the snow will be to deep but I will try to go if I can. Excuse my short letter as my hand trembles. But I remain yours  truly yours
Miss Marietta Boizard

*Throughout this letter, there are pencil corrections that have been made over lower case letters that should have been capitalized.*

**Chicago and Glen Arbor 1864-1870**

From Oliver to Eleanor & Marietta

Chicago Ill's
Sept. 13th 1864

My Dear Wife,
I send you by the "**Young America**", 1 Shoulder, 3 lbs. Cheese, 3 lbs Candles, 4 packages of "Extract" and a Jar of Butter. I also Send to Mrs. Tucker 10 yds Plaid and Braid & 2 Dolls. Worth of Green Tea with the Bills attached to her Packages  I felt Sorry that I could not See you but it was Lucky Enough to get off so soon. I went to work on Monday and to day I made out a large Muster Rolls Satisfactory to the Captain -- Excuse this writing as I am writing it on the Head of a Barrel, on the Wharf -- I had to hurry up as I just quit work, and the Boat being ready, to start Mr Fishers files are aboard with the Cap't. I have a Slight pain in my Side I presume it is cold, from the Lakes as it was pretty rough, give my regards to all Enquiring friends. I hope that dress wont get greased. Kiss Etty for me and receive my Blessing
Your Husband
Oliver


Note: Write Soon J.O.B.

Butter 48 cts a pound



From Oliver to Eleanor

Chicago Ill
Oct 3rd 1864

My Dear Wife,
I just received your letter, and I had made all my purchases, and it took all the money I had Except the $5 Doll's enclosed. I am Sorry that I cannot Send Mr Tucker his oil, but if he can make out till next month, I will Send it to Him. I send you by the Steamer "**Maine**" the following Articles of Provisions & c. 2 Bll's Flour. 15 lbs. Dried apples, 3 lbs. Tea, 5 lbs. Coffee, 10 lbs. Sugar. 12 lbs. Parched Rye, 5 lbs. Prunes, and Cod Fish 1 Platter, 40 lbs Bacon, 2 Prs' Shoes (which I hope will be big enough) 1 Iron Tea Kettle & c. And Some Reading Matter, and Ettys "**Day School Bell**" which I hope She will improve in it.   Your letter must have been overlooked at the post Office, for I went every day. Still no letter, and then I thought of McCarty's Dock, and then I saw the Captain of the **Young America** and he told me he delivered every thing right. Had I not got your letter this morning you would have had to do without money until the End of this month, however 5 Dolls may suffice until the month of November, and then if nothing happens I can send you some money  My pay has been raised to 100 Dolls. per month Commcg. The 1st October, 2 ½ Dolls. for Tax, leaves me $97.50 and that is good enough for an old Soldier  The articles are well packed in 2 Boxes, and the Shoes, Papers & Ettys Books and the letter in the hands of the Captain of the Boat. Kiss Etty for Me and Receive my blessing.
Your Husband
Oliver

**Long Distance Love 1855-1870**

From Oliver to Eleanor

Chicago Illinois
Nov. 4th, 1864

My Dear Wife,
I Send you by the Propeller **Empire** the following articles of Provisions & c. Butter, in a jar 20 lbs, 20 lbs Lard, 3 lbs Candles, 1 lb Yarn, 1 Shovel, 1 Rake, 2 yds Flannel, 2 Cakes Chocolate, 1 Dos. Extract Coffee, Sena, Oil 1 can, 3 galls. {gallons} 1 Bll. Flour  1 Bll Corn Meal.  1 Day School Bell, 1 Steel Thimble, 1 broom, 100 lbs Pig Feed,  1 Hind Quarter Fresh Beef. I should like to have Sent those things on the **Maine** but as the month was not out, and the Captain having been gone to Cincinnati, I could not do it. I suppose you will have them to haul up from McCarty's pier, as I understand the Boats all wood there. You will please find Enclosed the Sum of $10 Doll's, which will probably do for November, the Boats are not insured for running later than November 15th. I hope Mr. Fisher has surveyed your Land, and gave you the Deed for it, if not you must demand it of him, as you have no voucher for it at all, don't neglect it, and as I pay the installment on the house take the necessary receipts for it. I am not able to purchase that Sheeting for Mrs. Tucker as I have purchased Some articles for myself and the expenses which takes all my funds at present, the price of Sheeting per yard from .30 to 80 cts. Enclosed you will find a list of Prices paid for the different Articles. I am glad you are comfortable for the winter and also that the Shoes am sure that they are not the first rate Article but I guess they will do. Tell me how you like your Shoulders & side meat and cod fish, do you think that you will have Tea, Coffee, Sugar, enough  if not I must try to send you  more before the boats stop Running. Try to be careful of your provision, for there is not doubt you will have visitors this winter. You say you want **Sena**   has Etty worms. Kiss Etty for me and tell her to try improve herself in writing this winter. Tell her to take her time and write plain. Give my best wishes to all Enquiring Friends and please accept my blessing.
Your Husband
"Oliver"


N.B. Etty will find enclosed a little ornament for her hat, which I found in the Street. J.O.B.



From Eleanor and Marietta to Oliver (Written by Marietta)

Glen Arbor, Mich
Nov 11th 1864

Dear Papa
We are well and I hope that you are the same  the things came in at McCartys but we have not got them home yet owing to bad weather  it is a snowing   If you can send anything more in Please don't forget Mrs Tuckers muslin don't pay more than 40 or 50 cents a yard. we got 10 bushels of potatoes at $1 doll per bushel from Mr. Tucker and he worked 6 days on the house plastering at a $1.25 per day. you may send us eight yards of dark calico for aprons as we are entirely and you may send dicky some more seed  one night the mice broke dickys leg and mama splintered it up and it got well and so you see that she is quite a surgeon  you asked if we would have tea enough I don't think we shall as I had to part with a pound of it for to get corn for the piggy  you may send me some sugar get it cheaper don't get it so white. we liked the cod fish  shoulder and side meat very well  we are sorry that you didn't get it all side meat as the side meat was the best  you might Send us a barrel of apples if you can  coffee we have plenty of it and some matches  Ettie would like to have a Bottle of **Dr Hooflands German bitters** and send me 1 lbs of salts and some Ind corn or wild turnip and some bitter aloes not the powder that what looks like {?} when you break it  as the people all around has the fever either the **Typhoid** or **Billious** and we want to have some medicine in case we get it  Mr. Tucker has had it going on three weeks  don't be frightened as we are all well  Ettie

**Chicago and Glen Arbor 1864-1870**

is as fat as a little piggy. And I am not far behind  mamas shoes is to large for her she thought they would fit her but as she came to try them on she found out that they was to large  Mrs. Fisher thinks that she will take them if mama can get another pair because they just fit her  they are no. six  mama wears wide fives but don't get them so broad across the toes  mama says don't be frightened because we send for so much as we cant get any thing more untill the first of May  now for the village news they have been drafting  Dorsey is drafted and Parker and I don't know how many more  they have to go Traverse the 16th.  send me a box of pens **Gellots 303**

Mrs E M Boizard
Miss Ettie Boizard


*Written on the back of this letter was the following:*

Nov 12 1864

Dear Dada

I am going to finish my letter  we got our things home today and they was all right and we got the letter and the money  we did not find the thimble  the beef was very nice  Ettie likes her flannel  that yarn is very coarse and I don't think that it is very good  Mrs Fisher got some just like it and she says that it is a mixture of that stuff that they call shoddy.  Mama says that she expects that she will have to pay $2.00 for getting the things hauled down from McCartys  I saw Mrs Fisher and she said that Mr Fisher would come and survey the land tomorrow if the day was fit  No more at present

write every two weeks and we will do the same



From Oliver to Eleanor

Chicago, IL
Dec. 1st. 1864

My Dear Wife
You will please find Enclosed $15, it was my intention to Send you more, but I found the expenditures So much, I could not do it. I bought a new hat and a pair Shoes for myself. I See the last Boat Started yesterday "**City of New York**" I Send you Apples and a Box of Sundries on the "**Empire**" with a letter with Ettys thimble Enclosed. I hope you will have provisions Enough for the Winter, the weather is very mild. I Should have liked for you to have More, but everything is So high that the months pay Soon goes, but now the Boats stop I will not be able to Send you any more provisions, except your Monthly Amount of money. We must try to pay Mr. Fisher from this month out, December, I find you will have to be quite Economical with your Winter Stores, as the Meat part of them may not hold out. However I think if you occasionally buy Some fish, you can do well Enough– I would like to Know how you managed your Quarter of Beef – it Cost $10 - I should like to Know how you stand with Mr Tucker  I Send him 1 Bll. Flour, 1 Can of oil and 15 yds sheeting at 50 cts per yard. You Say you got 10 bus. Potatoes, $10.00.  6 days work at 1.25 per day 7.50 in all $17.50. The Flour I think cost 11.50. The Sheeting 7.50, The oil & can $4.00 and 45 cts for Braid, making in all $23.45 cents His Bill against you would be – deduct 17.50  due EMB 5.95 Besides what the Freight cost.  I Sincerely hope I Shall be able to Keep my place as there is 7 Clerks and I don't know whether the Capt. will keep us all or not. Patrick told me that he had a talk with the Captain about me and the Captain Said I was all right for the winter as long as I choose to stay with him. Let me Know whether the Snow beat in the house or not, and how the Pig stands the cold weather, and also the Chickens. Tell Mr. Fisher that I will Commence paying him Sums Every Month hereafter.  I forgot Etty's pens, I am Sorry, the vagabond will think I

# Long Distance Love 1855-1870

neglect her but Kiss her for me and that I know will pay her for the neglect. I Saw the Steamer **Allegheny** coming down with Some Blue Jackets aboard her, She touched at Traverse City – and I thought of Mr. Dorsey and Parker. I suppose they were among them. Dear Ellen I had a Strong notion of Coming to See you, on the Empire, but I Know it would not do if the Capt. had give me leave. However you must keep up a good heart this winter, you must not be lonely. I hope you will have Enough to Eat and you have Enough to Keep you warm. Answer this letter as Soon as you can, as it takes fully 2 weeks to come & go. I hope you will put Dick where the mice wont Kill him. Give my best respects to all Enquiring friends   And receive my blessing.
Your Husband
"Oliver"


Pffifer has raised the Board to $5 per week.


Kiss Etty for me and tell her she must not forget her schooling



From Eleanor & Marietta to Oliver (Written by Marietta)

Glen Arbor Mich<br>Dec 14<sup>th</sup> 1864

Dear Papa
We received your letter & was glad to hear that you was well   we got the money   there is about 1 foot snow   you asked if the snow blew in the house   it dont and the house is quite comfortable considering as there is no carpet on the floor   you said that you wanted to know how the pig got along she gets along very well   when you write tell us how much the first shoes cost that you sent in as we didnt know whether they cost $3.00 or not as they were different from the others   Mr Tucker cuts our wood and we dont burn any small quantity either   Mama says that when you write dont send so much paper when you write   one of them big **fools cap** sheets of paper weighs a good deal and we have to pay more postage   Sarah Tucker is very sick they dont expect her to live   Mama set up night before last and I expect that she will have to set up to night again   Dorsey & Parker ate supper at the **soldiers rest** and then they took the cars and went to **Jackson**   you spoke of paying Fisher all along untill we get the house paid for I will be better satisfied as we want a kitchen built   Mama wants to know what you sent that thin stuff in for aprons   it is not fit to make up   when it is washed there wont be nothing of it but a rag   that she would rather had two yds of good calico   when you come in will you fetch me a christmas gift   no more at present But remaining yours Truly Yours
Mrs Eleanor M. Boizard
Miss Marietta Boizard


PS dont get mad at us about the calico

**Chicago and Glen Arbor 1864-1870**

From Oliver to Eleanor & Marietta

Chicago, Ill's
Dec. 16th 1864

My Dear Ellen
Your letter came to hand this morning it has been 12 days on the road, it was post marked December 3rd. I was getting uneasy, I went to the Post Office everyday, and this morning I got it. the Snow must be very deep on the roads in Michigan, hence the delay. I am glad you are well and also Etty. I am also pleased to hear that Mrs. Tucker has partially recovered. I am sorry that the House leaks. I expected it would. I Send you a letter, on the 30th of November with 15 dollars Enclosed. I Suppose you have received it before this. After the 1st January I will Send you money, and then you must pay Mr. Fisher 25 Doll's. for the 1st Installment, you did not Say, whether he had laid out your 10 acres or not or whether you had got the deed or not. I am in moderate health at present. the weather has been intensely cold, but it has moderated Since. I Bought me a new Hat and a pair of Shoes everything is very high (provisions particulary) It will be good Enough to be frugal with your winter Stores, as you wont have much to Spare  I am glad that you got So many Candles off the Beef, and I hope the Beef was nourishing to you. As Regards taking that Boy I hardly know what to Say about it   You will be obliged to Clothe him & c. and you Know we have our house to pay for, and a number of other Expenses, however do as you like about it. You must tell me in your next letter whether the house is cold or not   you must try to Keep the Snow off the Roof. have you bought any fish yet, or do you think that you can fish during the winter when you want them
and now Ellen I must close this letter hoping that you will Keep well, also Etty, tell me how She liked her Thimble I forgot her pens. I am sorry   Give my best wishes to Mr Fisher and Wife   Mr Tucker and Wife and all Enquiring friends  Truly yours
 your  husband
  "Oliver"

N.B. Enclosed you will find a few lines from Emma Bridges with no date or place, the Envelope was Post Marked Nov. 11th New York   it was directed to me   J.O.B.



From Emma Bridges to Marietta

Dear Eta
it is with pleasure i take my pen in hand to set you a few lines to let you know that we received your leter and was glad to hear you were all well as this leaves us all at present   for chrismas stuf your fat turkey  make your good diner *{dinner}* for we are all a comeing   the wether is very moderate now but i guess we will have very cold now for it snowing hard   we keep a litle *{little}* store   I go to the city every morning with 30 dolers *{dollars}* to buy apeels *{apples}* belove*{?}* cheese. and you used to be afrad *{afraid}* a dolers *{dollars}* for fear she would lose it.   Ma and me have made a hundred and 20 dolers *{dollars}* since we comenced *{commenced}*.  mrs donelson is at the same buy *{by}* a fortune she is goin away soon- for he had an ordnace *{ordnance}* apoinment *{appointment}*    sergant galuger was sent away recruiting but him and vater was sent in the other day and put in the recruits and sent to the field   they don't know what for   and my father is at the same truble *{trouble}* geting drunk every day. He reenlisted and got 7 hundred dolers *{dollars}* and i want you to tell us how land is for we are comeing there to buy   you must have the house to buy and ma say she wishe your mother was here to go to the thater *{theater?}* and mr boizard in front with the umbrela under his arm and my fater *{father}* behind bringing up the rear   jiney and tomy goes to school and tomy got on his first hats and thinks himself quite a man and i think its is time to quit as i have to go

# Long Distance Love 1855-1870

down to the dock to get the pies   my mother gives her love to you and your mother and farthe *{father}* the same yours truly  Emma Bridges


From Oliver to Eleanor

I wrote this letter on the 30th Dec. but dated it on Jany 1. '65  

U.S. Mustering and Disbursing Office  
Chicago, IL  
January 1st 1865

My Dear Wife  
Your letter came to hand, on the 29th Dec '64 and I was glad to hear that you and Etty was well, but was sorry to hear of the Illness of Mrs Tucker's daughter, but it is to be hoped that ere this she is well.  Enclosed you will please find ($35 doll's) which amount you will please pay Mr Fisher the Sum of 25 Dollars, as the 1st Installment on the House and take his receipt for it.  You did not State in your letters, whether he had Surveyed your land, or gave you the deed, these things should be attended to, and if you have done so why not let me Know.  It being New Years, I have not the pleasure of Knowing how you May Spend yours.  I don't think I will spend mine with much Satisfaction.  I went to St Charles, Ills for 3 days, the Capt. Send me up there to take the Estimate of Public Property & c. as the Barracks are about to be Sold – I found it cost me $10. to live notwithstanding the Government paid the transportation on the Cars and Back – the answer of letters come Slowly from Glen Arbor, are there no Speedier way of getting letters from there.  One of your letters I see was dated the 30th of Nov. and the Post Mark was Dec. 3rd.  It appears letters are irregular in that Post Office Dept.  As regards to the price of them Shoes, the 1st pair was $2.75 and the other was $2.75.  I never enumerated freight for articles I Send up, you did not tell me whether the apples were as <u>miserable</u> as the apron stuff.  I hope they were Satisfactory   as for the Calico I thought that Lake Street <u>Gentleman</u> was not honest as poorer folks are.  Well now I suppose I have Said more than I Ought to (with propriety) but hope you and Etty may keep your health and it would be good Enough not to lose your rest <u>to much</u> as you are Subject to <u>Coughs</u> in that climate particularly – Give my best respects to all Enquiring friends, and Kiss Etty for Me and tell her, (If I live) I Shall buy her Something for a New Years <u>present</u>.  
Your  Husband  
"Oliver"

answer as soon as possible


From Eleanor & Marietta to Oliver (Written by Marietta)

Glen Arbor Mich  
Jan 6th 1865

Dear Father  
We received your letter and was sorry to hear that you are not very well but this leaves us well as the pantry shows Mama says for you to get one or two blankets for to keep you warm at night and keep yourself clothed warm   It is not very cold here and the snow in not any deeper than it was   you wished to know if we bought any fish   no they dont catch any now but I got some pork and had to pay 25 cts per pound.  you wanted to know if Mr Fisher surveyed the land yet as he is not at home he is at **North Port** he is a Judge or some thing but he will when he comes back

you wanted to know whether the house is cold or not   no   but it is as comfortable as can be expected as it is   we was to a party Monday afer *{after}* New Years.  it is right lonesome here   I liked the thimble very well.  Dickey is well and sings very loud   no more at present   but remaining yours  Truly Yours
Mrs Eleanor M. Boizard
Miss Marietta Boizard



From Eleanor and Marietta to Oliver (Written by Marietta)

Glen Arbor, Michigan<br>Jan 20<sup>th</sup> 1865

Dear Papa
We received your letter by the last mail and the money also 35 dollars. Mama says that she will give Mr. Fisher $30 so that we can get out of debt as soon as we can   for then I can get the shingles made for the house.  Mr Fisher has not surveyed the land yet as the snow is so deep that I don't think that he can as it is two feet deep but it is not very cold.  It takes Mr Tucker one day in the week to cut us wood.  we received a letter from Emma Bridges last mail and it had neither date or anything and I made out that they was all well and Mr. Bridges has reinlisted for seven hundred dollars **bounty.**  the mail only goes once every week we write every other mail.  those last shoes that you sent Etty the uppers are all ripped to pieces and she only wore them a week and I will have to go and pay $3.00 for her a pair for it will cost more than they are worth to get them mended for they ask $1.00 for putting just a couple of little soles on. Mama says for to tell you that she is a baking bread and pies our coal oil is all most gone we will have enough to last untill we get another letter from you. Mama has not had a bit of cough since she came in.  when Mr Tucker or any man comes in dicky will commence singing just as he used to when you were home.  no more at present. But remaining yours Truly yours
Mrs. Eleanor M Boziard
Miss M E. Boizard

Post Script  We are well and I hope that you are the same.



From Oliver to Eleanor

U.S. Mustering and Disbursing Office<br>Chicago, IL<br>Jany 21 1865

My Dear Wife
Your letter dated Dec'r 26<sup>th</sup> came to hand about 14 days after it was written, and I received the other one dated 6<sup>th</sup> Jan'y.  I am glad you are well.  I am not So well, as I might be.  I Send you a letter dated Jan'y 1<sup>st</sup> with $35 dollars enclosed, in order to pay Mr. Fisher $25 for the 1<sup>st</sup> Installment on the house.  the weather is very mild, at present I expect we will have rain.  I will Send Ettys Almanck in February, after I get paid off – I expect nothing else, but Some of us will be discharged the end of this month, as our work is pretty well Squared up, Should I be discharged I shall try to Come up and See you   I Shall have to foot it up there.   I hope the Captain will Keep me until we get out of Debt.  You Spoke of being at a party.  I hope you enjoyed yourself. I spend my Christmas & New Years like all other days, except we had Some little extras for dinner.  I read Bill Browns letter, but did not answer it, as I get tired of writing.  I hope You have received that Money, $35– You Say you paid 25 cts for Pork per pound, I hope your

## Long Distance Love 1855-1870

bacon is not used up – I have nothing more to add, Give my respects to all Enquiring friends and please receive my blessing,
Your Husband
(Oliver)

Kiss Etty for me
and take Care of Dickey
Tell me if you think your provisions will hold out


From Eleanor & Marietta to Oliver (Written by Marietta)

Glen Arbor<br>Feb 2<sup>nd</sup> 1865

My Dear Father
We are well and I hope that you are the same   we received two daily papers   Mama gave Mr Fisher the Money and took a recipt.  you must be right saveing this winter as we must have a new set of chairs in the spring as these are comming all to pieces   they cannot be touched but they come to pieces. Mr Tucker has been sick but he is better. I go to school and the weather is very mild   Mr & Mrs Goffart was down to day and they sent their best respects   we are making soap and the cat is in the box asleap and the pig a squealing and the rooster is a crowing and dicky is a calling for more seed   our house is very cold   no more at present but you must try to come home in the spring. We remain yours Truly yours   Write soon as you get this
PS You spoke of my New Years Gift   Get me something Nice
Mrs Eleanor M Boizard
Miss M.E. Boizard


From Oliver to Eleanor

Chicago, IL<br>Feby 3<sup>rd</sup> 1865

My Dear Ellen,
I received your letter dated, Jany. 20<sup>th</sup> acknowledging the receipt of the 35 Doll's. I became quite uneasy, as I had written the letter Jany 1<sup>st</sup>. However I Suppose the delay, is on account of the roads. You will please find Enclosed $30 – as Soon as you received it answer immediately. I don't Know of any thing that hurt my feelings So much as the Death of that Girl of Mr. Tuckers. She was an affable and Kind girl and then so much Company for Etty, truly I can not help thinking about her. You Spoke about Etty's Shoes and the Coal oil – try to make out the best you can until the Month of May. I am glad to hear that you are So well also my <u>Big Dudu</u>. You think of having the Shingles made, well act as you think proper, and probably we will get along By and By – I bought Myself New Books, and Some Clothes, which Cost Considerable, at the present prices, for Board, Washing & c. a person Cannot Save much, however after the property is paid for, it will be ours, and a home for you and Etty – You Spoke about getting a letter, from Bridges, there are Big bounties on hand at present, however that don't Effect me. We are busy now, as there are new Reg'ts raising.  There are negotiations now for peace, and it is to be hoped that it will be Satisfactory. Gen. Sherman is moving on to Charleston S.C. and likely there will be heavy fight in course of 2 weeks. Gen. Lee is still about Richmond, and Grant is watching him. However we will change the Subject. I am glad to hear that

your Daughter & Self is well. May you Keep So. Tell Mr. Tucker and Lady that I feel quite hurt about the loss of the Girl. However it cant be helped. "All must die, who live, passing from nature into Eternity." [10] Give my best respects to Mr. Fisher & Lady  Mrs Dorsey and all Enquiring friends.
No more at present
Your Husband
"Oliver"

N.B.  Kiss Etty for me Twice

I Send you Some papers


To Marietta from Emma Bridges

Fort Columbus New york harbor<br>Feb 4 1865

dear Eta
your leter came to hand this day in wich we were glad to hear that your were all well and in good sprits {spirits}   as you say you goin to the party i am happy to inform you we were all wel and i trust the pen line may find you enjoying the same to   i dont have to go to the city so often now as they have stoped the people from selling now for the sutter {**sutler**}.  Dear Eta we hope that as soon as the weather gets a litle {little} beeter {better} that you wil come to see us. and take giney home with you.  it is not very cold here no more. i supose things is very high every were {where}  we pay {?} cents for calico & 50 a barel of potatos
Eta  sarah is not here but her fathe {father} is phildelphia recruiting   i hope your dream may come true for i want you to come as soon as the weather is fine and so does Austin Newman. try and come. i send you by this male {mail} a rich valentine wich you will pleas acept. tommy says he will writ to Eta   I guess i will have to stop to start the fire  you must write the minute you get this. my father and mother send their love to your mother and father and my father to write to him now for he has got nothing to do and he can write   giny and tommy send their love. no more at present   do try and come.
Yours truly
Emma Bridges



From Eleanor and Marietta to Oliver (Written by Marietta)

Glen Arbor, Michigan<br>Feb 10th

Dear Papa
 We received your letter and was sorry to hear that you are not very well but I hope that you may be well by the time this reaches you. you spoke of coming home if you are discharged I hope that you will not be discharged untill we get Mr. Fisher paid   if you should come get a large pair of boots so you could put on two pair of stockings and dress yourself warm   you wished to know about our provisions   our butter meat and lard will be out first   we have over a barrel of flour and a good deal of cornmeal   we will have to feed it to the pig. we guess that we will have enough of other things to last us   Ettie is growing so that I have to put a piece to all of her dresses you must save all of your

---

[10] Shakespeare, William;  Hamlet Act 1; Scene 2

**Long Distance Love 1855-1870**

old clothes and bring them home   we can allways get wood cut or something done   no more at present  But remaining yours
Truly yours
Mrs. Eleanor M. Boizard
Miss Marietta Boizard

This is Dickys picture but the artist didnt draw it very well
*There is a hand drawn picture of Dicky with a text bubble that says "more seed"*


From Oliver to Eleanor

> Chicago, IL
> Saturday  Feby. 18.'65

My Dear Wife,
Your letter dated Feby 2$^{nd}$ Came to hand yesterday, and I am glad to hear that you & Etty are well.  I am in moderate health at present, now and then my Side hurts me, and then again it feels well enough.  Business is very brisk in regard of Recruiting, at present we are busy in the office, we worked all day Sunday last, and I suppose we will have to work Tomorrow.  You spoke of being Saving in order to get ½ doz chairs, I will try to purchase ½ doz chairs, in order to Send or bring them to you, in May.  I bought me a coat & pants, as my old pants were getting Shabby.  I will have to pay for the Coat at the End of this month.  The next installment I Send up, let me know, how much more we will have to pay for the house.  I think another payment of $30 ought to close the Bill.  I suppose I will have to bring up Some Provisions with me when I come to See you.  Let me know what you have left in the provision and whether that pig is worth anything.  I Send you $30 Doll and a number of Papers.  I suppose you have received them.  I must order 2 pair Shoes for you & Etty, (Calf Skin) before May.  I have still the old ones for measure.  Everything is very high.  I have to pay $5 a week for Board, and $1 for washing a dozen pieces.  I bought me Boots, cost $9.00.  The coat will cost $20.00 Pants $4. And then with other Expenses I cant save much.  However after the House is paid for that much will be Saved during this year.  Etty is quite amusing, in her letter, I showed her letter to the Clerks, and they Spoke highly of her, the cat asleep, the Pig Squealing, the Rooster crowing and you making Soap, it was quite a Programme.  Kiss her for me and receive my best wishes.
Your Husband
"Oliver"


From Eleanor & Marietta to Oliver (Written by Marietta)

> Glen Arbor
> Feb 26$^{th}$ 1865

Dear Papa
We received your welcome letter and the money $30 and was glad to hear that you are well we gave Mr F $20 we needed the other 10 dollars  mama says that she would like for you to send her $50 the next time and then we can pay Mr Fisher all and have done with it   Mr T is working at the shingles and then we will have him to pay after.   we had to kill our little pig as we could not get feed for it and we wanted the meat anyhow   Mama's shoes is not worth anything she has paid $1.00 for getting them mended   the leather is rotten for are all going into holes.  I want stout gingham domestic for dress   get one green and white and the other brown and white   narrow bars   9 yds   you

can get them in the spring as I am all in rags   mama is not very well that whatever it is a bout her heart trouble her dreadfully   I go to school and the teacher's name is Miss Cooke   Mrs Tators Sister   Mama thinks that the rye coffee hurts her and our other coffee is all most out   we received the papers   save all the books and papers that you can for they come good here   save me all the cards and gift paper that you can find   No more at present But remaining yours
Truly Yours
Miss Marietta Boizard
Mrs Eleanor M Boizard


From Oliver to Eleanor & Marietta

Chicago<br>March 3<sup>rd</sup> 1865

Dear Ellen,
I am well, and hope <u>the</u> <u>tall</u> <u>girl</u> and yourself are well.  You will find Enclosed <u>Thirty five</u> (35) We are very busy.  We have Sent off <u>two</u> Regiments *{the letter has a hole in it, causing words to be missing on both sides of the paper}* and a large portion of another Regiment *{missing word}* organizing.  I received a letter from Mr <u>Dorsey</u> and I Enclosed it to his <u>Lady</u>.  Please ascertain how you Stand with Mr. Fisher and let me Know the particulars.  I have been Somewhat uneasy about you, I dreamed that we met, and also Etty and you told me that you had to go home, as you feared the water was coming into the upper room-- I hope you are well and also "<u>Dudu</u>"   try to get the shingles, made if Mr Tucker is well.  I hope Mr. Fisher is well, as I understood in the <u>Dream</u> that he was not well.  Try to take everything particularly and I have no doubt, but we will get along in another Year.  The weather is very mild, at present, and I hope the navigation will be opened early, however you cant get passage much before the month of May.  I know it requires a great Economy to make your provisions hold out, I hope *{missing words}* not want.  By the By, how does your Pig, will *{missing words}* a barrell of meat, in time, Beef is *{missing words}* per Hundred on the <u>Hoof</u>.  Pork is cheaper than beef -- Coffee is about the Same, Sugar some few cents lower   I must try to get your <u>Chairs</u>, I would like to get a number of things for you if nothing happens.  I have not received an answer from the last letter, but I Suppose it will arrive tomorrow, the Post Office is Closed to day, on account of the Inauguration of <u>Old</u> <u>Abe</u> an <u>Honest Heart</u>   The Rebels are getting <u>down</u> in <u>the mouth</u>.  Wilmington N.C. and Charleston S.C. being lost, and nothing remains much except Mobile, and Galveston, on the Texas Coast and it is to be hoped, <u>Everything is gone up.</u>  I shall close this letter, hoping you are in excellent health and also my Big Dudu.  Give my best Respects to all enquiring friends and receive my fervent wishes.
Your  Husband
"<u>Oliver</u>"

## Long Distance Love 1855-1870

From Oliver to Eleanor

Chicago, IL<br>
(Sunday) March 12<sup>th</sup> 1865

My Dear Wife,
Your letter dated 25<sup>th</sup> Feby. 1865 came to hand on the 9<sup>th</sup> of March and I have felt quite uneasy about you since. I hope you are better, by this time. I cannot rest easy, when I know that you are Sick. and Etty tells me that She is all in rags I thought that She had Clothes enough to last her till Spring, as for Shoes wearing out that cant be helped, as the Shoes that you buy already made are not worth much. Although you pay a big price, for them. Etty tells me that you had to Kill the pig. I find it takes a quantity of provisions to last all winter,. I cant brag much about my health at present. I feel no appetite and my stomach hurts me frequently it is something like "indigestion" I set so much we are So busy that we are obliged to work till 6 O'Clock in the Evening, we have been at work including this day, four consecutive Sundays. Two of the Clerks are Sick, and the work comes heavier on the remaining Six. The Captain works very Steady himself. We will get off another Regiment in 3 days. And there is nearly another full regiment not yet organized. I Send you on the 5<sup>th</sup> March $35 I hope you have received it. Keep up Courage and all may go well. Kiss Etty for me and tell her I will bring her some gingham for dresses. Maybe in the month of May or June. Give my best respects to all friends, and receive my best wishes.
Your Husband
"Oliver"


From Eleanor & Marietta to Oliver (Written by Marietta)

Glen Arbor<br>
March 24<sup>th</sup> 1865

Dear Papa
We received your letter the 20<sup>th</sup> and we received the money and was glad to hear that you are well as this leaves us at present. all but mama   she has the headache. Mrs Dorsey received the letter and they are all well   we got a copy of the times from Emma Bridges. Ettie was at a childrens party at Mrs Fisher's last week. I got eight pounds of meat for $2.00 as our butter and Lard is out   they dont catch fish yet but as soon as they do we will buy some. We will pay Mr. Fisher $25 dollar's.   we will have to get some sugar. We have payed Mr Fisher $75 out of $98, we will have to keep $10 to pay the school bill and other expenditures   I hope we will be able to pay Mr Fisher all in another month   Fisher's folkes is well. but Mr. Tucker is not very well.   When you come in fetch in a mate for Dickie and bring it in a square cage as he is calling for young birds all day   when you write next time tell me what flour costs outside   we have bread stuff enough untill you come in in May. Come in as soon as you can   if they have any paper boxes at the office bring in some as we have use for them. Bob Oliver is married   he is married to a Miss Smith that came in last fall and Mary is married to that Miss Smith's brother. and Sallie was married to James Kilderhouse, when you get lard get it in a pail that has not painted in the inside.  no more at present but remaining yours truly yours.
Miss Marietta Boizard &
Mrs Eleanor M. Boizard
Both of Glen Arbor Mich


How is Heopshies or Whatever them German folks names was that used to live in the same house with us that live on pope st

**Chicago and Glen Arbor 1864-1870**

From Oliver to Eleanor

Chicago, IL
March 31st 1865

My Dear Wife
Your letter dated the 18th March, Came to hand this morning, but it appears that Etty did not State whether you received the $35 or not. I see by your letter that you have to pay Mr. Fisher 48 Dolls. Enclose you will find $35- (Dolls) and when the **Maine** Starts from here, which will be about the 20th or 25th April, I will Send you Some Coffee, Sugar, and Meat. I may not be able to See you until the 1st June as we are very busy, and I think there will be a change before the month of June, but I would like to come up about June, if nothing happens. I feel moderately well at present, but for 2 days last week, I was quite unwell about the middle of this month, my nose took to bleeding, and I bled the part of one day about 5 times, and once in the night, but it Stopped by itself. Mr Pfeiffer Boy "Emil" 10 years old got his leg fast in a wagon and made a hole in his Knee, that took place today at dinner time, and his father is gone to the Country till Tomorrow. I hope you will keep your health, as I can't brag much about Mine. Give my best respects to all Enquiring friends. Kiss Etty for me, and receive my best wishes.
Your Husband
"Oliver"


From Oliver to Eleanor & Marietta

Chicago Ill
April 16th 1865

My Dear Wife
I Send by the propeller **Maine** 1 Bll.{Barrel} Flour, and a Box of Groceries, which I had put up in good order. I also Send you a copy of the News, which you will find deplorable news, as regards the murder of the President. The whole Country is placed in Solemnity. All Buildings in the City of Chicago are decorated with crepe. Old men weep in the Streets, men appear to be infuriated at the dastardly act. **J. Wilkes Booth** the actor is Supposed to be the murderer -- **Sect'y Seward** was also stabbed in Bed, but his death requires Confirmation his Son was also wounded badly by the Murderer   I will write again the 1st of May   I Shall not be able to See you before the 4th or 5th of June -- I hope you are well and also My Big Dudu   Kiss her for me, and receive my Blessings.
Your Husband
"Oliver"

**Long Distance Love 1855-1870**

Chicago Ills
April 16th 1865

My Dear Wife

I Send by the propeller Maine 1 Bll. Flour, and a Box of Groceries, which I had put up in good order, I also Send you a Copy of the News, which you will find deplorable news, as regards the Murder of the President. The whole Country, is placed in Solemnity, All Buildings in the City of Chicago are decorated with Crape, Old men weep in the Streets, Men appear to be infuriated at the dastardly act, J. Wilkes Booth the actor is Supposed to be the Murderer. — Secty Seward was also Stabbed in Bed, but

his death requires Confirmation
his Son was also Wounded
badly by the Murderer

I will write again the 1st May,
I Shall not be able to See you
before the 4th or 5th June —

I hope you are well and also
my Big Sadie Kiss her for
me, and receive my Blessings

    Your Husband
      Oliver

Mrs E. M. Bajand
 Glen Arbor
  Mich

**Long Distance Love 1855-1870**

From Eleanor & Marietta to Oliver (Written by Marietta)

Glen Arbor<br>April 24, 1865

Dear Father
We received your letter and the money but was sorry to hear that you was not very well but this leaves us very well at present   I have paid Monsieur Fisher the last $20 on the house   I have got 1,800 feet more lumber from him.  we paid $5 for drawing lumber & logs  we can pay him   I have paid over $3.21 school money for Ettie   there were three or fore {four} Propellers in yesterday up at Macks dock and we dont know whether there was anything on them or not for us.  and they brought the news of the assination {assassination}  of P Lincoln.  now for domestic affairs we are very glad that the Lake is open so that the boats can run as we have to pay $2.00 for 8 pounds of meat and that wont go very far where there is not butter or lard.  our tea is allmost out as I let Mrs. Tucker have a pound of it in the winter.  Please send Ettie in a pair of shoes as hers is so much worn out that she gets her feet wet every time she goes or comes through the swamp.  if you can send them in by the next boat.  I have made about 10 or 12 lbs of maple sugar   we have pretty near two barrels of potatoes.  if you can I would like for you to send me in some dryed beef   we will have to have some kind of a fence around the clearing before we plant.  no more at present  but remaining yours truly yours.
Mrs. E.M. Boizard


From Eleanor and Marietta to Oliver (Written by Marietta)

Glen Arbor, Michigan<br>April 25 1865

*Written at the very top of the letter.*
 Mr. Fisher is not very well he is troubled with **boils**.  When you send things in send them in at Todd dock as it costs so much to send up to Macks dock as it takes a man and a team a whole day  we guess the buffalo boats will stop here at todds dock but we don't know yet for certain

Dear Papa {*crossed out*} Oliver
We are well and I hope that you are the same.  We received the things  a box and a barrel of flour we was very much pleased to get the butter and Lard as we had got tired of fat meat we was very glad to get the tea as we were just out  I guess that we will let Mr. Tucker have the flour as we will have enough to last us untill you can send us in some more as he is out.  When you write tell us the price including the freight   there is a letter and a paper over at Mr. Fishers but we have not got there yet   please excuse the blots   you may get this letter before you do the other and I will tell you about my shoes. please send me a pair of shoes as soon as you can   you may get it quicker as we are going to send it by a boat if we can   by the teacher as far as Milwaukee any how on the boat   they are expecting a boat any minute   Please send me in some writing paper and a box of pens.  paper is so dear   6 sheets for ten cents.  I just finished you a shirt.  Mr. Tucker will finish the shingles in a couple of days and then he will put them on the roof.  no more at present but I remain your affectionate wife.
Mrs. Eleanor M Boizard

# Chicago and Glen Arbor 1864-1870

<u>From Eleanor & Marietta to Oliver (Written by Marietta)</u>

*The top of this letter is missing, so we cannot see the date or the salutation. Based on the contents of the letter, I believe that it fits in here chronologically.*

We are well and I hope that you are the same. the kichen is up and part of the roof is on. they are working at it now it takes six thousand shingles.  we got the sash down at the store enough for three windows and six pounds of meat & the sash & meat cost 5 dollars. we had the ham but it would not go far where there is work men. please send us 4 or 5 pounds of putty as Mr. Tucker says it will take that much. Mrs Tucker wants 4 pound of tea. send Ettie 9 yds of pink calico you will find a sample in the letter & send Charity Brotherton 10 yds of the same piece that you get Ettie but have them measured seperate and two yds of plain **jackonet** you will find a sample of it also and one yd of white **drilling**Error! Bookmark not defined. as mr. Brotherton is working here helping Mr. Tucker   please send an ink powder   Mr Fisher has been very sick he has had a **carbuncle** on the back of part of his neck   I don't know what to do about planting as I cannot do it   yesterday I set out a few currant bushes and to day my heart pains me dreadfully   but I will have to try to put in a few garden seeds if I can get them   no more at present   But yours with respect
Mrs Eleanor M Boizard
Miss Marietta Boizard

Please come home as soon as you can. this is the last sheet of paper and there is not more at the store


<u>From Oliver to Eleanor & Marietta</u>

Chicago Ills<br>May 3<sup>rd</sup> 1865

My Dear Wife,
I send you by the Propeller **Granite State** a small package containing Some Garden Seeds, Etty's Shoes, and Gingham for a Dress, also a Spade, you Stated in your letter which I received this morning "post marked" Milwaukee, that I should Sent things to Todds dock. I Sent them by the Maine supposing they would land there, it appears there is antipathy arising about the Quality of the wood and the Boats wont stop there. Consequently, you are obliged to pay high to get them from the other Dock. **Booth** the Murderer has been Killed by a Sergeant of New York Cavalry. They fired the barn, arrested his accomplice, and exterminated the Murderer. President Lincolns remains will reach here Sometime on Monday and all business will cease, in regard of public offices. Capt Pomeroy leaves here on Sunday night, he goes South to transact business for the Government, he will be gone about 3 months. We have got the hurry of business over and 3 Clerks will be transferred from this office. Which leave 5 in number left. Government has issued a General order to reduce the force of Employees, also Stopping Recruiting for Volunteers   Many officers will be dropped, as the war is coming down to a point. Gen'l Johnson has Surrendered all the forces of Georgia & North Carolina, and there is another army (Rebel) west of the Mississippi, which will have to give up.  I paid for Flour $7.50 and $1 for Freight 50ct's for the Box of Groceries. I am glad to hear you are well, also Etty. Mr. Fisher I hope will get clear of his Biles *{boils}* Soon. I know what they are.  Ettys shoes cost $2.50 and hope they will answer her, as it is the most difficult thing to get good Shoes. I could have ordered them made, then I dont Know whether they would fit her or not, they are number "3's" they are large Enough, that's a sure thing, I think if her foot has grown much. I Suppose her foot is like the **Oldest of the Wimmens.** I enclose you $10 Dolls. My Expenses has been large this month. I paid 35 doll's for Provision, and $1.50. Freight.

**Long Distance Love 1855-1870**

I Shall try to Start from here about the 1st June, and then I will try to bring you 6 chairs. I am Glad Mr Tucker has the Shingles ready, and hope he will be able to Shingle the house as soon as possible. I met the young Goffart, moving up to Glen Arbor on the **Young America**, and now I will Close for awhile. Kiss Etty for me, and receive my blessing.
Your Husband
Oliver
John O Boizard


From Eleanor & Marietta to Oliver (Written by Marietta)

Glen Arbor
May 12th 1865

Dear Oliver
We received the letter and a package also the money $10. I hope that you will come home soon. We are out of flour and have baked the last baking   We received the shoes and the dress Ettie foot has not grown much and so her shoes are full to large No 2's are pretty large for her. the roof is on the house   Mr Fisher is better. We hope you will stay more than a day or two this time. Etty says you promised to bring her a present and she says She would like to know what it is going to be   there is no school yet and we guess it wont commence untill the 1st of June   we expect the teacher that taught last summer will teach, Mrs Tator.   we got one hen setting. Ettie has found three or four nests this spring today she found a nest with 8 eggs in it. Mr. Goffarts folks Says that you and me and Ettie has to go up there to their house when you come in.
You did not send me in any onion sets
no more at present
But I remain your ever affectionate wife
Mrs Eleanor M. Boizard

Write soon or come in soon I dont care much which you do but I would rather you would come in.


*{I believe that Oliver came home for a short visit}*


From Oliver to Eleanor & Marietta

Chicago, Ills
June 22nd 1865

Dear Ellen,
I arrived here this morning at 7. all Safe. I went immediately to the office, to report and found Capt. Hill, all right, go to work tomorrow, plenty work, office full. I Send you by the boat, **"Empire"** 1 box containing clothes & c. which I presume will Suit. The Calico prints I could not well find, and I thought I would Suit my own taste and I hope it will Suit the rest. I paid 26 dolls. for two coats $6- for pants, 4 dolls for vest and $1.75 for Hat. (20 yds of Calico $6.00) in all $43.75 without the price of the freight, for Mr Brotherton's family. they owe you 75cts -- it amounts to $43.75. I send you 8 spools of white cotton, also **skeleton hoops** for Etty, cost $2.50 the salesman told me a Lady shed tears, because she could not find any of the same kind.   at that time he had none on hand. I think he lies--   I do not Know how Miss Charity and Etty will like their dress patterns & c. But I did the best I could -- I

could not get Mrs. Brotherton's pattern of calico, and I chose that quality. After the 1st month if nothing happens, I will Send your little necessaries. I left Mrs Akeu about to look for her Sister. Give my regards to all
your Husband
"Oliver"



From Eleanor and Marietta to Oliver (Written by Marietta)

Glen Arbor, Michigan<br>July 1st 1865

Dear Father
We received your letter and the things and all the things were right but the stuff for the white waist   it was **paper cambric** instead of **Jaconet**  it was stuff for linings.  it has rained more or less since you went away and I guess you took all the mosquitoes away with you.  the old hen has all of her little children. Jenny has little birds and they are just like a nest full of worms as the man says but his was a mouth full.  I go to school and I wish you would send me the **History of the United States** as the Teacher says I must study it.  Mrs Tucker says if you cannot get photographs to get them on plates and get them varnished   but not in cases as she wants to send them away in letters to her people.  perhaps we will send this out on the boat   Dorsey has not come home yet   his regiment was sent back to Louisville KY and he says there is no knowing when he will come home.  Mr Tucker planted the rest of the potatoes.  Harrison Brotherton finished the fence.  I like the ribbon very much   I guess this is enough for tonight so no more at present but write soon. Yours forever
Mrs. Eleanor M Boizard
Miss Ettie Boizard

*there is a drawing of a bird with a text bubble that says   "more seed more seed"*


From Oliver to Eleanor & Marietta

Chicago Ills<br>July 3rd 1865

Dear Ellen,
I Send you by the "**Young America**" a Box containing Groceries, Hardware, and also your Dress, Shoes for you & Etty, which I hope will Suit, also a Small pocketbook, containing $15 Doll's. (all I could Spare). I hope you are well also Etty, and will Spend your 4th July, agreeable, without any disaster. The Captain has not returned yet. Expect him daily, dont know how things may turn out after his return. I hope I shall be Employed, this Summer, try to get along as Economical as possible, as we dont Know what May turn up. I will Send Mrs. Tucker's pictures during the month July -- I have nothing of importance to relate.  Give my regards to all Enquiring friends.  I Sent Mr. Lindsleys papers down for Signature.  I expect to hear from Mr. Dorsey shortly from Louisville, Ky. I Send a letter from him to Mrs. Dorsey --  Truly yours  Your  Husband
"Oliver"

By the By how is Miss Charity's dress   write in answer also Ettys

NB How did the clothes answer of Brothertons

**Long Distance Love 1855-1870**

From Eleanor and Marietta to Oliver (Written by Marietta)

Glen Arbor, Michigan<br>July 9<sup>th</sup> /65

*written at the very top of the letter:*
We owe Brotherton's 5.25 and they want you to send them 1 pound of tea the same kind we have and the rest in unbleached sheeting the same you sent Mrs. Tucker not to coarse don't pay more than 41 cts

Dear Papa
We received the things and the letter and the pocket book with $15 in it. I like the pocket very well. Ettie's shoes does but mine is very large but I guess I can change them. I liked my dress very much. I got the flour at Mr Field's. The next things you send try and send them in at Todd's dock. I paid Harrison $4 for making the fence and cutting some wood. When you write next time write and tell me whether I can get my winter wood cut. Please send me two yards of white **drilling** lining and send Ettie two round combs. two doz of glass with colored buttons with eyes in as large as a cherry. Mrs Tucker wants you to send in Willies pants one pair any how as that pair that Mr Tucker bought that day is allmost wore out. The young birds are all dead I guess the old bird did not feed them as she ought to. The day that we went to see about the things the fox came and took the old hen that Ettie had the little chickens and the little chickies go all around crying after her. the potatoes are growing nicely and what cucumber we had left we enjoyed the fourth very much. what few there was down at glen arbor dock they went a boat riding on the Caldwell. over to the south Island and they paid $.50 for the trip but we didn't go we went up to Mr Macks as there was a team down and we had a very nice time as every thing went off quietly Don't forget my **History of the U.S.** Mr Lloyd was here to clear up the log's off of the lot but I would not set him to work on it untill I know what you was going to do whether you was going to stay with the Captain or not Send me in a Flour Sieve our butter and Lard will be out by the 1<sup>st</sup> of August send me a jar about 4 or 5 gallons with a lid and put either the butter or Lard in it as it will do me as a churn have the lid so it will fit down in the inside no more at present But I remain yours truly yours
Mrs. Eleanor M Boizard


From Oliver to Eleanor

Chicago, IL<br>July 14 1865

My Dear Wife,
Your letters dated respectively the 1<sup>st</sup> and 9<sup>th</sup> July, are now before me, and in reply, I have to State, that I am glad to hear that you and Etty, are well and passed your 4<sup>th</sup> July, happily without any disaster. I am sorry that your shoes, did not fit you, for I took the precaution to have them made for you, thinking they would give Satisfaction. I paid $3.75 for your Shoes and $2.25 for Etty's. You spoke of getting your winter wood cut, you might Employ <u>Lloyd</u> to clear your logs from the clearing and make Fire wood of them for 1 week and I will pay him at the End of the month. The Captain has Come home and we are busy, but I do not Know whether he will remain here during this Summer or not. However I will let you Know if any Change takes place. Employ Lloyd for one week if you can get him and I will pay him in August. It wont cost more than $10.00. I will try to Send all the articles required for yourself and Mrs Tucker, Mr Brotherton at the End of this month. I heard McWickham had a fight with Bailey the 4<sup>th</sup> July – So the fox got the old Hen at last. I am Sorry, I would soon have lost 5 Dolls- than that old hen – Tell Mrs. Tucker I will Manage her Pictures this month, I have not been to See Mrs Kuntz yet with the Bag for Goffart, I

**Chicago and Glen Arbor 1864-1870**

forgot I happen to See the Bag under my Bed – Kiss Etty for me and tell her to be a good girl. I sent a letter to Mrs Dorsey from her Husband. I will close this letter as I am down hearted–
Good Bye
"Oliver"


From Eleanor and Marietta to Oliver (Written by Marietta)

Glen Arbor, Michigan
July 18th/65

Dear Papa,
We received your welcome letter and the papers and we was very glad to get them as reading matter is very scarce. You spoke of getting Mr. Lloyd to cut wood and clearing up the lot if we was to get him now he could not clear it up untill fall  the hemlock logs that are on the lot we could not burn as it will our stove out in- no- time.  Mamma has spoke to one of the Brothertons boys for to cut it by the cord and we can get (Lloyd) to clear the place up this fall. Tucker's want 1 lb Tea  I got 14 lights of glass at 15 cts a light.  I changed my shoes and I had to pay 50 cts for getting them changed they was (no) 6 but 4 will fit me if they are high enough in the instep and they are wide enough.  We have eight more little chickens. The Old Waddler is their mother we have the other eight and some of them crows and they go in with the other chickens   Harvey says the young chickens that is a week old lays eggs every day.   Papa will you get me a strand of Amber beads don't get them if cannot get amber as they say that amber will keep my neck from getting any larger as I am getting a large neck like Mrs. Tucker's   no more at present but remaining yours Truly Yours
Mrs E. M Boizard &
Ettie Boizard

Write Soon    PS send me three or four spools of colored cotton 2sps 40 & 36


From Eleanor & Marietta to Oliver (Written by Marietta)

Glen Arbor
July 28th/65

Dear Father
We are well and I hope you are the same   Mr Lindsley got the money and handed us the letter but he never said as much as thank you or anything   but you could not expect anything better from them the low lived set that they are  I will give you a specimen of Mrs Parker (our news carrier) You know when you were in here I had the prickly heat very bad and she was here and she saw it on my neck and she asked Mama what it was and mama told her what it was and she went around and told that I had the itch   I am not the only one that catches her tongue as you will see in the end of this letter but everybody.  Mr Tucker is working at the house and he wants you to send in a trowel   we are out of cornmeal and we would be glad if you would send us in some for the little chickies   if you can please send in some rice as our potatoes are out and we have nothing to put on the table but bread and butter and fat meat  our butter is out   also the lard   the little chickens crows   no more at present  but remaining yours
Truly Yours
Mrs. Eleanor M. Boizard

**Long Distance Love 1855-1870**

Miss Ettie Boizard

*{There is a picture drawn of a lady with a text bubble-- with the following words:}*
John Dorsey has deserted and he got as far as chicago with a cow and he was caught and taken back.  this is another one of her lies. Mrs Parker our news carrier

P.S. Dont show this to anyone


From Oliver to Eleanor
$\hfill$ Chicago, IL
$\hfill$ August 5$^{th}$ 1865

My Dear Wife
Your letter came to hand, dated the 28$^{th}$ July, and I find that Mr Lindsley received his money.  I am Sorry to hear that he did not Even thank any body for the Kindness bestowed.  However let it now.  I would have Sent your little Stores before now, but as the Boats (Northern Transport) do not land at Todds wharf, I Send a Box containing sundries, also a Can of Kereosene, and a jar of Butter.  I found the jar you required, but the weather being so hot, I though I would not Send the Lard this month, as it would be all Solution.  The corn meal I will try to Send up during the month of August.  I tried to find Amber Beads for Etty, But I could not find them.  The original Amber Beads are costly.  And the idea of her wearing about her neck for Cure that's all Bosh.  Apply friction of Iodine or Liniments if you have them, and if not, I will send them at the Earliest opportunity – You will please find $10 Enclosed.  I could not Send you any more but will try to make it up next month.  I bought a pair of pants & c.  You will find (I hope) the articles well packed.  Groceries are Somewhat higher, Tea is about the Same $1.80, Sugars higher, I also Send you 2 cans peaches which I suppose you will relish –  The Photographs are pretty well taken and hope will answer.  Give my regards to all Enquiring friends
Your  Husband
Oliver

Kiss Etty for me and tell her to Keep her temper


From Eleanor & Marietta to Oliver (Written by Marietta)
$\hfill$ Glen Arbor
$\hfill$ August 13th/65

Dear Father
We received the things   butter and money and also the photograph and they were well pleased with them.  Mr Tucker has worked Eighteen days on the House and he is not near done yet   I guess you forgot the Trowl as you did not send it in.  We had to get 5 bushels of Lime and five lbs more nails.  Mrs Dorsey has got the **Typhoid Fever** and she is at Tuckers.  Mr Collins oldest Daughter has it also and they dont expect her to live as the Dr. has given up all hopes of her recovery   We was not out of tea and Mr Tucker took both pounds of teas as they owed a half pound.  but we had enough to last untill the last of the month.   Mr Tucker wants you to send in a iron tea kettle like ours   but get it no. 9 or 10   and send Mrs T a **skelaton hoop** skirt the same as Etties but get it larger around the top if you can and send us in a barrel of flour as ours is allmost gone and it is not fit to pay Tuckers with   we have to

feed the chickens with it (as we have twenty four young chickens) and Mr T is boarding here and it takes a great deal where there is no vegetables and we have no cornmeal to feed the chickens with   we like the cans of peaches very much but I would rather have had pickels.  we have picked 20 quarts of whockle *{huckle or whortle}* berries and I am drying them   most of them for winter.  I got four pairs of colored hose and I had to pay 60 cts a pair   two pair for me and two pair for Ettie.  Mr Tucker would like for you to Send him a barrel of flour as he is almost out   you could send the things in at todd's dock for it costs as much to get them down from McCarty's as it does from chicago.  We got the wood cut and we will have to pay for it at the end of the month   we got nine cords cut   will you please get me one of Sarah's photographs if the artist has the negative as I would like to have one   no more at present But we remain yours truly.
Mrs Eleanor M. Boizard

*{It appears from July 31, 1865 letter that Mrs. Tucker was having prints made of Sarah Tucker's picture to send to her family.  Sarah died in January 1865. Eleanor & Marietta wanted one of the pictures.  There is a picture of Sarah Tucker in the back of this book.}*


From Eleanor and Marietta to Oliver (Written by Marietta)

Glen Arbor, Michigan
August 20th

Dear Father
We are well and I hope you are the same.  Mrs Dorsey is no better and she took a whim that she must go down home and Fisher took her home in his wagon.  we have one of the children up here.  Collinses daughter is no better she may linger along for two or three months but the Dr. says she cannot get well as she had the hemorage of the bowels and stomach.  Harrison says he wants you to send him in $7 worth of blue **drilling** and Hickory blue and white  9 yards blue drilling and the rest in Hickory don't pay more than 40 or 50 cts a yd as it is towards cutting the wood   don't forget the flour as both families are out as it takes so much to feed the chickens that we have to bake every day as we have nothing to feed them   our potatoes is not large enough to dig and there is so few in a hill as the ground is so hard   it not being worked any   we have to buy them from the neighbors   potatoes is going to be very plentiful this year.   when you get these things send the bill   as people asks us what the price is   we cant tell them   they asked us the price of willies pants and we could not tell them   papa I would like you to send in my chain and pin as you might lose it.  If you can please send us in some casteel **{castile} soap**   no more at present. But we remain yours truly yours
Mrs. Eleanor M Boizard
Miss Ettie Boizard
Glen Arbor


*{Oliver visited Glen Arbor}*

**Long Distance Love 1855-1870**

From Oliver to Eleanor

Chicago, IL<br>October 12<sup>th</sup> 1865

My Dear Wife,
I arrived here this afternoon. We had a very Stormy time this morning about 5 O'Clock it lasted about 3 hours, just when we left Milwaukee, I thought it would become Serious, however it got Calm. I gave Mr. Sheridan $5 dollars he went off the Boat at Milwaukee and was going in the Country about 12 miles– and he told me he was a going to buy Some Butter and I gave him the Bucket, and he told me he would do the Best he could   he thinks he can buy Butter for 30 cents in the Country. I went to my grocer and he told me he was retailing Butter at 45 cents a pound. I will be obliged to get my Shoes mended it will cost me 75 cts and I think I will look around for one day and if I don't find anything to do I will be obliged to go to Springfield. I hope you and Etty are well. Keep up a good heart and don't be uneasy. If I go to Springfield I will write to you as Soon as I get there. If I can't get nothing to do there, I will try to go to St. Louis, if my money holds out. I paid 5 dolls, on the Boat and 5 dolls for the Butter and my shoes may cost me $1 and then it will cost me something for Board and I wont have much left  Mrs. Tator got off at Milwaukee. I expect Mr. Sheridan will go down on the same Boat, if So, you will get your Butter Sooner. I Send this letter by the **City of Boston.** No More at present But remain yours with respect –
your husband
"Oliver"

Kiss Etty for me.


From Oliver to Eleanor & Marietta

U.S. Mustering and Disbursing Office<br>Springfield, Illinois<br>Saturday October 14<sup>th</sup> 1865

My Dear Wife,
I arrived here this morning, from Chicago Ill's, and I immediately went to the Captains Office, he had Sent for Mr. Truesdell and me to Chicago, but being in Michigan, he could not find me  it was the Same day I left McCarty's Dock. I found Mr. Truesdell at work, and another new <u>Clerk</u> consequently, he filled the vacancy. however the Capt'. has given me a Situation in the State Armory, he has charge of the Ordnance but it does not  pay so well, it will pay $2 per day (Except Sundays) but he told me that he would do better for me, as Soon as the opportunity offers. Enclosed you will please find <u>Three Dollars.</u> all that I could possibly spare, until the 1<sup>st</sup> of next month, and then it will take till the 16<sup>th</sup> Nov. before you get it, leaving out Sundays it will be about $50 per month, however I am glad I got this job, as the winter is coming on. the Capt. used me very well. It happened that a young Soldier want to quit work this day, and that just left a vacancy for me, for the Capt Said he was glad I come. There is a man & wife by the name of Hartmann here, they Stopped at Pfeiffers Some 4 months ago, he had just left the Army, at that time, and I became Somewhat acquainted with them, and I am not Staying with them at present. She owns the Brick House, She lives in, and he is a machinist and I may probably board with them, but I am afraid it is rather too far from my work -- I Suppose the Board will be $5 per week, I have not asked them yet. I go to work on Monday. Dear Ellen have patience, I will not be able to Send you any provision, but I will try to Send you money monthly. Mrs Pfeifer and Lizzy is on a visit to this family, and will go back on Monday next. I will write again on the 13<sup>th</sup> of the month (November) if I live. Kiss Etty for me, and give my Compliments to all Enquiring friends, and receive my blessing. I hope you got your Butter.

**Chicago and Glen Arbor 1864-1870**

Your Husband
Oliver

Direct your answer to John O. Boizard
PO Box 107. Springfield. Ill's –


From Eleanor & Marietta to Oliver (Written by Marietta)

Glen Arbor
October 17<sup>th</sup> /65

Dear Papa
We are well and I hope that you are the same  we have not had any snow yet  only once and then it was only a little spit and now it just like Indian summer. I have 14 quarts of **beechnuts** gathered for winter. our house is plastered upon the outside and it is very comfortable. our flour is out and we will have to eat cornbread untill we can get the means to get some  it will cost us almost as much again to get our things in here this winter as every thing is so high but we will have to do the best we can. Mr Lloyd has cut our wood so far. I got half lb of tea since you went away and had to pay $1 and it is not very good at that  I would not know what to do if it was not for my chickens as we dont have any meat  no more at present
But remaining yours  Truly Yours
Mrs. Eleanor M. Boizard
Miss Ettie Boizard

P.S. write soon

October 18<sup>th</sup>

This letter was written last night and this morning we received the letter and the money which will go towards getting a barrel of flour. we have not got the potatoes from Mr. Miller yet as he is waiting for snow to come so he can get them here with the sleigh and ponies. we was glad to hear that you was well. we got the book and two papers and was glad to get them as we haven't any reading matter  we dont know whether we can get the stove as Dorsey has not moved yet and cant untill the man gets out of their house but we can get one from Tucker if we could get pipe any where



From Oliver to Eleanor & Marietta

Springfield, Ills
Oct 31<sup>st</sup> 1865

My Dear Wife,
Enclosed you will please find $12. I Signed the vouchers for $28, but I could not wait till they were Sent to Saint Louis and back, as the amount is paid by the Chief of Ordnance, and So I borrowed it from the Clerk, for a few days until the money comes. I have to pay 12 dolls. for my Board & 1 Dollar for Washing for part of the month of October. which will leave me $3. for expenses during the month of Nov. I hope you will be contented and also hope that your provision will hold out till you can get this money. There being no vacancy for a Clerk in this Dept. I am reported as Laborer, but I dont do any thing but write.  Capt Pomeroy is not a Major by **Brevet**, and I expect he will be the Principal Must'g officer and then I may get $3 per day for he told me that he would give me the first

**Long Distance Love 1855-1870**

chance   I am at Present in his Employ, only I am at the Arsenal which belongs to the State of Illinois   only that there is Government property on hand, which the Captain is accountable for as he is the ordnance Officer -- I wrote you a letter from Chicago Ill also one letter from Springfield enclosing $3. which I hope you have received.  It takes so long before a letter reaches here, it would be much better for you to Send your answers on the Propellers while they are running as it Saves about 10 days -- I hope that you will Keep your health also Etty.  Tell me in your answer about Mr. Lindsley whether you got any more Potatoes or not and whether Mr. Miller paid you in Potatoes or not -- Tell me whether you have had any cold weather and what chance there is for Mr. Dorsey's Stove   I will close for awhile   Give my regards to all Enquiring frinds, and Kiss Etty for me.  Please write Soon So you can put the answer aboard the Boat before the Navigation Closes   I am yours, till death closes the Scene
Your Husband
"Oliver"


From Eleanor & Marietta to Oliver (Written by Marietta)

Glen Arbor
Nov 1st 1865

Dear Papa
We received your welcome letter and was glad you had employment at Springfield Ill.  it is not very cold here yet as we hadnt any frost untill the 27th of October   everything was as green and as nice as it was when you left.  I am digging my large crop of potatoes   I have about a barrel.  Flour is $14 a barrel down at Todds & meat is 28cts per lb   we got the butter 12 lbs. -- Mr Lloyd is got so that he can be around.  I have been up to goffarts   we had our first chicken today and we wished you were here to have a piece of it   they are in good order   I traded a quilt for potatoes and corn as I was out and Miller did not bring them   they owe us them.   we got only a bushel of potatoes and a bushel and a half of corn that made about $1 from Lindsley.  I hope that you will get a good boarding house and a good wash woman.  I sent to Traverse for $1 worth of tea by Mons. Brotherton   no more at present But remaining yours truly
Mrs. Eleanor M Boizard
Miss Marietta Boizard

P.S. We are well.


From Oliver to Eleanor & Marietta

Springfield, Ill's
Nov 8th 1865

My Dear Wife
Your letter Came to hand this morning and I am glad to hear that you and Etty are well.  I am Sorry that you were obliged to part with your Quilt.  I hope you will not be obliged to Sell any more --   Enclosed you will please find $4. and I hope that you have received ere this the 12 Dollars which I enclosed to you in a letter dated the 31st October.  You Spoke of the weather being good, the weather has been very favorably here   we have had no Snow yet.  Last Sunday I went to Oak Ridge about 2 miles from town, and I Saw the Vault of Mr. Lincoln he lies there in view, with his Son Willie aside of him.  he is Enclosed in a Metallic Coffin, and there is also a Square Walnut Box outside, also the Son   the doors are Stone and Iron grating inside.  4 persons are allowed at a time to look at the

Boxes, through the iron Grating. The Place is the most Beautiful I See   there are a Squad of Soldiers Stationed there  the Sentinel walks in front of the Vault. they are about commencing the monument, and then they will remove him, only a few rods, where they now lie. I am in hopes you will be able to weather the winter, by Sending you Small Sums of money every two weeks -- Boarding cost me 22 1/2 dolls. per month my wash Bill amounts to 1.50 and I dont have much left at the End of the month   I shall have to get Boots for the Winter, Clothing is higher here than any part of the Country I have See yet. An overcoat is worth from 40 to 80 Dolls. pants 15 dolls, prices are awful. Have you received your <u>Deed</u> from Mr. Fisher yet. By the time you get this Navigation will be closed, and then I will have to wait a good while for an answer. I shall be quite lucky if I can retain my Situation this winter  Kiss Etty twice for Me, and receive my blessing Give my best respects to all the neighborhood-- (I send you some reading matter)
Your Husband
"Oliver"

From Eleanor and Marietta to Oliver (Written by Marietta)

Glen Arbor, Michigan<br>November 24 1865

Dear Father,
We received your welcome letter dated the 8th of the month and the money also. We are well and I hope you are the same. I got the barrel of flour and it cost $12 and when it is made up it looks as though it had molasses in it, it is so dark. the weather is very mild and we have not had any snow   it has hardly froze yet   some of our hens lays and one of this years pullets lays   she is only 6 months old and she lays the cunningest little egg   we have killed 5 chickens and we will have some more to kill when they are large enough   my Tommy cries after me every place I go as soon as he finds out that I am going he begins to cry. dicky sings as loud as ever and Jenny she prates for some one to talk to her   mama is knitting and she says she don't know what she will do for yarn   school has commenced and I don't know as I shall go or not but I would like to go this fine weather   no more at present   But remaining yours
truly yours
Mrs. EM Boizard
Miss Ettie Boizard


From Oliver to Eleanor & Marietta

U.S. Mustering and Disbursing Office<br>Springfield, IL<br>December 1st, 1865

Mr Dear Ellen and Big <u>Dudu</u>
I received your letter this morning and was rejoiced to hear, that you were both well. The answer was two weeks a coming, I am glad you got the $12 about the 4th or 5th of December, as Soon as I can get Some money, you may expect it about the 20th of this month, as it takes 15 day to reach you.  Try to hold out and I will try to Spare you all the money possible  I have had a rather bad cold, and have not get rid of it yet. I am glad your house is plastered, and you are comfortable   I wish you had Some Pipe for the Stove.  I Send you Some reading matter, be patient   I

**Long Distance Love 1855-1870**

think I will get more pay in January 1866 if nothing happens. Give my best regards to all Enquiring friends and receive my best wishes (Kiss Etty for me)
Your Husband
"Oliver"


From Oliver to Eleanor

Springfield, IL
Dec 8th 1865

My Dear Wife,
Please find Enclosed $20.  We did not receive our money until this morning, as Lt. Col. Pomeroy was away in Chicago, and yesterday being "Thanksgiving" there was nothing done.  My pay will be raised this month, and if nothing happens, I will be able to Send you $40 in January.  I hope you have been able to hold out, it takes so long for letters to reach each other.  the weather has been Cold for 2 days past but today it is quite pleasant.  I hope you have had no very Severe weather.  It will be not So hard for you to get along after this month, December.  I have had a bad cold for about 10 days, but it got better without any treatment.  In order to raise my pay 25 Dolls, the Capt gave me and the other man the job of watching the Arsenal, we have to Keep awake half the night and I suppose that gave me the Cough but now it is better.  I Send you a letter a few days ago with Some reading matter.  I Suppose I Shall receive an answer from a letter written a month ago containing $4.  I Send with this letter a Magazine directed to Etty.  I hope you are well I have Changed Boarding house, on account of the distance.  I Sleep at the Arsenal when I am not on Watch, Answer this as Soon as possible, Kiss Etty for me and give me all the particulars, and receive my best wishes.
Your Husband
"Oliver"


From Oliver to Eleanor

Springfield, IL
Dec 20th 1865

My Dear <u>Ellen</u>
Enclosed you will find Five Dollars.  I am well and hope you and Etty are also well.  I Suppose you received $20, which I enclosed on the 8th December.  Before you receive this letter, Christmas will be over, and another year will Commence.  Still nearer the <u>End</u>.  I am Sometime quite uneasy about your welfare, this Winter.  The weather has been moderate So far, until this day, Snowing has Commenced, which reminds me of your Situation this winter, in that Solitary Abode, however I hope you will get through without much Suffering.  I frequently Send you reading matter.  I had Some notion of Subscribing for **Peterson's Lady Magazine** it is $2. Payable in advance for <u>one</u> <u>year.</u> I Suppose you will have to pay 3 prices for your provisions this Winter.  If I can remain in Employment I will try to remit you money to carry you Safe through.  I am afraid you will get Sick from the Cold.  Especially if you have no heating Stove.  In your answer tell me what you have to Eat, and tell me whether your Chickens will hold out.  I will close this letter and receive my best wishes.  Kiss Etty for me, and try to Keep her warm and Comfortable.  Give my best respects to all Enquiring friends.
Your  Husband "Oliver"

N.B.  Direct your answer as usual Box 107  No. of Bill No. 549175
My pay has been increased I watch the half of Every night beside my daily labor J.O.B.


From Eleanor & Marietta to Oliver (Written by Marietta)

Glen Arbor<br>December 22<sup>nd</sup> 1865

Dear Father
We received your letter dated the first of this month but we did not get it untill the 19<sup>th</sup>   I am sorry that you have a bad cold but you must keep yourself dressed warm. we have had very cold weather for about two weeks and the snow is about 6 inches deep.  we have got the stove from Dorseys and the pipe from Burdicks  Charity and George and I go to school down town to Mr. Smith  I hope that we will get the letter with some money in it as everybody is thinking of christmas but us and we have not anything to think about   but we will have our Christmas when you come home   Mr. Fisher has not gone to northport yet but when he goes he will see about our deed as he has got several deeds to see about   send us two almanacs for 1866   no more at present  But remaining yours
Truly yours
Mrs Eleanor M. Boizard
Miss Ettie Boizard
both of Glen Arbor



From Eleanor & Marietta to Oliver (Written by Marietta)

Glen Arbor<br>Dec 29<sup>th</sup> 1865

Dear Father
We are well and I hope that you are the same   we never spent such a poor christmas as this christmas was   we did not know it was christmas but we thought it was sunday and we went down to Mrs Dorsey's to spend the day.  every thing is very high   tea is eighteen shillings per pound and butter 50 cts when we can get it to buy and everything accordingly   it takes one man a day every week to cut us wood enough and that costs $1 1/2 but that is nothing to what it would be if we had to buy it at $12 or 15 per cord I made a pair of pants for one of the Millers and I got $1 for it and a vest also and I guess that will be 75 cts  I will have to get Ettie a pair of shoes made as it is better to get them made and then they will be worth something they will cost $2 as she is almost barefooted.  try and have a christmas Gift for us   I would like to have a set of new knives and forks for my christmas gift small ones  Ettie says she would like a pair of black bead bracelets   you can get them for about $1.  We got the money and the letter and reading matter also.  no more at present  But remaining yours
Truly yours
Miss Ettie Boizard
Mrs Eleanor M. Boizard
*{There is a drawing of a bird with the words 'Dick or Jenny', also a picture of a person on a pig.}*

**Long Distance Love 1855-1870**

From Oliver to Eleanor

Springfield, IL
Jan 12th 1866

My Dear Ellen,
You will please find Enclosed Thirty Five (35) Dollars. Which will Enable you to pay a portion of your debts. I enclosed you on the 8th December 1865 Twenty (20) Dollars which letter I have received no answer. I also Send you about the 20th of December the Sum of 5 dollars, however it is hardly time for that letter to be answered, but the letter which I wrote on the 8th Dec I am Somewhat uneasy about it, however I may get it Tomorrow, or next day. I hope it has not been Stolen, for to lose 20 dollars, would be too hard for us. I Send Etty some papers & Books, with the two fifty cents currency in them. I hope She will get them. I had Some clothes made for Myself. The Stuff I bought at Auction. I also bought Myself a Hat & Boots, I Send you with this money, Some Reading Matter, I Suppose the Roads are Blocked with Snow, which detains the Mail. However the letter which you Sent, dated the 22nd Dec. came to hand in 14 days. I was in hopes that the letter dated the 8th Dec would reach you about Christmas. So to Consider it a Kind of Christmas Gift. Tell me your answer, how you get along whether you Suffer for any thing, or not. Also tell me how often the Mail leaves Glen Arbor. Tell me all the particulars about your Potatoes, Provisions & c. If you receive this Sum of Money, in good Season it will help you along, the Col. (Pomeroy) has

just returned from Cincinnati where he took his Wife (who was Somewhat rounder than usual) and he returned this morning So we did not get our Money untill to day.  My Shirts, are getting Much worn, and I am getting myself 2 pairs of drawers made.  And now my Dear Wife I will Close this letter hoping that you and Etty may Keep your health, and tell Etty Mr Smith must learn her how to **Cypher.**  Kiss Etty for me and tell her not forget her Dada. Give my best Respects to all the neighbors and receive my blessing.
Your Husband
"Oliver"

N.B.  If our work holds out to the month of April, I will consider it lucky.  J.O.B.


From Eleanor and Marietta to Oliver (Written by Marietta)

Glen Arbor, Michigan<br>Jan 26<sup>th</sup> 1866

Dear Father
We are well and I hope that you are the same. the weather is very cold the snow is so deep that it covers a barrel when it stands on the end so that you can use it. it keeps me making fires. it is very lonesome here I have not been out since New Years and I hardly ever see any one this winter.  Ettie goes to school when ever there is a road broke. I got her a pair of shoes made and I had to pay $4.00.  we burn half a cord of wood per week and so you see that there is no danger of us freezing this winter.  our kerosene is out and we will have to get some   we had not any candles and so Ettie went to the store and paid 30 cts a pound and they are made out of this stinking lard and one of them would not burn an hour.   coffee is 50cts per lb   I am making a new dress for Mrs Tucker to pay for some butter    if ever you get a chance I wish you would get some yarn.  but don't get that nasty shoddy stuff   you can keep it in your chest or trunk   we have to pay $3 a pound in here and then it is not very good at that    get it a dark blue gray   if you get it get a lot of it as we all will need stockings.  Robinson and Hatch have not been heard of yet. I received some reading matter and the book you sent is continued and I wish you would send me the continuation of it which is entitled. Clara St. Johns or the mystery solved.  We had not had any letter since new years day and I think it is about time to have one.  no more at present.
 But remaining yours Truly yours,
Mrs Eleanor M. Boizard
Ettie Boizard

Dicky and Jennie are both well and prating away like every thing


From Eleanor and Marietta to Oliver (Written by Marietta)

Glen Arbor, Michigan<br>February 2<sup>nd</sup> 1866

Dear Father,
We received your welcome letter and the money also. we were glad to get the letter and the money also. I paid Mr. Tucker $15 which makes $20 in all that I have paid him.  I have a barrel of flour to get and some other little things in the house and I have to finish paying for Etties shoes.  We have got the deed it is recorded.  you wanted to know how often the mail went from here it goes out but once per week   we got the Almanac's and the reading matter also.

**Long Distance Love 1855-1870**

You spoke of your clothes being wore out. I am sorry to say that ours is wore out to   we must have some coarse unbleached sheeting and you must have some fine unbleached for shirts.  but however we must try and get out of debt for we owe Brotherton's some for the little things that we got from them also for the wood they cut for us last summer.  you wanted to know how our potatoes hold out we have enough to last until spring but we will have to get some seed potatoes in the spring.  The weather has been beautiful and mild for the past week we have not had any snow.  The crust will bear us we can walk all around on it.   our hens has commenced to lay this fine weather   I am very sorry that I haven't the stuff to make your shirts now so I could have them ready when you come in the spring no more at present but remaining yours truly yours.
Mrs. Eleanor M Boziard
Ettie Boizard


From Eleanor and Marietta to Oliver (Written by Marietta)

Glen Arbor, Michigan<br>Feb 9th 1866

Dear Father
We received your welcome letter dated the 29 of Jany. and the papers also.  I have not received the bracelets yet.  I did not want you to get me a pair of costly ones I only wanted you to get me a pair of black bead bracelets and they would only cost about $50 cts or 75 cts at the farthest.  I wanted a pair as all the rest of the girls had some.  I got a barrel of flour I was not quite out but I would not had enough to last untill I got some more money.  it cost me $12  I got half a gallon of kerosene at $1.25 cts per gallon and I got half a pound of tea at 18 shillings and it was not very good at that and a few lbs of meat.  I signed for the **rural new yorker** at $2.50   I had to get some more yarn to knit Ettie some stockings as she is almost barefooted and I paid Mr. Tucker $15 (after I finished paying for Etties shoes) now I have told you all my purchases and I have the large sum of 20 cts left out of $20   no more at present. But remaining yours truly yours.
Mrs Eleanor M. Boziard
Miss Ettie Boizard

Chicago and Glen Arbor 1864-1870

Glen Arbor Feb. 9th 1866;

Dear Father

We received your welcome letter dated the 19 of Jany, and the papers also I have not received the bracelets yet. I did not want you to get me a pair of cuffs one I only wanted you to get me a pair of black bead bracelets, and I thot it would only cost about 50 cts — or .75 at the farthest. I wanted a pair as all the rest of the girls had some. I got a pail of flour I was not quite out but I would not had enough to last until I got some more money. and I thought it was best to get it while I had the money. it cost me $12. I got half a gallon of kerosene at 50 cts per gallon and I got half a pound of tea at 18 shill[ing]s and it was mighty good at that. and a few lbs of yeast. I signed for the usual newspaper at $1.50 I had to get some more yarn to foot Ettie wips stocking as she is almost pin footed and I paid the shoemaker $1.15 now I have told you all my purches and I have the large sum of $1 left out of $10 no more at present but remaining your truly yours

**Long Distance Love 1855-1870**

From Oliver to Eleanor & Marietta

Springfield Ills<br>Valentine's day<br>Feby 14<sup>th</sup> 1866

My Dear Wife
I Send you by mail a Small Box containing a Bracelet, which I hope will please you as every body expects Something in Shape of a New Years Gift. I hope this will Suffice -- Your letter dated the 26<sup>th</sup> Jany 1866 came to hand. I thought it might be an answer to the letter containing 35 dolls. We have not been paid off, for January yet, as I expect, they have run out of funds. So Soon as we get our Money, I will Send you $50 which will Enable you to get out of debt and then you will be able to Save Some money, that is, if my Employment, Keeps until May. There are but 7 Illinois Regt's. to be mustered out, and when they turn in their arms, I think the work about the arsenal will close. I also Send you 2 Papers, 1 with the picture of Gen. Grant which will do to nail against the wall of your Log Cabin. I hope the Snow will Soon disappear about your neighborhood. this day it is blowing and the Snow drifts very much. Kiss Etty for me, and give my best respects to all Enquiring friends, and receive my Blessing –
Your Husband
"Oliver"

N.B. answer this immediately


From Oliver to Eleanor

Springfield, IL<br>Feby 20<sup>th</sup> 1866

My Dear Wife,
You will please find Enclosed a <u>Fifty Dollar Treasury note</u> which money I hope will Enable you to pay Some of your debts. you might pay Mr. Fisher a portion and also Mr. Tucker, but be Sure not to let yourself out. I have not received any answer from the letter dated Jany 12<sup>th</sup> which contained 35 dolls. I answered your letter dated 26<sup>th</sup> Jany and Enclosed you a <u>Bracelet</u> also Send you Some reading Matter. We had no mail from Chicago, for 5 days. The Snow blocked up the Railway, but now it is open. I Suppose by the time you receive this letter, the Snow will be mostly gone. I Suppose the Snow must be very deep, between Grand Haven and Traverse. I am in moderate health, and I hope you and Etty are in the same state of health. Although I have been uneasy, as you told me in your last letter, that you were lonesome, and you had not Seen any body Since New Year I wondered how you could get any thing for to Eat, Such Weather -- I hope our business will last till May and then if the Capt or Col. is not ordered away, I think he will let me go for 20 days. My Shirts are nearly gone. I will have to get two made up. Give my best respects to all Enquiring friends
Your Husband
"Oliver"

P.S. I looked for that <u>Clara St Ive</u> but could not find it. Kiss dudu for me. J.O.B.

**Chicago and Glen Arbor 1864-1870**

From Eleanor & Marietta to Oliver (Written by Marietta)

Glen Arbor
March 2nd 1866

Dear Father

We are well and I hope that you are the same  We have not had any letters from you for almost a month  any how we have not had a letter since January the 19th 1866 and we are beginning to feel anxious about them. Dicky and Jenny are both dead  they both died the same time I broke a basin full of oil and the scent went all through the house and I expect that was what killed them. It is dreadfull lonesome   if it was not for a party occasionally we would not know what to do.  there was one the 23rd of February there was one the 21st & 22nd but we did not go to them  one of them was at Mr Todd at the hall and two at Mr King  the 23rd there were 26 couples at Mr. King's and we went. I wish that you would get 2 lbs of yarn you will find a sample in the letter dont get it any coarser than the sample and get it as near the color as possible   you can get it cheaper out side then you can in town  they charge $3 a pound in here and you can get it outside for $2. I am quilting Ettie a skirt  she does not go to school as her eyes began to hurt her and so I thought I would not let her go any longer.  she got her bracelets and she says she would rather waited a while longer and got another pair  she say that they are not worth the wait and she says that she can never have anything like any person    I am in hopes that by this month and another one we will be out of debt  it cost so much to live and it seems that we dont have much to eat  the meat that we got down at the store is not fit to eat and they charge 25cts per lbs  we get an egg occasionally   the weather is very fine but the snow is very deep  where there has not been any path broken the snow is 4 feet deep  Charity B has had that fever but she is getting well now  no more at present but remaining yours truly
Mrs. Eleanor M. Boizard
Miss Ettie Boizard


From Oliver to Eleanor & Marietta

U.S. Mustering and Disbursing Office
Springfield, Illinois
March 7th 1866

My Dear Wife

You will please find enclosed $40 (Two 20s) Feb'y being a short month my pay was considerably less. I Send you 1 Bill of $50. on the 20th Feby, but have received no answer So far, also Bracelets for Etty and one nice one for you. This money will Enable you to pay Mr. Fisher, and all your debts, I hope, for we must try to Save Something for next winter, for fear I should run out of work for I think our job will close about May, if So I Shall be obliged to Come and See you, and then I will require money to take me out again. I Know you are Saving, Still it requires to be careful, for I dont want you to be so pinched as you were this Winter for provisions & c. I bought myself a hat, and 2 new Shrits as my old one's are worn out. I have bought you a dress and Some yarn, and I purpose buying Ettie one also, and Keep them in my trunk. I want Some clothing but I will try to get a Suit about the month of May or June. I hope you will receive the Money Safe. let me Know whether you Suffer for anything or not. Tell me all the news and give my best respects to all Enquiring friends –
Your Husband
"Oliver"

Direct your letters as usual Box 107

**Long Distance Love 1855-1870**

From Eleanor & Marietta to Oliver (Written by Marietta)

Glen Arbor<br>March 9th 1866

Dear Father
We received your welcome letters one dated the 14th and the other the 20th of Feb. one contained $50 and I was very glad to get it as I could pay some of my debts   we did not get them untill the last mail I got the bracelet and the papers also   I was very much pleased with it and the picture of Gen Grant   if only had a Frame for it I would be glad.  I am in hopes that the next remittance will put us out of debt and then we have to get the lot cleaned up. You spoke of coming home in May I hope you will   and you say that your shirt being worn out you must save money enough and when you send us some more money   get a bolt of muslin   get it fine unbleached shirting and get it over a yard wide. and get two or three yards of fine Irish linen for the bosom. get a couple doz of pearl buttons for the bosoms and some Coats & Cotton No. 30 & 50   there is not any muslin in here and when there is it is three prices and it is all gone as soon as there is any brought in from outside   by the time you get this I expect we will have another remittance and that will be enough to get us out of debt and after that you need not send us so much send us about 10 or 15 dollars monthly.  for I am tired of buying things in here, save as much as you can to bring in provisions and things with you.  the weather is very fine and the people are commencing to make sugar.  I will not try to make any as I do not feel strong enough and if I did I have not got any kettle to boil it in.  it would cost me as much to get the wood chopped as it would to buy the sugar   let lone all the trouble to get the trees tapped and carry the sap and everything   we would give anything for a piece of beef.  I have not got any lard and I dont think it pays to pay 50 cts for butter to shorten pie crust or anything else and I will have to have some lard.  I have got fifteen dollars worth of butter this winter from Mrs Brotherton at 50 cts per pound and we did not eat much meat as it so rancid that we cannot eat it.  I have paid Mr. Fisher $15. and I want to pay Brothertons what I owe them.  the remainder I will need about the house as I need several small articles about the house   no more at present but remaining yours Truly yours
Mrs. Eleanor Boizard
Miss Ettie Boizard


From Eleanor and Marietta to Oliver (Written by Marietta)

Glen Arbor, Michigan<br>April 6th 1866

Dear Father
We are well and I hope that you are the same.  The weather is very stormy at present it storms every other day   but the last two days have been very warm   we have not had any sugar making yet as the weather has been so stormy. The snow is going off very fast   our hens lay every day we get 3 eggs sometimes it is very hard to get any butter you have to all most beg for it and pay very dear for it 50 cts per lb is about what we have to pay.  I will be glad when you can come to bring in some provisions   if you can I wish you would bring in a large handled scrubbing brush like they used in the army because we cannot mop the kitchen with the mop the other scrubbing brush is wore out   bring Ettie in three yards of pink ribbon a little wider then the sample you will find in the letter don't get the kind they call {? } ribbon get it the same kind as the sample but get pink. no more at present.
but  remaining yours truly yours.
Mrs Eleanor M. Boizard
Miss Ettie Boizard

Chicago and Glen Arbor 1864-1870

From Oliver to Eleanor & Marietta

Springfield, IL
April 7th, 1866

My Dear Wife,
I hope you will find every thing I send you Satisfactory, about Ettie's dress, I looked as Some Lawn but it looked So flimsy, that I thought I would not buy it, but you will find I have bought her a good gingham dress, which cost 55c. yd. I think it is very genteel and more durable, it is very much worn here by women. the other two dresses, I do not Know how you will like them, they cost 35 cts. yd. the bolt of muslin cost 29c. by the Bolt. I think it is very Strong for Shirts, the linen cost $1.00 yd. I Suppose it will answer, there are 3 yds. I bought you Some fine and Coarse Yarn 2 dolls. there are Some other little traps, Etties' pennies and c. I Suppose they will Send you the Groceries. I Send the Grocery men $35. and that will pay for Freight. I cannot Send you any money, as it nearly cleaned me out. We are working hard Shipping all the Stores to St. Louis Arsenal. I cant tell you exactly when we will be done but as Soon as we get through, there will be no further use for us here, and then I Suppose we will be discharged. I expressed the little trunk to the Grocers. I have got me a new chest made, and have had it Stained and varnished it looks like walnut. I hope you and Etty are in good health.
Give my regards to all Enquiring Friends  Your Husband "Oliver"

N.B. After you receive your things try to get the answer on a Boat  JOB


From Oliver to Eleanor

Springfield, IL
April 11 1866

My Dear Wife
Your letter dated the 23rd March, came to hand on the 6th of April, and I would have answered it before but I was awaiting for Col. Pomeroy, to return from Cincinnati Ohio. I find he will not return until the 17th the consequence is that we will get no money until he returns. I must get me a Common Suit of Clothes, as my clothes are getting quite shabby. I am glad that we are out of debt. I been looking for that announcement for a great while. Try to get along until I shall be able to remit you Some money. I have spoken for 2 dolls. worth of good Seed, of different Kinds, from a Dutch woman who tells me they are all good and fresh Seed. I rather think our Arsenal will Close on the Govert. Account about the latter of May, and then I don't know what will turn up. I have been writing at Cols Pomeroy's office this last month (March) and Still kept watch at the Arsenal at night. I am well and I have gone to my old Boarding house, where I still get my washing done. I Suppose by the time you get this letter the Snow in your neighborhood will have all melted away. I hope so for you must be tired of So much Snow. Tell Etty I will try to get her **Lawn** dress when I go to buy Some clothes for myself. I have two **Merrimack** prints in my trunk. I propose getting Some domestics and provisions about the last month, as this job may run out in 2 months – I would like you to try to get the lot cleared up – in order that you may plant – well I have nothing Strange to tell you of any interest, this day the Election takes place for Mayor and City officers & c. Give my best respects to all Enquiring friends, and receive my best wishes– Kiss Ettie for me.
Your Husband
"Oliver"

**Long Distance Love 1855-1870**

To Oliver from Higley & Huntley

Chicago<br>April 17/66

Mr. Boizard
Dear Sir Yours of the 16th is just rec'd  in reply I would say that we are still located as when you were in C- {*Chicago*} and were much pleased to hear from you and to know that you were enjoying health and happiness. Enclosed I send you the list as you request and should you order goods of us and the market have declined you can depend upon the market price. Hoping to hear from you soon. Feeling confident that we will give you satisfaction. We are truly yours   Higley & Huntley

codfish 10cts
Best Sugar cured hams 22 cts choice
Best Sugar Cured Shoulders 17 cts
Flour winter white $11 $12 $12.50 (choice)
Flour Spring 6.50 com 7.50 fair   8.00 good 8.50 choice
Butter today is worth 35 cts
teas Japan $1.00 to 1.50 good
green teas 1.40 1.60 1.80 good 2.00 choice
good Rio cof 30 cts
Kerosene oil 60 cts
sugars
brown 12 ½ - 14 & 15
yellows 15 & white 16 cts
Hard Sugars 18cts.


From Eleanor and Marietta to Oliver (Written by Marietta)

Glen Arbor, Michigan<br>April 18th 1866

Dear Father
We received your welcome letter dated March 23rd we were glad to hear that you were well but we were sorry to hear that you cant come home in May.  I will be glad when you do come to bring some provisions in with you.  I will have to get another barrel of flour before you come in.  I am not feeling well this spring my heart troubles me a great deal.  You spoke of having the lot cleared up.  The snow is not all gone yet   there is over a foot of snow on the ground and there has not been very much sugar made yet.  Ettie was at a little sugar party last evening which the young folks had at Mr. Wells Miller.   We are out of debt now I guess.  Ettie will soon be 14 years old and it seems but yesterday that she was a little baby.  She is almost as tall as I am.  Mr. Fisher was up at the marsh after hay and he cut his foot   it rains more or less every day and the snow is going off fast.  I would like to have a beefsteak for dinner as I have got tired of eating pork such as it is.   I don't know whether there will be any school this summer or not.  I have just got some more pickles from Miller   I should get potatoes from Tuckers for seed.  no more at present.  Truly yours
Mrs. Eleanor M. Boizard
Miss Ettie Boizard
Please write soon

**Chicago and Glen Arbor 1864-1870**

From Oliver to Eleanor

Springfield, IL
April 20, 1866

My Dear Wife,
You will please find Enclosed $20 doll's. The Col. Has just arrived from Cincinnati with his wife. I have written to the Grocers in Chicago and they had Sent me a list of prices of provisions & c. and I expect that the Boats will commence running Soon, however if nothing happens you may Expect to get Some provisions about the 10th May, 1866. I think our work will Soon be over, as there are only 3 Regt's of Vol's in the field yet, and when they turn in their arms I suppose the Arsenal will close then. I am about to purchase Some Summer cloth, and get a Suit of Clothes made. The articles that I have now in my trunk and what I will buy next month, I will Express them to my Grocer, and he will Ship them with the Groceries to you, I am well, hoping that you and Ettie are also well. Give my best Respects to all Enquiring friends, and receive my best love and wishes.
Your Husband
"Oliver"

P.S. Write soon   should a boat stop try to get a letter aboard. J.O.B.
I have purchased a stuffed squirrel, for Ettie it is in a case.

*Written on the back of the letter*: Since Writing the within I received your letter dated 6th April '66. I will get Etty's ribbon also Brush   J.O.B.


From Eleanor and Marietta to Oliver (Written by Marietta)

Glen Arbor, Michigan
April 27th 1866

Dear Father
We received your welcome letter dated April 11th and we were very glad to hear that you were well as this leaves us at present. We are very sorry that you cannot be at home for Ettie's Birthday as we expected you would as it is the 15th of May. That little boy has gone back to the shanty   that we had all winter   I thought I could not keep him any longer as the snow has all gone off. I spoke to Mr. Brothertons about clearing up the lot. I will have to get the land plowed as I will not be able to dig it. There were some passengers come in last Sunday on the boat for this place. I do not know what to do as I shall be out of flour before you come in and I don't care about getting another barrel in here as I have not had any good bread this winter out of the flour they bought in the fall. Try if can to send in some lard with you. Ettie was over the lake she went Friday and came home Monday. Charlie & Frank Fisher went over Sunday and they had a nice time as there were two girls over there. Mr. Freeman and Mr. Baldwin's daughters. Ettie is going up to Goffarts tomorrow as she has not been up there this winter. Mr Fishers foot is better. You spoke of having a couple calico dresses I am very glad of it as all my calico dresses are almost all worn out   all my dark ones.  be sure and get Ettie the kind she wants, either one with white ground and purple or pink figures   very small figures.  you must come home as soon as you can.  if it were not for our hens I don't know what we would do   we have eggs every day.  No more at present but remaining yours
Truly yours.
Mrs Eleanor Boizard
Miss Ettie Boizard

**Long Distance Love 1855-1870**

From Oliver to Eleanor

Springfield, IL
April 30th 1866

My Dear Ellen,

Your letter dated 18th April is now before me, and in reply I have to State to you, that I am quite troubled about your illness, about the Heart, but I hope Ere this letter reaches you, you Shall have got over it. This coming Month (May), I am Sorry to Say, will be my last Month for Employment here. We have received an Order to Ship all the Government Ordnance and Stores to St. Louis MO, I Suppose it will take the whole of May, then good bye <u>John</u>   I watch the **Chicago <u>Marine List</u>** and I can See when the Boats arrive from your country. I See the "Cleveland" has left for Ogdensburg, some time ago, She wintered in Chicago. Ere you have received this, you shall have received your provisions, as I intend as Soon as we get our pay, to Send 40 dolls. to the Grocer and he will attend to it. You Say Ettie has grown So big. I am very anxious to See you both, I hope She is a good Girl, and has not forgotten her precepts of morality and Goodness. I Expect to Start home in June. Give my best Respects to all, and Kiss Ettie for me. your husband
"Oliver"

N.B. I am Sorry Mr. Fisher has cut his foot My best regards to Mr. & Mrs. Tucker (J.O.B)

I send you some reading matter J.O.B.

*{This previous letter actually has the date of April 30, 186<u>5</u> but it is a response to a letter written in 1866 and it fits chronologically here in the story. He is about to be let go from his job. He is also writing from Springfield, IL. I feel like he just made a mistake in his date when he wrote this letter. So I have opted to amend the date and place it here where I believe it actually belongs.}*


From Marietta to Charlie

Please do not let any person see this

May 6th, 1866

Dear Friend,

As you have requested me to choose you a name instead of Andrew I have thought of three, the first is Charles Alfred, Charles Edward, Charles Fredrick. If neither of these work out I shall try and think of some more. It is rather hard to get a name that will suit and go with the name Charles. Please excuse this short note and this poor writing no more at present.

Yours until death,

Miss Maitie E Boizard

Constancy
I seek a mind from guilt refined
And know of none so pure as thine
A form and face of gentlest grace
And thine are such

Accept this as a valentine

I saw two clouds at morn
Tinged with the morning sun
At dawn they floated on
And mingled into one
*{This is a verse from the poem "Lovers" by John Gardiner Calkins Brainard (1795-1828)}*

Loves First Dream
Tis a fairy scene, where the fond soul roves,
Exulting in passions warm beam
Tis sad to think we should wake with a chill
From Loves first dream
But it fades like the rainbows brilliant arch
Scattered by clouds and wind
Leaving the spirit, unrobed of light
In darkness and tears behind
*{This is a verse of "Loves First Dream" written by Eliza Cook.}*

Please don't laugh at my nonsense
Miss Maitie E Boizard


From Higley & Higley to Oliver

Chicago
May 10, 1866

Mr J.O.B.
Dear Sir  We shipped your goods today on board the propeller **Brooklyn** which left this am at 7 oclock    Enclose find your bill and bal. 90c your due  Many goods have {?} much since your letter enquiring price was rec'd.  Hoping all will be satisfactory and that the goods may reach Glen Arbor in safety we remain as ever thanking you for your patronage
truly yours
H & H


From Eleanor and Marietta to Oliver (Written by Marietta)

Glen Arbor, Michigan
May 11th 1866

Dear Father
We are well and I hope you are the same.  We received your welcome letter dated April 20 1866 and the money also.  Mama has gone up to the other dock and I am staying at Mrs Fishers this week   I expect mama back Sunday. the boats stop here almost every day.  The **Brooklyn** stopped her last Tuesday   She is the new boat that was

**Long Distance Love 1855-1870**

launched last February. The mosquitoes are so bad that I can hardly write they bother me so   you must excuse this short letter or note.  no more at present but remaining yours truly yours.
Miss Ettie Boizard


From Eleanor & Marietta to Oliver (Written by Marietta)

Glen Arbor<br>May 18<sup>th</sup> 1866

Dear Husband
We are we well and I hope you are the same   We received the trunk and box and one barrel of Flour. I found your likeness and I think it looks like you   There were three dresses. I would rather had a dark calico instead of the blue {?}  I shall have to take the Gingham one but is almost to good to wear every day. Ettie wanted a light dress  the kind she sent for  as all her dresses are dark. The muslin is entirely to heavy for shirts. There would not any person wash it as it will full up so. You sent sheeting instead of shirting. But I can make use of it. You will find a sample enclosed. There is not any shirting in here  when there is you have to pay two prices 40 & 45 cts a yard. You ought to try and bring in some stuff for shirts   bring me in a large kerosene lamp with a marble bottom as those that have a glass bottom tip so easy. You will get a nice big one for about two dollars   I borrowed one from Mrs. Dorsey and it has a glass bottom   I am afraid to move it for fear it will tip over.  What provisions we got we could not get for $50 in here  we had to pay 50cts for butter  I just paid $5 for some that I had got.  The things that we got from Chicago as near as we can guess  Tea 4 lbs  sugar 5 lbs   coffee 5 also  Butter & {?} pail about three parts full   Lard a 3 gal crock full   Smoked meat 20 or 25 lbs  we are guessing on the amount but we don't know for certain. I had to get Ettie a pair of shoes and I paid $3 for them   if you get my muslin get it as wide as you can  don't get it less than a yard wide  I got Ettie a {?} for $1  I got some tea  I was out and I had to get some and some other {edibles}  I have not got the lot cleared up yet as it is so hard to get any person as they are all so busy.  Today is Ettie's birthday she is Fourteen. No more at present   But remaining yours  Truly Yours
Miss Eleanor M. Boizard
Miss Marietta Boizard


From Oliver to Eleanor

Springfield, IL<br>June 7<sup>th</sup> 1866

My Dear <u>Wife</u>
Enclosed you will please find ($40) Forty Dolls I presume we will be discharged this month, I do not Know, whether we will be kept all the month or not, the stores are nearly all Shipped to **St. Louis Arsenal**, I have worked harder Since the 1<sup>st</sup> May, than I Ever did, there was such heavy lifting all Lead, Balls & c. Try to Save one half of this money as I will be out of Employment, I will Start for home, as Soon as I can, probably about the beginning of July (if nothing happens) I may bring in some more provisions.  I would like to work out this month, but thing's look like a close. Col. Pomeroy is getting ready packing up & c. expecting some orders. I have not been as well as usual, these last two weeks, but I still worked, I took medicine, am better, Give my best respects to all Enquiring friends, and Kiss Ettie for me.  I will try to bring her <u>Squirrel</u>, <u>Safe</u>, also my dog "<u>Charlie</u>" No more at Present
Your  Husband "Oliver"
N.B. Answer this by a boat if you can. J.O.B.

**Chicago and Glen Arbor 1864-1870**

*{Oliver makes a trip home sometime in July or August}*

From Marietta to Charlie

*{This letter is actually two letters, and both written sections are crossed out. I am not sure Charlie ever received them.}*

Glen Arbor<br>June 18th, 1866

My Dear Friend,

I had my fortune told by Miss Baidie. It was a cheat for sure. I am going to meeting next Sabbath. I was _____ staid last winter at Mr Fishers and I was employed in the kitchen helping the hired girl cook potatoes and pork for the menfolk.
Your sincere Friend
Maitie E. Boizard


My Dearest Love

I received yours dated June 19th stating that you could not think of anything more to write   you told me to write soon   I am answering this as soon as I can   Oh if I had the wings of a dove. (Remember)  How soon I should come to thee my love.
Yours until death
Miss Somebody

Remember me when this you see
Though many miles apart
Remember me when this you see
And press it to your heart
M.E.B.

Remember me my love, yes my dearest


From Marietta to Charlie

Glen Arbor<br>Tuesday Eve. July 16th

Friend Charlie,

I received your note and was somewhat surprised. You must know that I thought something of you to give you the answer that I did when you asked me that question  I will try you once more providing it never transpires again. I have always tried to keep my name untarnished, but we can talk about it better than I can write about it. I don't know which one feels the worst, you or I  have both had the blues for two or three days past. You may consider it all right between us and never let it be mentioned for my sake.  I hope you done as I requested in burning up that

## Long Distance Love 1855-1870

note. Will you please come over tonight and stay overnight as Mrs. De Latour and myself will be alone for my ma is going up to Mr. McCarty's docks. You requested me to try and think that you loved me the same as ever, I will try to and you may do the same by me if you will. Well my dear Charlie (if you will permit me to call you that) I shall have to draw my note to a close as I can't hear myself think as the folks are talking so.
I remain yours until Death,
Maitie B or MaGill




From Eleanor and Marietta to Oliver (Written by Marietta)

Milwaukee
Sept 8th 1866

Dear Father
We are well and I hope that you are the same,  I am in Milwaukee as you see by the heading of this.  Mrs. Grandz wanted me to go out and help her take care of her two children, she pays my passage and so you see that it will not cost me any thing I shall stay about a week   Mama gets Charity or some of the children to stay with her at night   I shall not be able to write any more   excuse this poor writing as I am in a hurry   no more at present  I remain yours
Truly your Daughter
Ettie Boizard



From Eleanor & Marietta to Oliver (Written by Marietta)

Glen Arbor
Sept 15th 1866

Dear Father
It is with much pleasure that we received your welcome letter, we were glad to hear that you were well as this leaves us at present  you need not worry about us because we don't stand in need of anything  our potatoes are yielding very well we got fourteen out of one hill, and they were about as long as your little finger  Ettie has been out to Milwaukee, but she has got back, she went out to help Mrs Grandz take care of the children and they paid her passage there and back and it did not cost Ettie any thing  we got all the potatoes out of one hill of those that were planted last  I guess that I will not be able to write any more as they expect the **Brooklyn** in and I shall have to take the letter down to send it out by her  give our love to Mrs Pfeiffer and the children and a part your self  no more but write soon
Mrs. E.M. Boizard



From Eleanor & Marietta to Oliver (Written by Marietta)

Glen Arbor
Oct 29th 1866

Dear Father
We received your letter and the butter which we were glad to get as we had not any butter in the house and hardly any meat. I am just going to bake my last baking of bread   there is pipe for the stove but we shall have to get

**Chicago and Glen Arbor 1864-1870**

elbows  we shall have to get two   you will find a measure in the letter for the elbows  as quick as you can get it you must send a barrel of flour and after you get the flour you will have to get some more butter and lard   groceries also as soon as you can, because we cannot get butter in here and that butter wont last us all winter   I am just done digging our potatoes and I am very tired   I have six bushels   we have got the corn from Dorsey   you must send us a dog chain because we cannot have that dog following us every where that we go   we have not got the potatoes from Dorsey yet and we wont need them as we have plenty of our own   and what we had are splendid and I wish that you were here to help eat them.  the school commenced today but I shall not go  I shall have to learn at home, please excuse this short letter as I am in a hurry   no more at present but write soon  Yours truly
Mrs Eleanor M Boizard
Marietta Boizard

send us two elbows 5 inches round

Mrs Fisher let us have one elbow and you need not send but one


From Eleanor and Marietta to Oliver (Written by Marietta)

Glen Arbor, Michigan
Nov 6 1866

Dear Father
We received your welcome letter dated the first which we were glad to get.  We were glad to hear that you had found employ for we were all most out of every thing to eat but we have plenty of potatoes and squash.  Mr Tucker wants you to send him in a 7 inch elbow.  The weather has been quite cold for about two weeks and its rained all most all the time but has moderated some, and we are having fine weather now.  I am taking music lessons at Mrs. Fishers on the **melodeon**.  I help Mrs Fisher when she wash and irons and I don't have to pay anything for learning.  I am making a pair of pants for Silas Miller.  Our chickens don't do us any good this fall, because when you were at home you fed them so well that you stunted them and they have died and the hawks have carried them off.   Lloyd has cut all the wood.  The dog all that he is good for is to bark and eat.  he wont eat anything but bread and meal and it costs more to keep him than it would a pig.  I don't know what I shall do for soap grease I have just 5cts left.  don't forget a chain for the dog.  No more at present but write soon.
We remain yours Truly
Mrs Eleanor Boizard
Miss Ettie Boizard


From Eleanor & Marietta to Oliver (Written by Marietta)

Glen Arbor
November 16th 1866

Dear Father
We have got the flour home from the store house, and it is splendid   it is the same that they charge $14 and $15 for in here   the sugar and all the rest were good   we have got the stove up  it burns the wood out very much because we have not got any elbows for it   if you can you may send us in two 5 inch elbows  you need not send in any for Mrs Tucker   we had one that we got from Fisher but it was to small   we will have to get Lloyd to cut some more wood

## Long Distance Love 1855-1870

and pay him when I can   if you can you might send Ettie in a pair of calfskin shoes number three and have them come up high on the ankle   those that I had just riped {ripped} on the back   The soles are good yet of both pairs but the rip on the side and on the back and there is not any person in here to mend shoes.  I will try and send this by boat so that you can send my shoes by the **Brooklyn** if you can send them in   no more at present  but write soon.
Yours Truly
Mrs. E.M. Boziard
Marietta Boizard

PS.  We have got the potatoes from Dorseys  MB


From Eleanor & Marietta to Oliver (Written by Marietta)

Glen Arbor<br>Nov 28<sup>th</sup> 1866

Dear Father
We received your letter and the provisions  which we were glad to get  I have not been very well for a week past but I feel much better  now   Ettie is as tough as ever. the weather is very fine now but for a week past we have had very disagreeable weather. the clock wont go and we are so lonesome that we dont know what to do   I guess that when the cat knocked it down off of the shelf that it injured it some how   I guess that as soon as I get a pair of shoes that I shall go to school  I guess that it will be very lonesome here this winter   We will have enough to last us 4 months if we had some kerosene for lights  Mr Tucker has not plastered up the kitchen yet but I expect that he will come this week.  McCarty has failed   all the girls have gone out to go to school but two or three   I have been troubled with job's plague   I had some of his boils   one of the Brothertons boys has got the fever   no more at present but write soon.
Yours  & c.
Mrs. E Boizard

I got the shoes and they were quite large, but they will have to do.  I will write you a longer letter when I get some paper  This is the last piece of paper that I have  Mamas hair is all coming out  every time that she combs her hair she combs out great hands full.  We are well and hope you are the same  Ettie can play three pieces on the **melodeon**  no more at present but write soon.


From Marietta to Charlie

Glen Arbor<br>December 4, 1866

Dear Charlie Friend Fisher

Though long neglected but not forgotten by me. I now avail myself of missing your welcome letters    you insisted me to write you   I don't know what kind of letters    and I guess I shall have to   I rather think that I shall go home tomorrow whether my mother comes home tomorrow or not    you must excuse all from writing and bad spelling as Frank is bothering me considerable   I hardly know what I am writing.   Charity Brotherton has gone home and I guess that she feels quite bad because you do not go up and see her.   I rather guess that I have written about enough

nonsense don't you    yours until death
Ettie Boizard  Maitie E MaGill

Burn as soon as you read this


From Oliver to Eleanor & Marietta

Dealers in Paints, Oils, Varnishes Glass & c.<br>
Office of Heath & Milligan<br>
167 Randolph Street<br>
Chicago, Ills. Dec. 16 1866

My Dear Wife,
Enclosed please find Two Doll's   I received Etty's Letter dated Glen Arbor, Nov 28 and Post Marked Milwaukee, Dec. 14. I did not understand how it was, as the Boats are not running. Etty acknowledges the receipt of her shoes, but Says they are large, they are number Three. Etty states that you have been unwell but getting better. I hope you may Keep well this winter. I have a rather tight time to get along, my pay is so small, that I dont know what I shall do for clothes. My clothes are getting shabby, and my Stocking's are getting very much worn. You must try to get along with the small sum of Money  I Send you, better Small Sums than none. You must Keep up a good heart, and try not to Worry. I hope your chickens will do you some good. Give my regards to all the neighbors and receive my Blessings.
Yours "Oliver"

This is the 3rd remittance    How about the Dog


From Eleanor and Marietta to Oliver (Written by Marietta)

Glen Arbor, Michigan<br>
Dec 18th 1866

Dear Father
We received your welcome letter dated the third of this month we received $1 also which we were glad to get. we are all well with the exception of colds which every person has. The flour is just the same as the first barrel. Charlie Fisher is clerking in the store for Mr McCarty. The snow is about a foot deep and it is real lonesome. They are finishing the Hotel that they commenced in July. Since I commenced my letter Austin came and he says that he is going to stay until after Christmas. I wish that you were here to spend Christmas and New Years with us. I do not think, that I shall go to school this winter as they say the school teacher is crazy. My mother is getting dinner. Mr Fisher hauled up our wood for winter We have not had a letter from Mr. Bridges yet. Have you heard from Browns lately. I guess that I shall close as it is getting late and I have some work to do. Write as often as you can and we will do the same. no more at present but write soon.
Yours truly
Mrs Eleanor M. Boziard
Marietta Boizard

**Long Distance Love 1855-1870**

*Written on the bottom of the letter:*
Ettie & her mother said that I might write a few words so I will wish you a happy New Years hoping that next winter you will be some where nearer home enjoying yourself.  You and Charley had quite a time together so he said.  Good bye till we meet.
Austin Newman



From Marietta to Charlie

Glen Arbor<br>Dec 22 1866

Dear Charlie
I will keep my promise to you about going to the Party as Mrs Tucker told me that you left word for me about the party.  Mr. Newman is here and I guess that he will stay untill after Christmas but he is going to take my ma.  If you and Frank can I would like for you both to come over Friday and spend the day or evening as I would like to see you.  You may consider it all right about the party.  I am going to your house to spend the evening and wish you was there.  I remain yours untill death.
 May Bee



From Eleanor & Marietta to Oliver (Written by Marietta)

Glen Arbor<br>January 4$^{th}$ 1867

Dear Father
We received your welcome letter which we were glad to get and we received two $1 bills also.  we got a letter Christmas with two dolls in it also. We are well with the exception of colds.  It was quite lonesome Christmas & New Years   Austin stayed untill after Christmas    and New Years morning mama and myself went down and spent the day at Mr. Dorseys  The snow is only shoe top deep   we have got both the corn and the potatoes from Dorsey  We get along very well.  The stove that we have in the room takes a great deal of wood as we have not any elbow for it   you must get yourself some clothes and keep yourself dressed comfortably.  I have two pairs of stockings here that I wished you had   I wish I had plenty more yarn so I could knit you some more socks and plenty muslin so I could make you some shirts. Mr. Lloyd has gone to live on his homestead and I have to get Mr. Tucker to chop my wood for me.  I have one hen that lays.  The dog is here, he lays around the stove and barks when he hears any person at the door, stamping the snow off of their feet   he flies at them as though he would tear them to pieces and barks   we have not heard from Bridges yet. I don't know what Ettie shall do for her schooling as the snow is too deep in winter and the heat is so great in the summer that it makes her sick   she ought to be at school she is growing up without any learning   Goffarts were here today and he sends his regards to you.  There was a Tug here last saturday with a crew of sailors from off some vessel that was {?} on the coast some where below here   I am knitting Ettie a pair of stockings out of that fine blue yarn that you sent in May   There is a stage that comes through from Traverse, every week it brings the mail in every week.  We wish that we had some apples   They have them down at the store for $6 per barrel   if you can get any book save them and bring them home   and save all your old clothes and I can take them for carpet rags   my kitten has grown so large that you would hardly know it if you was to see it.

**Chicago and Glen Arbor 1864-1870**

The dog and kitten sleep together and they play like two cats I cannot write any more at present as I have to go and get supper and wish you were here to drink a cup of tea with us   no more at present but write soon
Yours Truly
Mrs. E.M. Boizard
Miss M. E. Boizard

*The previous letter had the date of January 4, 1866 written on it, but taking the letter in context, it follows chronologically to actually be January 4, 1867.*


From Marietta to Charlie

Glen Arbor<br>Jan 10<sup>th</sup>/67

Dear Charlie,

I received your welcome letter and the belt and buckle also with which I was <u>very</u> much pleased. I was very glad to hear from you also. When I see you I will tell you how much I thank you for the belt and buckle. I would rather have a dark blue belt. I will you give you the other the next time I see you. I have changed my mind about going over the lake next Sunday. I shall not go over until the 20<sup>th</sup> of this month. I shall let you know the week before I go. I was over at your house this week and your folks are all well. Your ma was plaguing me, but I didn't care much as she didn't plague me very much. Charlie do you know whether Jerry McCarty found himself or not the day after New Years. I rather guess that Mrs. Tucker is one of his enemies now as she was very angry after she came home. I had a letter from Ellie Cook today and she told me to tell you to come over when you come home again. I shall try to send this to you before mail day. Charity – she sends her love to you   Harrison Selers and Charity spent the eve Saturday evening – and there was one person smiling and it was you. I have the words of Pretty Little Ellie and I will write them off for you when I get time     Now dear Charlie I shall have to close as I have no more at present to say.  From your true Maitie   I remain yours Truly
Your Gypsy Queen

P.S.
I asked the kitty if she wanted to send her love to you and she answered yes. When you read this nonsense you can rub it out as I don't want any person to see it.


From Marietta to Charlie

Glen Arbor<br>Jan 22<sup>nd</sup>/67

Dear Charles

I arrived here safe and have had a great deal of fun.  I wish you could be over here. I shall come home Friday. Thursday I will ride over with Mr. Goff's folks. If you can I wish you would come up on early Saturday evening as you can. I went over to young Mr. Millers and had a very nice time   I will have to hurry as Kennsington wants to start so he can get home   no more at present   but answer this as soon as you can if you have time I wish you would write and send a line by Kennsie'

## Long Distance Love 1855-1870

I remain yours until death
Maitie B.

Politeness of Master Kennsie' Miller



From Eleanor and Marietta to Oliver (Written by Marietta)

Glen Arbor, Michigan<br>Jan 25

Dear Father
We received your welcome letter dated the 5th and two dolls also which we were glad to get. We are well but mama has two boils on her foot and she cannot wear her shoe   her blood is very much out of ordinary. The snow is very deep it is very lonesome in here this winter. You must keep up courage as there are several Fisher kin a great deal worse off then we are. Mr. Lloyd he is worse off then we are, he had but one small quilt to put over him and two children untill Mrs. Dorsey and mama went around amongst the neighbors and got things enough for him a quilt. save all of your old clothing and they will do for his little boy as he is almost naked. Mrs. Dorsey & mama made the quilt on mama's birthday. Mr Fisher is not very well. What is the name of the person in that picture that you sent to me in the last letter we know her name is Bertha but we don't know her other name. Mrs Aikens has had the Ergsiplos *{Erysipelas}* but she is better now   it is hard to get anything to write as we answer every letter that we get if you can get any papers send them in as we don't have very much to read. no more at present. But write soon.
Yours truly
Mrs. E.M. Boizard
Miss Ettie Boizard



From Marietta to Charlie

Sleeping Bear City<br>Feb  3rd/67

Dear Charlie,

It is with much pleasure that I include a few lines to you to let you know that I am going over the lake to Mr. Baldwins and shall not return until next Sunday. I presume you will think that I commenced my letters rather old fashioned but I hope you will excuse me as I am about crazy and do not know what I am about. I received a letter from you since I commenced this which I was very glad to get   I heard that there was not any   Frank told me Wednesday when I was over there after the mail.   I shall be very happy to accompany you to the party My Dear   I did not attend the Old Folks party as I heard it was especially for them.  I have something to tell you that will make you laugh, I shall tell you when I see you   George is up to the Brothertons to see Charity and Charity is very much tickled   I am going over the lake to see your intended A.B.   I presume you know who I mean.  I will take that back if you don't get angry. You spoke about me answering those questions   One is   Will you marry me   The answer is Yes, my Dear   The other is     Stir up, be lovely the sweet one     I will try to be the best what I can.

P.S.  Please excuse this short note as I am in a hurry, and poor writing also.
Ettie MaGill

I remain yours until death, Ettie Fisher  (don't take my head off)

**Chicago and Glen Arbor 1864-1870**

From Eleanor and Marietta to Oliver (Written by Marietta)

Glen Arbor, Michigan
Feb 15th/67

Dear Father
We received your letter dated the 16th and two Dolls which we were glad to get. Mama has not got any better of her cold. I was coming down stairs and had my hands full and one of my ankles turned and I fell and hurt one of eyes it is black and blue. the snow was so deep that we could not get any mail for two weeks from Traverse City. there is something killing all our chickens and we will have to get another chicken house built. You say provisions are getting cheaper I wish they were in here. Meat is 25 cts sugar 20, muslin is 45 & 50 cts per yd as quick as you can you must put some money away to get some muslin for your shirts. It has rained for about twenty four hours. Mama has not been out of the house since New Years only to a funeral. you must send the muslin as soon as you can after the boats run. I will take this two Dolls that you sent and get yarn for to knit you some stockings. I am sorry that you fell and hurt yourself you must be careful, we would like to be out there be we could not live and pay rent and buy wood. We will soon have to have some dark calico dresses as we are almost naked we have plenty of others though. The tea at 20 shillings in here is not near as good as that tea you sent us in the fall, our butter is almost out we can get it at the store but it is 40cts per pound. we have browned the last of our coffee. Give our regards to Mr & Mrs. P. no more at present but write soon.
Yours truly
Mrs. E.M. Boizard
Miss Ettie Boizard


From Eleanor & Marietta to Oliver

Feb 21st/67

Dear Father
We received your letter dated the second of this month which we were very glad to get. We received the two dolls *{dollars}* also. Mama is a little better of her cold and my eye is a little better. The last money that you sent us I took and got some yarn to knit you some stocking It is only $2.40 a pound and not good at that. it is half dirt. I should have to take this two dolls that you sent and get some sugar and other things that we need about the house. shoe strings are only 5 cts per pair and every thing accordingly Ray is in the store and he sells every thing dearer than ever. Mama is knitting. The dog does nothing but bark. we are having very pleasant weather but it is very lonely here. I have attended but two parties this winter and there is not any church to go to we have not got any thing to read and so you see that time drags along very heavily. I have written all the news to you and so I shall close no more at present.
Yours Truly
Mrs E.M. Boizard
Miss M.E. Boizard

PS I have to pay 20cts for a bottle of ink that I used to get for 5cts outside.

**Long Distance Love 1855-1870**

From Eleanor & Marietta to Oliver (Written by Marietta)

Glen Arbor
Feb 29th 1867

Dear Father,
We received your welcome letter dated the 9th of this month and $2 also   we are very glad to hear that you are well as this leaves us at present.  When you write let me know whether you will want any stockings before you come home, if you do I shall try and send them by the first boat that goes to chicago  save your old ones for they will do to {? }  Your dream was true about us being ragged   we never wanted dresses as bad in our lives as we do now.  You will have to get some muslin for your shirts and Ettie some underclothes   I would like to have it so I could make your shirts by the time you come home, you can get it either bleached or unbleached which ever is the cheapest.  Dont get it less than a yard wide get it as much over a yd. wide as you want to   you will find a sample in this letter.  *{There is a sample sewn to the top margin of this letter.}*  We have had another snow storm  it snowed Saturday and Sunday. We have two hens that lay every other day we are glad of it as we can have some eggs to eat occasionally.  Mama is knitting all your socks   I have written all the news so I shall have to close.  Write soon.
Yours Truly & c.
Mrs. E.M. Boizard
Miss M.E. Boizard


From Eleanor & Marietta to Oliver

Glen Arbor
March 8th 1867

Dear Father
We received your welcome letter dated the 16th of last month and two dollars also.  We were very glad to hear that you are getting better  this leaves us well at present.  You wanted to know what we have to eat   we have plenty of potatoes and flour and tea  we have, good coffee enough for one meal   we have had to buy butter sugar & meat - it just takes the $2 for to get things for the table as everything is very high in here.  I gave Mrs. Tucker some tea for the use of the stove as I had the tea to spare and not the money.   I suppose Mr Tucker will soon want the money for cutting the wood.  You must get a dog chain and send it in as soon as navigation opens for we cannot have him following us everywhere we go and fighting every dog that he meets.  The chicks has commenced  to lay and we have some to eat occasionaly.  The weather  is very mild at present and has been for quite a while back   it is thawing today.  Mama has got rid of all her biles *{boils}* but two.  I wish that the boats were running so that you could come home   We have never heard anything from Bridges and I presume you have not either.  will you send in some cabbage & cucumber seed as soon as navigation opens.  I guess that I have written about all the news as we have not any to write in here   it so lonely   no more at present   write soon. Yours Truly
Mrs. E. M. Boizard
Marietta Boizard

**Chicago and Glen Arbor 1864-1870**

From Emma Bridges to Marietta

Mary Cooper Wells {*Maricopa Wells*}
March 11 1867

dear Eta
i set down to write you at last after a long time but i no you will forgive me when you hear the reason i did not write sooner   dear Eta we have seen a great deal of hardships since i wrote you last   when your letter came to **fort grant** we were expecting everyday to leave so i thought i would not write to you until we herd where we going   we were at **fort grant** a little while when we got orders to leave for **camp reno**   then the order was countermanded in 2 weeks   we were ordered to **fort Macdowl** and we left and had a hard road to travel.  when we got Macdowl we were wore out and had to live in tents in the broiling hot sun for 3 weeks before we got a house to go in to   now dear friends i got something to tell you.  i was maried on the 27 of December   you will be surprised i supose   i was married in tuson *{Tucson}*   my husband is solger *{soldier}* now but when his time is out i see citizen life to   dear friends i know you wish me a great deal of hapiness   my Mother told me to tell your Mother she did not let me throw myself away on a drunkerd   she says your mother knows what trubel *{trouble}* she has seen   she says i never will have such trubel   she says to tell your Mother that she has been very happy since i ben maried but she often thinks of her and cries to think she is not with her   my Mother is at **fort Macdowel** now and I am at Mary Cooper *{Maricopa}* Wells about 45 miels *{miles}* away from Macdowl   my husband is comasary Agent here   my Mother is comeing down to live with us   jenie has grown very big and so has tomy   he often speaks of your mother   you never say anything about dick how is he getting along   i suppose you had a pleasant time on chrismas day   we had not anything but rations to cook   we are hundreds of miles away of civilaztion   out here amounst hostile apaches   all we ever see is  two companys of solgiers   a couple of women.  i hope you will never come to such a county of arizona   Eta i wish you would send me something to read   you cannot even get a newspaper   you promised to send me your photograph i wish you would   i will send mine and my husbands as soon as we get where we can get them taken   write often and i will write oftiner as well   i must say Mother told me when i wrote  to send her love to all   i give my love all and more   you try write to me soon i shall be anxious to hear from you   direct your letter   Mrs Emma Brown  Mary Cooper Wells AR
i remain your own dear friend
Emma.

# Long Distance Love 1855-1870

Mary Cooper Wells
March [?] 1870

Dear Ella

I set down to write you at last after a long time but I no you will forgive me when you hear the reason I did not write sooner dear Ella we have seen a great deal of hardships since I wrote last when your letter came to fort grant we were expecting everyday to leave so I thought I wouldnt wait to [answer] untill we knew were we were going we were at fort grant a little while when we got orders to leave for camp reno then the orders was countermanded a week we were [ordered] to fort McDowel and we left and had a hard road to travel. when we got to McDowel we were wore out and had to live in tents in the broiling hot sun for [a few] weeks before we got a house to go in to now dear friends i got something to tel you. I was married on the 29 of December you will be surprised I supose I was married in tuson my husband is soldger now but when his time is out I [see] citizen life to

122

**Chicago and Glen Arbor 1864-1870**

From Eleanor & Marietta to Oliver (Written by Marietta)

Glen Arbor
March 15th 1867

Dear Father

We received two letters by the last mail  one was dated the 23rd & the other the 25th  one had $2 in it  we were very glad to hear that your health was improving  we are both well at present. Our barrel of flour is half gone  it will last until the first of May  it begins to look like sugar making  I wish I had muslin so I could be making your shirts. I am working at the last pair of socks and have got them almost done. you might send us an almanac as we have none, and the Ledger, no 52  in 1867  will you get any bounty  I never heard you say any thing about one and I thought I would ask you  I have just had a letter from Austin  Newman  and he wanted to know how you were. Mr Tucker has been here sawing wood today  he has *{chilblarins ?}* on his heels  when you write be sure and let us know whether you want me to send you your socks out or wait untill you come home  we got a paper also by mail I shall have to get butter & coffee with the two dolls that you sent us. I wish that I could buy a beefsteak. There has been a tug running from South Manitou Island every week this winter  it will soon start for Chicago. The Dog still barks at the least noise that he hears  we have the best cat in the country  it will sit up tall like Tuckers dog. Charlie Fisher thinks that it is the best cat that he ever saw  he says it will do everything but talk. it is hard to get anything to write as we have not any news and it is very lonely  we wish that you were at home. No more at present  write soon.
Yours Truly & c.
Mrs Eleanor M Boizard
Ettie Boizard


From Eleanor and Marietta to Oliver (Written by Marietta)

Glen Arbor, Michigan
March 22 1867

Dear Father

We received your letter dated the second day of this month and two dollars enclosed. we are well and hope this will find you the same. You spoke of getting some dark calico dresses when you get them get eleven yd in each, and you spoke also about being almost out of debt. I am very glad of that  we must pay that bill of $7 at the store  if we don't they will begin to think that we are not going to pay them. if I should want anything on credit I would be ashamed to ask it. I am glad to hear that your eyes are better. If they should trouble you again take chamber **lye** and rain water take half and half  we have had three or four days of very cold weather but it is thawing today. Mr Fisher is not well at all this winter  they will soon commence to make sugar. when you have the money to spare I wish that you would get 3 or 4 yards of crush toweling as we are out of dishcloths and tea towels  do you think that you can come home soon  save all of your old clothes for carpet rags if nothing else. we cannot find anything to write as we don't have any news in here  write soon.
Yours truly & c.
Mrs E M Boizard
Miss M E Boziard

**Long Distance Love 1855-1870**

From Eleanor & Marietta to Oliver (Written by Marietta)

Glen Arbor
March 29th

Dear Father
We received your letter dated the 9th of this month and the money also   Mama is not well and has not been for about a week.  she has done nothing ever since she has been so unwell but lie around.  when navigation opens send her in some good brandy or whiskey  as she wants to put some raisins in it and take it to strengthen her.  She had a spell with her heart and she has had weak spells ever since and chills & fever   but she is a great deal better today    it still keeps snowing   it seems as though we are never going to have any spring  we dont think that we will have any sugar making this year   I think that our flour will last - untill the first of May    I see by those papers that you sent us that every thing is a great deal cheaper out there then they are in here.   excuse this short letter as the mail goes out today and I have to take this down today  I could not leave mama very well during the week and so I had to go down today with the mail.  I shall have to close now for I must hurry write soon.
Yours Truly
Mrs. E.M. Boizard
Miss M E Boizard


From Eleanor & Marietta to Oliver (Written by Marietta)

Glen Arbor
April 4th/67

Dear Father
We received your welcome letter and the $2 also which we were glad to get and 4 papers also two Republicans, Times and the Police we were glad to get them as we were lonesome.  Mama is better but still she is not well enough to go around the house to do any work    if it not be asking to much I would like you to get me just a common wooden rocking chair as she is not strong enough to sit up all day   She wants a strong one.  one that wont come all to pieces.  she feels like she did when we were in Newport  she dont have any chills now but is very weak.
The snow is going off very fast   you ought not to have bought your stockings  it costs more to buy the stockings than it does the yarn and after they are bought they are not worth anything  Mr Fisher has quit using tobacco   our hens dont lay as much as they used to they have stopped to rest a while   we write so often that we dont have any news to write   there is a **grist mill** William Burdick owns it   it has been running since last fall.  no more at present write soon
Yours Truly
Mrs E M Boizard
Miss M E Boizard

**Chicago and Glen Arbor 1864-1870**

From Marietta to Charlie

Glen Arbor
April 8, 1867

My Dear Charlie

I received your welcome letter which I was very glad to get   I got it in this weeks mail   My mother is somewhat better than she was on Sunday when you came over but still she is not able to go around the house yet   I think I will go down to the city today as I have not been there yet   I wish that I could see you as I am lonely and feel like crying I want to see you so bad   You must be sure and come down next Saturday night and stay all night if you can and I shall try and beat you playing exercise (only I won't miscount)  But I shall beat old smart face by playing it smart don't you think I shall   I was over at your house yesterday after the mail and I met Mrs. Goff and she went home with me to see my ma   she wanted to know how you and I  proposed and I told her I guessed that we got along just best   what do you think about it   I have not seen anything or heard anything of Charity since Sunday evening and so I don't know whether she sends over her love to you or not.  Have you seen anything of Eddie, the little rogue, since Monday morning.   I don't know whether Charity has passed the question but I rather guess she has not   don't you   I guess that you will get disgusted at me and my nonsense  and think Charitys words are true about me being a fool   if you don't write   I don't want you to whip me the first time you see me   and Dear Charlie I must close as I have written  five letters and have 8 more to write   I will try to write more next time   Please write soon    I remain your one true love
Maitie MaGill

Love is like a little bee
Bearing honey joyfully
But the bee its honey brings
With its mummer and its stings
I'll complain not -- let me know love
With all its joy and woe

{*This is part of a poem entitled "LOVE" which was printed in the Harper's Magazine on March 23, 1867*}


From Eleanor & Marietta to Oliver (Written by Marietta)

Glen Arbor
April 12th 1867

Dear Father
We received your welcome letter the money and paper also which we were glad to get   Mama is a great deal better than she was but still she is very weak.  I was at the store and Mark Todd asked me about that seven dollars   he wants it by the first of May   I cant pay him any out of that two dolls that we get weekly as it takes all of that to get things for the house.  Mama has not been away from the house for about a month and she dont know how soon  she will be able to go away from it.  The folks are making sugar.  Brothertons have made 182 lbs and they sugared off twice in one day and made that much   the snow is going off very fast   we have had eight trees tapped and we are boiling the sap down for vinegar.  you spoke of calico being 18cts it is 25 in here and its hardly worth picking up muslin that is only three quarters of a yard wide is 45  50 & 55cts - butter is 40cts per lb.  I am sorry that I had to send for that bill of Marks   if I had know that he would have been so particular   I shall not have sent for the dresses we live on just as little as we possibly can.  but we cant complain as there are people worse off than we are.  Mr

**Long Distance Love 1855-1870**

Fisher has quit chewing tobacco and he is a great deal better   no more at present   I shall bring this letter to a close as it is nothing but a grumbling letter   write soon.
Yours Truly
Mrs. E M Boizard
Ettie B


From Marietta to Charlie

Glen Arbor<br>April 24, 1867

Dear Charlie

I presume you think I am not going to answer your letter but I hope you will excuse me as I have been quite busy and have just got this chance to write and I shall try to make it up.  I rec'd a letter from Sarah C by the last mail she talks of going out this summer and she wants us to come up there this spring  I will show you the letter when you come down. Try and come down next Sunday if you can    Charity and Geo. G were here Tuesday morning a little while. Charity went downtown with him   I don't know whether they went down to be married or not   but I guess they did not. George said that he had Charity under an arrest.    I was quite lonely on Monday after you went away. I am going down to the City tomorrow and I dread it on accord of the sand  it makes the walking so bad. Give my respects to Emma Barker when you see her if you please.   Charlie I have written  so much nonsense in all my letters or notes that I shall try to have a little common sense in this    since I rec'd Minnie's letter I am ashamed of myself but I hope that you will forgive me and think that I can't help it.  I am trying to be sober today but I see that there is no use for I can't   I am to giddy to be sober   I shall have to have you come and give me a lecture. I am going to bake some pancakes for tea and I wish that you were here to have some   You better call in the evening and see how we get along   I have not commenced farming yet   I shall have to wait until I come home from town tomorrow and then I shall have to commence.   I shall have to send you a dozen kisses if you will accept them  I will send them in the letter   but you cant receive them until you come down next Sunday as I would like to send a letter  up to go out on a boat if you will take it. How does that Mr. Porter and his betrothed get along   he has not committed suicide yet has he.  I guess that you think I have written enough such as it is    I shall close by sending you all the love that this envelope will hold and please answer this as soon as you can.  I remain your one true love

Maitie MaGill


From Eleanor & Marietta to Oliver (Written by Marietta)

Glen Arbor<br>April 26th 1867

Dear Father
We received the letter by the last mail   one had a one dollar bill in it.  we were glad to hear that you were well. Mama is getting better very fast   she is almost well but she has nervous spells sometimes   I am making your shirts and I want you to tell me whether I shall send you a couple when I get them made.  I shall make you three shirts out of the muslin.  we could not get such muslin in here for 50cts a yd.  It is time that we had commenced to plant potatoes but I dont know whether I can plant any or not as the ground is not plowed and it will be hard to work.  I shall have to take that dollar and pay for getting Etties shoes mended   I wish that you had sent me a few spools of

Coat cotton I use the numbers from 40 to 20 more than any other. Our hens lay very well now  we get 4 eggs sometimes.  I do wish that you would send us in a dog chain for I cant have Carlo following us everywhere he fights every dog he meets.  I got some coffee down at the store and payed 50cts a pound for it and when it is made it tastes like old rotten wood.  I shall have to close as I am in a hurry to go down town   no more at present   write soon.
Yours Truly
Mrs. E M Boizard
Miss M E Boizard



To Oliver from Eleanor and Marietta (Written by Marietta)

Glen Arbor, Michigan<br>May 1<sup>st</sup> 1867

Dear Father
We received your welcome letter dated the 22 of last month and the money also.  I made you a shirt last week and I cut another one this week.  I am a great deal better   I will make you three shirts and Ettie one under garment   in your next letter, write and tell us whether we shall send you a couple of shirts.  do you think that you could sell shirts if we could get the material to make them.  if you think we could and we could get the stuff we could help get our clothing (Ettie & I)  we have not got the barrel down from McCartys Dock yet as there are not any teams around that we could get  as Fishers have sold all their teams.   we have had three nice roses on our bush.  Brothertons hogs trouble us very much, and Charlie    the dog is so brave that he gets up on top of the house and barks at them.  we have had quite a shower today but it has cleared off very fine   have you heard anything of Bridges lately I am afraid the Indians have killed them all.  No more at present write soon.
Yours & c.
Eleanor M. Boziard
Marietta E Boizard



From Eleanor & Marietta to Oliver (Written by Marietta)

Glen Arbor<br>May 10<sup>th</sup> 1867

Dear Father
We received the letter and two dollars also   we did not get the provisions untill yesterday   Mr Brothertons folks did not go up untill then.  I will send you three shirts by Mr Newman and you may sell one if you can get $3   do so and you can get more muslin and send it in.  Dont send any more provisions on any boat that will land at McCarty's Dock  for they might just as well be in Chicago as up there   for there are not any teams here that we can get as the people are using their teams in plowing and dragging.  We did not get that book or letter from Captain Rosman as he did not leave at Glen Arbor.  I guess he must have forgotten to leave it at the store.  Mama is not very well today   I guess that she has worked to hard for a day or so.  I guess that Carlo will have to be killed for he eats all of the eggs.  no more at present  please write soon.

PS  All the neighbors send their best respects.
Mrs. E.M. Boziard
Miss Ettie Boizard

**Long Distance Love 1855-1870**

From Eleanor and Marietta to Oliver (Written by Marietta)

Glen Arbor, Michigan<br>May 17th 1867

Dear Father,
We received two letters one dated April 27th and May the 11th we received $4 and the book and braid also.  I feel a great deal better then I did when Mr. Newman was here.  I hope that you will like your shirts.  The next lot of Provisions that you send in I wish that you would send me in some kind of beef as I have a hankering for it.  Brothertons does my hauling and they want to know whether you can get any blue cotton stocking yarn   see if you can and write and let us know in your next letter   but you need not buy any  untill we send you a sample.  It don't seem worth while for us to plant any potatoes for the pigs   there are five or six pigs running   they are here most all the time and we have not got any fence to keep them out   it just keeps one person another time to watch them   I wish you would send me in some dried apples or some kinds of dried fruit   be sure and send all the provisions on the **Young America**.  no more at present please write soon.  I will take this down to day and try to send it out to you by the Captain of the **Young America.**
Yours truly & c.
Eleanor M. Boizard
Mary E. Boizard


From Eleanor & Marietta to Oliver (Written by Marietta)

Glen Arbor<br>May 27th 1867

Dear Father
 I have good chance to send a letter out as far as Milwaukee by Mr. Walker Cooke, as he is going out  he can send it by mail or send it by the Captain of the **Young America** or whatever boat he goes on.
Mama is well as usual   we had to have Carlo shot as he ate every egg that the hens laid.  for about four weeks we did not get an egg but since he was shot we have got over four dozen   he has been dead about a week   we would have had to pay a dollar taxes for him and he ate all our eggs.   when you send in anything more you must try and send us some more flour as I owed part of that that you did send.  I can't eat more than one meal of corn-meal at a time as it sours on my stomach.  I have not been to Glen Arbor or down town for over four months.  it is quite cold here   we have to have a fire most all the time   we have used all our wood up that we had chopped    there is an exhibition down town tomorrow night   I dont know whether I shall go or not as I dont go anywhere much since mama has been feeling so unwell.  no more at present  write  soon.
Yours Truly
Mrs. E. M. Boizard


From Eleanor & Marietta to Oliver (Written by Marietta)

Glen Arbor<br>June 7th 1867

Dear Father
We received your welcome letter the money and the papers also.  mama is not very well, she planted some potatoes and she could hardly get out of bed she felt so stiff and old   the least bit of work that she does it makes her sick  it is

hardly worth while to plant any thing    for there is five of Brotherton's hogs here most all the time and it keeps one of us running after them most all the time, as we have not any fence to keep them out.  I shall not try to plant any thing another year unless we have a fence for it will just be labor lost.  We had to borrow flour today as we were all out of flour.  Ettie received a letter from Mr Newman   he arrived home all right   we have two hens setting    eat a good lot of beef steak for us both   I have been to town once since the eighth of March and it nearly killed me.  We would like very much to see you in here no more at present   write soon
Yours Truly
Eleanor M. Boizard
Mary E Boizard


From Eleanor and Marietta to Oliver (Written by Marietta)

Glen Arbor<br>June  1867

Oliver,

I received the letter and the flour.  We had a letter this mail from Emma Bridges   she is married to a soldier   she was married the day before Christmas    Her name is Mrs. Brown    she was sixteen the 16th of May.  She is at Mary Cooper Wells, Arizona {Maricopa Wells}    her parents are at Fort McDowell    She don't say anything about her father    You can see the letter when you come home.  You speak about the dog.  I should not have had him killed had I known that you thought so much of him.  I did not think that we could keep a dozen hens to lay eggs to keep the dog on    although I might have killed the hens and ate them    he was not worth anything    for you might as well try to set the cat on anything    when the Brotherton's pigs came he would jump up on the house to bark at them and that is not all   he got to going to the neighbors to eat their eggs    all that he was fit for was to bark and eat    I am very sorry that he was killed being as you thought more of the Dog then you did of us    no more at present    write soon Yours & c.

Post Script

Willie Tucker has cut his knee


From Eleanor and Marietta to Oliver (Written by Marietta)

Glen Arbor, Michigan<br>June 10/67

Dear Father
We received your welcome letter and two dolls also you did not say anything about the yarn of Brothertons and they are on nettles about it    if you don't soon send it we will have to pay them the money for the hauling those things from McCarty;s Dock.  They wanted cotton yarn two pounds.  Do you think that you will stay out where you are and have the same employ as you have.  cant we come out and stay this winter so that Ettie can go to school as she is not getting any schooling here as the snow is too deep in the winter and it is too warm in summer and for her to walk six miles every day   she can't stand it.   you could rent a couple of rooms somewhere in the city I don't think that It would cost any more to do that than it would for you to pay your board pay your wash bill and keep us beside    they have a school teacher here but she is not much older then Ettie is herself and I don't know anything about her education    all the girls are going or gone out to school even Louisa Goffert    she was out all last winter and part of

the young men and boys also.  we would not want to come untill almost the last boats for we would have the potatoes to dig   we could bring what potatoes that we would want to use while we were out there and they would not cost as much as they would to buy them out there   we would not want to take anything with us excepting our clothing and bedding   when you write let us know what you think about it we are out of both lard and butter as I have to use butter most everything.  the weather is very warm we can hardly stay in the house, no more at present please write soon.  Yours truly

Mrs E M B

Miss M E B

PS I forgot to sign our names in the last letter EMB


From Eleanor & Marietta to Oliver (Written by Marietta)

Glen Arbor
Augt 22nd 1867

Dear Oliver

Yours of the 5th of this month came to hand this mail which was last Monday   there was $2 in the letter which we were very glad to get.  I have two very large boils on my arm but one of them are broke   they must make me sick   the potatoes are now as large as good sized hickory nuts   we wont have our seed from them and the ground not being plowed makes it worse   we are not going to have any squashes this year and we wont have any bean for seed.  if we dont go out we will have to have the house plastered   I shall have to get a pair of shoes before very long for that pair that you got me when you were here are almost worn out.   they may last through blackberrying   you will have to send the money to me so that I can get them here   for you will not be able to send the right size to me.  the wine is working very nice   I hope the butter and chickens feed will soon come.  you spoke of getting a house in October but if we come we wont come much before the last of October.  dont get more than two rooms.  no more at present   write soon

Yours &c.

E. M Boizard

M. E. Boizard


From Eleanor & Marietta to Oliver (Written by Marietta)

Glen Arbor
Augt 30th 1867

Dear Oliver

I received the cornmeal & butter and then I got a letter with $1.75 in it.  did you pay the Freight on the meal & butter   it was 40cts   we paid that here   we had a shower here yesterday but it did not do much good as it did not lay the dust - the potatoes look worse then they did last fall when I dug them   I guess that it is because the ground has not been plowed and this dry weather too.  Last Monday we got 18 quarts of blackberries and when they were dried we had over a gallon still.  Wednesday we got 21 quarts.  I was glad to get that bag that had the cornmeal in it   if we have any potatoes we will need some bags to put them in when we come up to Chicago.   when you get the house dont get it down on the sand amongst the Irish   it may be such a thing that Charlie F will come out and go to school to this winter   but we are not certain   they talk some of him going when we go.  no more at present   write soon

Yours & c.
Mrs E M Boizard
M E Boizard



From Eleanor & Marietta to Oliver (Written by Marietta)

Glen Arbor
Sept 12th /67

My Dear Oliver,
I received three letters by the last mail and one by boat   we got $8.00 in three of them. We have picked over a hundred quarts and we are going to pick some more blackberries tomorrow. Ettie got a letter from Emma her Fathers time is out  he has gone to California to reenlist -  Mr Lloyd cannot leave his homestead but we can nail this house up. we were very sorry that you have been sick. I will write more next week as I have no time  I am very tired I have been berrying all day   write as soon as possible.
Yours Truly
E. M. Boizard



From Eleanor and Marietta to Oliver (Written by Marietta)

Glen Arbor, Michigan
September 20th 1867

Dear Oliver,
Yours of the 9th came to hand in the due time. I was very glad to hear that your health was improving   there was $2.50 in the letter and a photograph. You spoke of getting a house for $10 a month we cannot get ready to come before the last of October or the 1st of November   you can get it if you can by that time. You spoke of selling this place that I shall never do untill I have a better place to go to. I have got it   now I intend to keep it as poor as it is. You spoke of bringing all our things and everything we had but I won't  for it would destroy the furniture more than it is and it would cost more to pay the freight on it –then it would to buy new   anyhow we want another bedstead and lounge. Get a house with two good rooms anyhow but don't get less than two rooms when you do get them get straw enough for two under beds and have it in the house when we get there.  for what few chickens we have it would cost more to feed them there then they are worth and we would have meat to buy   anyhow the hawks are carrying them all off.  it has been very warm for two or three day period. I don't know how many potatoes we will have as soon as they are ripe I shall dig them.  our flour is almost out but we can buy a few pounds here and that will do untill we come up to chicago. We were black-berrying the other day and picked 21 quarts I am going to go once more and when we get them all dried I shall weigh them to see how many I have. One of our little peach trees has three peaches on they are as yellow as can be.  They look so nice and they are almost ripe. Fishers will have about 50 bushels of peaches & Tuckers will have about 12 bushels. you spoke of letting Todd have the wood off of the place   if we do  it will only grow up to briars and weeds  we had better let the wood stand.  no more at present write soon. Yours Truly
E.M. Boziard
M E Boizard

**Long Distance Love 1855-1870**

From Eleanor and Marietta to Oliver

Glen Arbor, Michigan
Sept 24th /67

My Dear Husband,
I received your welcome letter dated the 19th of this month there was $3.00 in the letter & three newspapers also. Ettie and myself went blackberrying today and picked 24 quarts it is the last time that we shall go as we are both of us most sick from going a berrying.  we have had quite a good rain here but it is too late for to do the potatoes any good.  when we come up to Chicago you will be ashamed to walk the streets with us for we will look so rustic and shabby for we have not had any new clothing for almost three years.  Dick O'Donald I presume that you have heard about him   he is an Irishman he got drunk and built up a fire and laid down and went to sleep  the shanty took fire and they could not get him out before he was half burnt up   his head arm and the lower part of his limbs were burn off.  The shanty was burned down to the ground   he left a wife and five children the oldest is a girl about four months younger then Ettie   this happened last Tuesday.  I will write more next time.  I am very tired.  Write soon
Yours truly
E.M Boizard
M E Boizard

P.S.  If you have any old clothing send it in to us for Mr. Lloyd.  send me in three or four gunny bags to put our potatoes and if you can send me a pound tea and that will do me untill we go out.  EMB   MEB


From Eleanor & Marietta to Oliver (Written by Marietta)

Glen Arbor
Sept 28th 1867

Mr Dear Oliver
We received your welcome letter yesterday and were somewhat surprised to hear that you had not got any from us as we always answer them as soon as we get them  it will be impossible for us to come Chicago by the first of the month as the potatoes are greener now than they were a month ago and they are not fit to dig yet and if we were ready we have not got the money to come with   when you do rent the rooms get room enough   for Charlie Fisher expects to come out to school and board with us this winter   when you do rent them get straw enough for two beds - by the time we get there and have it in the house   we will not fetch anything excepting our winter clothing & bedding   I paid $3.25 for 50 weight of flour today as we were out.  I have to pay two dollars a pound for tea and it is not fit to drink   for chopping wood last winter we owed Mr Tucker $13 1/2 we have paid him $4.00  I suppose I shall have to pay him the rest before I go out. The nights are getting very cold  no more at present   please write soon.Yours Truly
Eleanor M Boizard
Marie E. Boizard

Please send us a {?} large {?}  we will want it very much before we come to Chicago
PS Since writing the above I have received $2 from Mr Ray.

**Chicago and Glen Arbor 1864-1870**

From Eleanor & Marietta to Oliver (Written by Marietta)

Glen Arbor
Oct 2nd 1867

My Dear Oliver
I received your letter yesterday by the Prop. **Brooklyn** you spoke of me bringing the stove  I am afraid of getting it broken   perhaps we can find a stove   if we cant we can get a parlor cook stove as we need one any how to put in the room.  I shall not bring any furniture with me as it will cost more to get them to the boat and all than they are worth   we wont need more than three or four chairs a bedstead lounge and a table.  we will have our potatoes to bring and they will cost a good deal.  I don't know how many I will have or anything about it   when we do come we want to come on the **Oswegatchie** so that we can leave this dock.  it would cost so much more to go to McCartys dock and I don't know whether I can get a team or not   we will be ready about her second trip  you can let us know by that time what we are to do   because if I have to move I wont come for the expense and trouble will be more than it is worth   we can not rent the house   we might get some perfect stranger in it   we can nail the door & windows up and get Mr Fisher to look at it once in a while   no more at present   write soon   Your & c.
E.M. Boizard


From Eleanor & Marietta to Oliver (Written by Marietta)

Glen Arbor
Oct 13th 1867

Mr Dear Husband
Your letter came to hand in due time  I was glad to hear that you were well as this leaves us at present.  You spoke of us bringing our furniture  I will bring our stove but not the table or chairs for they would not be fit to be seen.  The **Oswegatchie** will be here at this dock about the 27th of this month.  you need not buy the bedstead & lounge untill we come up to Chicago for I want to buy them myself.  I have no chairs to bring except those cane seated ones and I would not take them as a gift by the time they are taken to Chicago and back again   you may send the money to pay our passage or buy the tickets and send to us  just as you think best   I can't write anymore as I have to hurry for Ettie & Charlie are going up to the other dock and I want to send this up by them. Ettie is going to have her tooth pulled.  no more at present
Yours Truly
E.M. Boizard
M. E. Boizard


From Marietta to Charlie

Glen Arbor
Thursday Morning
Oct 24th/67

Dear Charlie
You must not be surprised at me writing to you but I forgot to ask you if you would write to me every week and I will do the same and then we can hear from each other oftener  if you should not come out this fall please come in the spring  but I want you to come down to the boat and see us off.
Yours forever
Maitie E. Boizard

**Long Distance Love 1855-1870**

From Marietta to Charlie

Glen Arbor<br>Oct 24th 1867

My Dear Charlie

I received your note and was very glad to get. I guess that we will go out tomorrow some time. I feel so bad I dont know what do   I want to see you very much but I presume that you will not want to come clear up to the other dock to see us off   but I should like to have you.  you may direct your letter to me in care of my Father, direct to No 93 South Canal Street Chicago Ill's


From Marietta to Charlie

Milwaukee<br>Oct 28th 1867

My Dear Charlie

I arrived safe in Milwaukee after a very pleasant trip. I was not a bit sea sick but I expected that I should be  some of the ladies were sick. I cried myself to sleep on the boat   I felt so lonely and I wanted to see you so much.  did you see me cry when I was waving my handkerchief. We are visiting at Mrs Cookes  the girls are all trying to find out who I am writing to but I will not tell them. Mrs Tator came home from Portage City yesterday.  she said she saw Herbert McCarty on the cars   he talk some of attending Commercial College. He is in Milwaukee someplace. There was a couple of Mrs. Tators Friends call last evening to take us to the Theater. (Mrs Tator & I) but it was raining and I could not go and anyhow I did not care about going  I would rather been where I could see you  then go to the Theatre. I feel so home sick that I dont know what to do  Today is Sunday and it seems a great deal lonelier then Glen Arbor  because I am not acquainted with any person here and there I am   I would give most anything to see you   if you are as lonely as I am I feel sorry for you    Well I presume that you think I had better write about something else by this time   how did you get home that day after the boat left. I had a dream about you last night and the night before   I guess that it will come to pass  I presume that you will like to know  so I guess I will have to tell you   I thought that you came to Chicago and you were at our house and you were sitting down by a window and you were holding a young lady on your knee   I shall judge that she was about 15 years of age   I was not acquainted with her  but perhaps you know her, but I dont   you called her your (dear Little Wife)  I have come to the conclusion that you know her   I would like to have an introduction to her.  remember I dreamed this all in two nights and if I dream it again tonight I shall begin to think that you are married or just about to be   I hope that you will send me a piece of the wedding cake and the card also.  I shall send a parcel by the Captain, the trimmings for your mother are in it.  Give my respects to all inquiring Friends and tell them I will write them as soon as I can. remember what you said about writing to me. My Mother sends her love to all of her Friends  she says she would like to see you all again   well I can not think of anything more  at present  but perhaps I can before I go on the boat. no more at present   please write soon.
Yours until death parts us
Maitie E. Boizard


P.S. Please excuse all mistakes and poor writing for I am very much confused the folks are talking and Kittie is playing on the Piano.

**Chicago and Glen Arbor 1864-1870**

From Marietta to Charlie

Milwaukee 29th 1867

My Dear Chas,

You see that there has been a great space since I commenced my letter but I had to lay my letter for a while as one of Mrs. Tator's friends called in.  I have been to the theater and a Ball all the same night   I did not dance but once and then went home  I wish that you had been here to go   May and I went in the company of a gentleman that was about 30 or 35 years of age he was ever so homely   When you answer please let me know if you will come to Chicago to spend the Winter or not   as I am anxious to know   I met Herbert McCarty on the street   but I guess that he did not recognize me   I will enclose a short note to Mrs. Tucker   My dear I am ashamed to send this to you   I had the letter in my valise and a bottle of perfumery and the cork was loose and I see that some of it got on this letter  I shall have to close as I have to write five more letters    My respects to my friends and much love to your own dear self.

Yours until death   Maitie E Boizard


From Marietta to Charlie

Chicago
Nov 6th 1867

Mr Dear Charlie

I received your welcome letter the day that I arrived in the City   I would have answered it before the later day but I had to help clean the house. I have not commenced to go to school yet but I expect to about Monday. I presume that you have rec'd my letter before this   I am looking for an answer and waiting patiently. I do wish that you would come up and spend the Winter. I have attended the Theater once since I have been in the city and once while I was in Milwaukee and when I *{thought}* we were going home we went to a party and danced one **quadrille**Error! Bookmark not defined., and then went home. I went with Miss May Cooke & Mr Anderson. I presume that you have attended several parties since I left Glen Arbor   have you been down to Mr. Tucker's lately   I wish that you would pet my Kittie and think it is me. I am so homesick that I feel like crying most all the time. My mother is not feeling very well. She has a bad cold   she coughs some   she looks almost as bad as she did when we went down to Glen Arbor four years ago. How do George & Charity get along   do you think that they will get married.  you must not think that I am inquisitive but you know that I am not in GA and I feel interested.   I dont know what to make of you   I dont know whether you are in earnest about that engagement.   My Mr. Newman is here   he has been here about two weeks   he starts tomorrow for Pine Lake.  when we came to the City he was at the House that my Father boarded at. My Pa says that we cannot board you any cheaper than Five Dollars a week and do your washing also. he had to pay this and pay for his washing also. Mr Newman is paying six for his board. we would board you as cheap as we possibly could   everything is very dear.  you ask me if I did  not see you waving your handkerchief yes my Dear I did and it seemed like taking part of my life to see you standing on the Dock   you looked so lonely   Mr. Newman says that I am heartless  but I told him that my Heart was in safe keeping and out of his reach   am I right, my Dear Charlie   My heart is in Glen Arbor. How are all my young Friends getting along and you especially  I would like very much to see you again but if nothing  happens I promise myself the pleasure of seeing you in the spring if you dont come up this winter. My ma sends her love to all the Family & all inquiring Friends   Give my respects to all the young folks and receive my love   please write soon  Yours forever and ever
Maitie E. Boizard

**Long Distance Love 1855-1870**

P.S. Please excuse all mistake and poor writing.  Maitie
Direct to 195 South Canal Street   Chicago Ills.


From Marietta to Charlie

Chicago<br>Nov 13<sup>th</sup> 1867

My Dearest Charlie,
I rec'd your welcome letter last sunday morning   my Pa went out and when he came home he brought me the letter he tried to plague me   he told me that he had none for me   My ma and I reached his pockets and we found one.  I am sorry that you are so lonely   but I am worse off than you are as I am not acquainted with any one.  you spoke about that party that I attended in Milwaukee and though that it was not much like the parties in Glen Arbor.  I agree with you there  as the dancing is not near as good as the dancing in GA.  You or I can dance a great deal better   it was for the Benefit of a dancing school but it was not to be compared with Mr. Kings school, I will say that much for old G_ A_.   You were right about me holding my head down and crying.  My Dear (if you will permit me to call you such endearing names) but I guess you will for I will anyhow.  you need not be afraid of me taking your dear head off as I will not for I think to much of it for to do that.  You were right about my dream.  You know what has passed between us and remember if you are true to me I am to you.  Mr. Newman has not gone home yet but he says that he will go in two or three days.   we went to the Minstrelles **(Minstrels}** last night they were not worth going to see.  I am so mad at him that I dont know what to do.  Has Mrs Tucker come home yet   I hope she enjoyed her visit   have you heard anything about that parcel yet   I hope that you have rec'd it ere this   I fixed your letter on the parcel and I dont see how they would get separated unless the Captain took the letter off of the parcel.  you mentioned a party at Mr Decker's who got it up  I am glad to hear you say that you dont attend such parties   not that I want you to stay away from them because I am not there   for of course you can do as you like about that  but I don't think such places are fit for young men or girls that think anything of their honor or themselves   take my advice and stay away from such places.   My mother sends her love to your ma and all the Family.  My love to all the Family and a good share for yourself My Dear   write soon   if you will permit me to sign my self,
Your own True Little Wife Ettie
P.S. Here is a note please hand it to Mrs. Dorsey  dont get mad at me for signing my name as I have  Ettie

N.B. My Mother is not any better   she has a cold in her head and a bad cough   she had a spell with her heart the other night   I am afraid that she will not be as healthy as she was in Glen Arbor  I have not been very well, one day I was sick in bed but I am much better   excuse poor writing as I have to get dinner now.   Ettie


From Marietta to Charlie

Chicago<br>Nov 21<sup>st</sup> 1867

My Dearest Charlie
I rec'd your welcome letter dated the 9<sup>th</sup> of this month and was somewhat surprised to hear that you had not rec'd any letters from me, as I have answered every letter that you have written   when I read your last letter  I had a good cry  it made me feel so homesick.  but if I could have had a good look at you I would not have felt so bad   when you spoke about my Poor Kittie I did not know what to do  I hope that you will pet her for me.  Is Mrs Ayres at Glen Arbor yet.   there are two letters on the road to you ahead of this.  I shall be very sorry if you dont come up here this winter  I have not commenced to go to school yet but I have been examined and the teacher says that she will send

**Chicago and Glen Arbor 1864-1870**

for me as soon as there is a vacancy. I am expecting a letter from you every day   it is just one month day after tomorrow since we left Glen Arbor.  but it seems more like six months than one.  but never mind if we dont have gay times when I come home it will be because we cannot    has there been any changes there since we left   how many young Ladies has come ther    I hope that none will steal my Dear Charlie's Heart away   if they should what would poor Ettie do  she would cry and break her heart   you may think that I am in fun  but I never was more in earnest in my life   please believe me Dear, your own through life. dont let any person see this  Mr Dodge is in the City  he was here yesterday. Mr Newman is here yet  he is expecting a boat in every minute they have been looking for five for a week  I am in hopes that he will start soon for I can hardly tolerate him   well my dear I must close as it is near noon and I have to get dinner.  Give our love to all the Family and friends and receive all my Love and that is just as much as the letter can carry and believe me your own Dear little Wife
Ettie

write soon   direct as before.
My Pa's address is 167 Randolph Street  that is where the store is it is a large Paint Oil and Glass establishment  I thought I would give you his address also  Maitie B


From Marietta To Charlie

Chicago<br>Nov 23<sup>rd</sup> 1867

My Dear Charlie
I have not rec'd any letter from you for over a week   I thought I would write and see whether you had forgotten me and again I thought that you were not at home. I did not know but you had take a notion to go away some where I did not know. I thought I might have said something in some of my letters that would offend you. If I have I am very sorry as I did not do so intentionally. Mr. Newman has gone home  he went last week. We are having very stormy weather it has rained for two nights and a portion of the day   it is very muddy. I see more mud in one half day than I have seen in four years. I was out last night with my pa and it was raining so hard as it could pour. I feel so home sick that I don't know what to do.  I never knew what it was to be homesick untill I came out here. If I ever get back to old Glen Arbor, I don't think that I shall leave it in a hurry. I have rec'd one letter from Sarah  she send her love to you & Frank, but I had ought to have got it before I left Glen Arbor. how many Ball's has there been in the place since I left. there will be a grand one in the city sometime during the month of December   only $20 a ticket   that is not very much.  what would you think to have the tickets so high in Glen Arbor. I guess that it would be the grandest Ball that ever has been in G.A. I have been to the matinee  they have them every Wednesday & Saturday afternoon. they are at **Woods Museum**   they are mostly for children but any person that wants to can go. I heard the Peg Factory was for sale, is it a mere rumor or is it a fact.  you know that there are so many false reports that you cant tell anything about what you hear. I tell you news fly very rapidly   I heard that you were surely going up to Chicago, but Mr Dodge told me that and a lot more but I wont tell what.  you know he has been a way from Glen Arbor most of the season but as soon as he landed at Mr McCartys Dock he commenced to take the news and what I have already told you amongst the rest. he needed to know if that was so I told him that I did not know for certain, what did you think about it.  how are all the young folks getting along.  I presume they are getting along nicely and never miss any of their absent friends but absent ones do not forget them.  I hope that you will not forget Ettie B. for she is a true Friend if nothing more to you.  don't be offended at me, I pray. I will enclose a note to Kate King will you be kind enough to hand it to her and I will try and do as much for you sometimes. Please give my Love to other inquiring Friends if there are any.  our love to all your Folks and please receive a good share for your own dear self.  Please write as soon as possible.

**Long Distance Love 1855-1870**

From your Loving
Maitie

Direct to 195 South Canal please excuse all mistakes and poor writing
your own true Wife

but I hardly dare sign myself that for fear it will offend you  if it does please let me know Mattie


From Marietta to Charlie

Chicago<br>Dec 2<sup>nd</sup> 1867

My Dearest Charlie
I rec'd your Welcome letter dated the 16<sup>th</sup> of Nov and you may be sure that I was glad to get it  I am expecting to get one either today or tomorrow  I hope that you are not offended with me for writing to you as I did in my last letter  but I had the Blues so that day  I felt as though every person despised me  I know that it is very wrong to entertain such feelings but I could not help it. I am very sorry that you cannot come out here this Winter as I shall be so lonely for I dont know any person. Mr Dodge has gone down to Ogdensburgh  he has been gone about a week. I have not commenced to go to school yet and I dont know when I shall as there is not any vacancy  but I am studying at Home  My Arithmetic is the most that I care about and my Pa can learn me that  if I only knew as much about it as he does I would do. I was quite surprised to hear about the Weddings that took place in Glen Arbor  I presume that when I go back home that there wont be any person there but married Folk and I will have to wear the {Willow?} what do you think about it  but you must not get married untill I come home for I would like to be some where  where no one could see me and look on and see you kiss the Bride. but you must not be like Tom Helm and forget to kiss the Bride for if I should happen to be there I will kiss you to put you in the mind of kissing her. please dont take my head off. Yes I guess that we will tell the Glen Arbor People some news in a few years  I rather guess it will make some of them open their Eyes  dont you think it will  My Darling Chas. Yes I will take good care of your Heart and it will be the best of care to  remember and take good care of mine  to tell you this candid truth Charlie I never Loved any one as I do you  nor ever shall. you spoke about Mrs Tucker and getting her dress  I am very sorry but Tell her if she dont get it we will make it right with her. How does my Pet get along  you requested me to tell you what boat we came on from Milwaukee  it was one of Goodriches Line the name of the boat was the **Orion**. we left the Parcel for Capt Rosman and your Letter also  the Letter was fastened on the outside of it  I slipped the letter in under the string that was around the parcel. My Ma says that she always knew that you were mischievous  and she says that she expects by the time we get back you will be so roguish that we wont know it is Charlie Fisher.  You are quite excusable but I dont care how many questions you ask  if I did not know you it would be different but as it is I dont care. yes I know what a great Fellow you are to ask questions especially when you asked me one question  I presume you can guess what one that was.  My Ma has not been well since we have been in the City she sends her Love to all enquiring Friends  here are some patterns for your ma  How does Frank get along  poor boy  I pity him since Angie has gone. but he will soon forget her  My regards to all and My love to your own dear self  please write soon  I remain your own true Wife forever & ever
Ettie

please dont get mad    I send two ledgers 37 and 39 we will get 38 as soon as we can  Please excuse all mistakes and poor writing as I dont feel very well today

**Chicago and Glen Arbor 1864-1870**

From Marietta to Charlie

Chicago
Dec 11th/67

My Dear Dear Charles
Yours of the twenty fifth is now before me   it was post marked Detroit Dec. 9th you dont know how glad I was to hear from you as it has been over two weeks since I heard from you last   I had almost given up as I thought you had forgotten me  but I presume that it could not be helped for I know how long it takes a letter to come from G A to Chicago.  I hope it will be so that you can come up in the spring.  I would like to have you come  I am very sorry it is so that you can not come this winter as I thought that we would have such Gay Times   but you may Bet if we both live to see each other again we will have just the Best of Times   You say that your Heart is mine   that I am most happy to hear and you rest assured that mine is yours as long as you wish for it   I dont think that there is any danger of any person winning my Heart as it is already given to you and I would sooner loose my Life then break the vows that I have given to you   although you may change your mind different from what it is now  I shall always remain true for it shall never be said that I broke my vows  not that I think you will and I hope that you will take no offense as I mean none, I will do as you said  I might in signing my name.   I hope that you will not go Crazy untill I come home and then after that I dont think that there will be any cause for you to   for I am as true to you as True can be.  I am not feeling near as well as I did when I was in Glen Arbor. I feel dull and heavy all the time just as any person would when they were coming down with the Fever.  I must tell you how much I weigh   when I left Glen Arbor my weight was 112 pounds and now it is 102 lbs so you may see for yourself how the city agrees with me and as far as my ma  I dont believe she has been well a day since we left the shores of Mich.  I am very happy to hear that you are having such a good school  and that you are progressing so finely in your studies   as I have not commenced to go to school yet   but I am studying at home  I am getting along very rapidly with my Arithmetic  I understand it better now then I ever did before   for I could not see into it very well before but now I can  but it is coming to me just like all others to  I presume it will be about Christmas when you get this   so I will wish you a Merry Christmas   if you attend any parties please dance a set or two for me  well I must draw this to a close as it is getting late and I shall have to write to Mrs Tucker yet tonight   Give my Love to Frank and all the Family and receive the greatest share for your own Dear Self  write soon and Believe me to be your Loving Little Wife
Ettie Boizard

PS  We will send two or three Ledgers   Tell your Ma that my Ma sent the beads in Mrs Tuckers parcel and she will make it right if you shall not get them  she sends her love to all   Ettie

Please excuse this poor writing as I am in a hurry

enclosed you will find a letter for Mrs Tucker   when you write please tell us how the House is and all around it.  You know what the color of this envelope denotes   please dont laugh at this letter I wanted to write all I could on it.
Ettie

# Long Distance Love 1855-1870

<u>From Marietta to Charlie</u>

Chicago<br>Jan 13<sup>th</sup> 1868

My Dear Charlie
Yours of the 4<sup>th</sup> of this month is now before me and you can not guess what pleasure it gives me, to hear from you but I was sorry to hear that had such an accident  but I hope that you will recover from it   I was glad that it was not any worse than it is   I was very glad to hear that you had such a Gay Time on Christmas and hope that you may enjoy your self at all the Parties especially the Fourth of July  but you had ought to take some of the girls   I request you to take some one to the next party if it is not untill the Fourth of July  please do take some one   for I know that you can find plenty up there to take   as for me I dont expect to attend any more parties in a very great hurry as there are not any here, that I would care about attending and dear only knows when I shall ever see any of my young Friends from Glen Arbor   as I dont expect that any of them will come out here to see me  unless you should take a notion to come as I dont know when I shall come home.  I do wish that you would try and come out or up  as it is so lonely that I dont know what to do   let me know when you have concluded {who} to take to the next party  if you have made up your mind when you answer this   you must be careful how you drive when you go out cutter riding but I am glad that you nor Frank, either were hurt.  you spoke of the numbers that were sold at the party  it seems that there are more Folks at Glen Arbor then ever.  you say that you wish that I was there on account of the Grand Skating   I wish that I was   if it would do any good but alas it will not   one reason is that I could not skate if I was there and there is not any likelihood of me learning.  I hope your Head is better   dont be offended at me or my poor letter as I dont feel very well and I am so homesick that I dont know what to do   when I think of what gay times I have had.  but I shall not speak of it for it makes me feel worse.  I hope that there is a good time coming tho. {though}  I came very near being run over today by an express wagon   Tell Frank that there is a Little Boy here, that is as great a hand to kiss as he is (not saying anything about Charlie) for I know that he dont like to kiss the girls.  I see that there is a blot on the paper   I did not notice it untill I commenced to write on this side I hope that you will excuse it.  I rec'd a Letter from Mrs Tucker the same time I rec'd yours   when you write will you please tell us if the house is all there.  today is wash day and I will not be able to write much more.  I will send your Ma a  list of prices.  our love to your Folks and receive a good share for yourself  please write soon   the weather is very strong and cold   it is snowing quite hard but the snow will not last more than a day or two and then the ground will be bare again.  Well I shall have to close as I have bread to bake and it is ready to mix up now   no more at present
but believe me your True Little Wife
Ettie


<u>From Austin Newman to Marietta</u>

Pine River Mich<br>Jan 16th/68

Dearest Ettie
Yours of Dec 20<sup>th</sup> reached me day before yesterday and oh was I glad to hear from you - that is I was glad to get a letter from my Darling.  but I think Ettie there was too much pepper in that letter; and I felt thankful that I was not near the writer when she wrote it -- But my Dear Little Girl  you are not very mad at me are you.  You dont think I have any right to lecture you.  Why that is just what you have been doing to me.
But please Ettie let us be Friends.  I agree with you them fellows are not worth talking to but if you make faces at them or look at them or give them the slightest chance they will take it.  they would do the same to me - a man  how much quicker to you a nice young girl as lovely and beautiful.  I <u>was</u> angry at them fellows for staring in the

**Chicago and Glen Arbor 1864-1870**

Windows and calling out to us -- but we will not say any more about them and I am sorry for mentioning it at all. So please accept my apologies for doing so. In my other letter to you the principal subject was learning music and I have spoken to you so often or written rather, that you might be angry sometimes  but I do like music so much and you are a pretty good singer; that I desired very much to have you learn; but I guess it is as you and your Father say too big an expense. I shall tell you all the news Ettie or anything that will interest you or you will care to hear. The snow here is nearly 2 feet deep and the **Sleighing** is first rate  We have had some splendid skating too  both before and since my last letter to you   Charlie and I and Harry too had great times on Pine Lake  the water so clear as you know it is on those little Lakes. The water 3 or 4 feet deep some places where we skated it seemed as if there was nothing between us and the bottom -- come across trout or schools of herring and chase them until they got into deep water  I wished very much you was there or here rather  It makes a person feel splendid to fly over the ice on water that way. Please Ettie did we not have a pretty good time in Chicago last Fall  I wish we had taken some rides  I mean in a buggy or open Carriage to go swift  it is some like skating -- well we will make it up some other time if you will consent or say so and will permit and allow and order and command –your very humble Servant -- please dont think me foolish E  for I would not like to have you labor under such a mistake. There is a Steamer advertised to run from Traverse Bay to Manistee touching at intermediate Ports  it will come to this place too and so forth and soon -- and likewise etcetera -- the last is supposed to be Latin  I am not in the enjoyment of the best of health same as I hope you all are. rheumatism bothers me some and sometimes low spirited  -- untill I begin to think of you then I feel better. that last letter was a first rate one; but Ettie there was only one leaf -- but then I know that it is hard work writing letters - at least it is for me.  it was a very neatly written letter. You say my Bird is well  Oh Ettie I thought it was your bird - but let me tell you please how we can manage it   You can get a Lady Bird and your bird and mine can go to keeping House  Dont you think that is a good idea Little One. Please Dearest dont be offended with me for calling you Little One for you know you are not very big or old either  We take the Traverse Eagle and I look over frequently to see if I can see anything about G.A. but up to this have seen nothing of the people or the place   Please excuse this poor letter   I will try and do better next time
With Love and respect
Yours truly
Austin C Newman


From Marietta to Charlie

Chicago
Jan 22nd 1868

My Dearest Charlie
I rec'd your welcome letter dated the 11th of this month and you may be sure that I was very happy to receive it  I was very happy to hear that you were well as this leaves me at present. I do wish that I could see you, as I am very lonely. Oh dear, my ink is so poor that I dont know what to do. you spoke of it being doubtful about your coming up here  I am sorry and wish that it would be so that you could come. you may look for us on Capt. Rossmans Boat as we intend to come on the boat that he runs if nothing happens more than I know of at present. My Pa tries to plague me by telling me that we will not go home this Summer but Ma says that we will go home in the Spring on the Capt's boat if he run   but I presume that he will   but please dont let any person know when we are coming as I want to surprise the Folks  but when you hear the Propeller whistle you may think   well that Ettie Boizard is on that Boat  she has come back to bother us all,  if you want to see me very much you will have to come down to the dock,  please excuse me for saying you must but you know that I dont mean it   but you can come down if you wish to.   My Dear is your Grand Father still in Glen Arbor. I did not know whether he was or not   as you had not mentioned him. how is our house getting along or dont it get along   please let us know when you write as my Pa is

**Long Distance Love 1855-1870**

uneasy about it   I rec'd a Letter from Charity and she says that Lottie Mason is a <u>Dear</u> <u>Good</u> <u>Girl</u>.  I used to be a dear good girl once in their eyes but now I am a dreadfull girl    I presume that you know what I mean   we will talk about skating when I get home.  I will send you my picture as soon as I get it taken    I should have sent you one like {Remnies?} but I did not want to offend you with one, as they was not like me   I just looked like a big Dutch Girl.  You wished me to finish my dream   well I will, I thought that I went up to Glen Arbor and we did not get off the boat in time so we were a way out in the Lake before we knew it and you were on the boat but we did not know it  and then I thought that I was married to Austin Newman    I thought that he forced me to marry him but still he was not on the boat  he got off at Glen Arbor and that was the last of him and then I saw you and commenced to cry and you wanted to know what was the matter and my Ma said that I married to Austin on the 10th of August   then you felt very sorry  you kneeled down on the deck near me and put your arm around me and my arm was around your neck just then the part of the boat that we was on  (you and I) sunk and you said it was better as that we should die together  we were at the center of the Lake and the Sea was very thick all around us.  I  for my part dont know what to think of it.  please excuse this poor Letter and writing but  I am very busy and have not very much time   I dont think  that you can read it   my ma sends her love to all.   I can think of a great deal more to write but you see that I cant write any more as the paper is not large enough  I guess that I shall have to get a foolscap sheet next time for I can think of enough to fill one.  How does my Kitten get along.  well I must close this Letter write soon
Your Little Wife Ettie B.
  to Charlie F.


you must excuse this sheet of paper as it is all that I have in the House.  You said that you loved me more and more  I will see about that when I come home   dont be offended at any thing I say to you.  Your L____W_____ Maitie



From Marietta to Charlie

Chicago<br>Feb. 12th 1868<br>Wednesday Afternoon

My Dearest Charles
Your  most kind and welcome Letter is now before me and you may be sure that I am very happy to hear from you My Dear Chas. please dont Laugh at my poor Letters.  I hope that you will try to come up here this Spring or in the Spring I should say.  yes, we will start for home about the middle of May if not before that if nothing happens.  I must confess that the Girls are rather high in your estimation.  you say that you wished I had been <u>here</u> <u>last</u> <u>night</u> as there was a party up to Brothertons  I think that they are going in on their nerves this Winter in having parties  but let them enjoy it while they may is all that I can say.  I think that Glen Arbor, is rather more lively than it was Last Winter at Least for the young Folks.  you spoke of me being so homesick and lonely   I might enjoy myself here if I could get acquainted with any young Gent's but I dont want to now.  I will not    you know what I have told you  there are several young Gents that are trying their very best to get acquainted with me, but I nix every ole ruse. There are a whole Factory full of them right next door to us   it is a Plowing Mill  & Box Factory   everytime that I go down stairs they can see me and I can see them    I guess you know how it is with all these young fellows if there is any young girl around       you say that you attended two parties    Both Dances or whatever they are called    you have done better than I have for I have not attended any    you know that I wont even attend any when I am at home and therefore I dont know what they are called.  Oh I must tell you of a very heavy crime I am guilty of  and I do wish that you would tell me how to get out of it    I have broke a couple of young Fellows Hearts as they say    but I say that I have only bent them    they are both strangers to me    but they told a young Lady that lives in the house that

I had broken their hearts  but I told her that I had only bent them.  please tell me what to do   I guess that they will get well when I am gone, dont you think so.  I pray that you will excuse this poorly written letter as I am not well and dont feel like writing or doing any kind of work.  My Mother and I am both just about down sick, with colds.  I know if you felt as I do you would not feel like writing  but I dont want to let the week pass without writing to you My Dear. for that would be breaking my promise to you.   Well I presume that Valentines Day will soon be along  long before you receive this   I will send one to Frank in your letter but you are not deserving of any as your dont write long enough letters  you <u>scamp</u>.  but I will see by the time I get another letter from you and if it is a good long Letter you may look for a Valentine  but mind I would say who it will be from.  I guess that by this time you are tired of trying to read my Letter or what ever you call it and I guess I shall draw it to a close.  please write as soon as you can   My Parents send their Love to all, and receive a good Share for your self from me. and believe me, your T____Little Wife Ettie


<u>From Austin Newman, to Oliver</u>

Charlevoix
Feb 17th 1868

Mr J O Boizard

Dear Friend Yours of Jan 31st came to hand on the 14th. Harry got 3 letters at the same time and I got 2 yours and Etties.  We are all in pretty good health here in the North Pole for it is almost too cold for comfort sometimes   as you will see by the color of this Ink it has been froze and refrozen consequently makes it look "kinder" pale as the American says.  As long as I get as good letters as this last my Dear Friend I shall be glad to correspond with you   I began to think that you would not have much to write but I guess writing is what you are used to and you mix business and pleasure so easily; that a fellow don't feel any hesitation about having you write   I certainly am much obliged to you for your kindness in doing that small favor for me  Harry got a letter from one of the old hands of the 10th  Harry wrote of a venture to Newport (the fellows home was close by there) calculating that it was about time for him to be out of money; the Gentleman wondered how Harry found out he was there; pretty well guessed wasnt it?  You quite surprised me when I read that you were out of debt I really thought that it would take till spring to clear off the amount you owed the company your wages are so small.  In a letter that I rec'd from Edward a short time ago he mentioned you and said that Army Clerks were hard to get so I wrote him 3 or 4 week ago and if there is any chance for better wages and enough to pay you to leave   I will let you know   for if you are to be absent from your home I should think the best way would be to go where you would get most wages   We can wait and see what they will offer.  Charlie has just got a letter from him (Edward) and he don't know wether he will come up here in the Spring or not but he says his wife wants to come and stay up here awhile; she has been here before  He says she wants to come and set out a row grape vines  About being pleased or looking forward to the time when navigation will open so I can go hunting  you mean so that I can go to Glen Arbor  for I believe I told you there was a Steamboat advertized to go there direct from here.  I am afraid I shall not be able to go to Chicago in the Spring because it will put me back in my spring work same as it did last spring  you see I want H & J to put in about 5 acres of Potatoes same of corn and 5 acres of other stuff good deal of work isn't it?  Come to Chicago  next Fall if living with a lot of stuff to sell   My Dear Boz (that is **Dickens** -- by the way has he been in your little Village this winter) you did not tell me wether you was giving "Young America" lessons in French though I suppose you are so please don't be angry with me for mentioning it.  I suppose Richard does 'make music all the day' and sometimes nearly deafen you   I told Ettie she ought to get a mate for him and raise some canaries she could go into speculation.  Does the shade of the Old Dog Troy ever trouble you  now I don't want to hurt your feelings but he used to bark so

# Long Distance Love 1855-1870

often peace to his ashes I have a mind to write a letter to Mother; but I know she has both yours and Etties my love to her and best respects to yourself and all inquiring Friends
yours Truly
Austin C Newman


From Austin Newman to Marietta

Charlevoix<br>Feb 23rd/68

Dear Ettie
Yours of Jan 31st reached me on the 14th of Feb. when I got the envelope containing the Valentine I thought it was your letter  I suppose I am in the enjoyment of as good health as most people -- but my dear little Girl I get very low spirited sometimes  but that last letter Dear One made me feel very happy  it was a real nice letter Ettie  very neatly written and I do love you so for it Darling and I have been four or five days not knowing how to answer it  I will have to get down on my knees or in an attitude of prayer begging your pardon for not answering before  you are or was so good to me when I was in Chicago last Fall and now this real nice letter and Valentine makes me so love you that I dont know what to say -- and the very pretty verse that you wrote on the Valentine -- it is beautifull; Dearest both the verse and the Valentine  Oh if I was only where you are  would not I have some kisses! I think Beloved I missed happiness very much in not corresponding with you when I was in the Field -- but it always seemed so long whenever I would think of you till I would think next {of} you  I mean that I thought of you as little as possible. That Valentine is very suggestive Darling  the nice little church on one side and the nice little cottage on the other  both embowered  among the Trees and Flowers, and Lambs skipping around; When is all this to be realized? My Sweet One  it seems so far away  causes me to feel so low sometime and everything seems dark and distant. We have a book here, "Tempest & Sunshine"  You are the Sunshine Dearest  dont you know I always compared you to a sunbeam "bright and warm"  Your letter is like a steel engraving  very neat indeed. So you are going to make it all up by and by are you?  For {?} now - well maybe I will have the happiness of being with you  You know there is a preference for your Valentine in all dances and Parties for a year  whoever the happy One may be -- but I dont suppose I need tell you anything about that for you know more of it than I do  and you promise yourself or rather think there are good times coming for you  I hope so Darling and I hope you will permit me to make myself happy by doing all I can to please and make you happy. When I came to where you say (in your letter) that you intend to go to all the Dances for 10 miles around  I thought it read for 10 night ahead  you would be getting ahead of Time and no mistake Dearest! I do hope next winter to have a Horse of my own then when I want a Cutter ride I can have it and so can someone else I know of.
Please Ettie will you permit me to tell you of some of the local news  though there is not much room left so I guess I wont mind it -- but we had a Dance here at which there were 48 tickets sold  there was twice as many as there ought to be - for comfort  I really hope to see you and Mother here next summer and hope to make it a very pleasant visit  I have some good times with Charleys little ones  I feel Dearest that I had ought to write you a longer letter than this but you will forgive me wont you? and I will try to make it right some other time. Please remember me to Mother. Beloved and kiss her for me please and Oh! Ettie have many kisses for your self  Your  most humble Servant and admirer  Austin C Newman

*Written in Ettie's handwriting across the previous letter is  "My Dear Friend Charles   Glen Arbor Mich" Apparently she forwarded the letter on to him.*

**Chicago and Glen Arbor 1864-1870**

<u>From Marietta to Charlie</u>

Chicago
Feb 24<sup>th</sup> 1868
Monday Afternoon

My Dear Fr. Charlie
Yours of the {?} of this month is now before me. I am most happy to hear from you and that all were alive and well. I thought that you joined in the Performances the night of the Masquerade Party   at least you had ought to have done so   when I told you to save your Money I did not mean that you should deny yourself the pleasures of Society for I am perfectly willing that you should attend all the Parties but above all dont deceive me. You spoke of sending me some kind of a present that was what I meant when I told you to save your money and I told you what I would rather that you should do with it   but as matters stand at the present time that can go with this {?}  you spoke of some large Fires in Chicago   there are Fires burning most of the time in some part of the city. last Friday there was quite a large Fire a little over a Block from us on the same street that we live on (Canal) from Friday Afternoon 4 oclock untill Saturday Morning at six oclock there was no less than five Fires and so you see that a Person is in danger of being burnt up alive   we often wish that we were back in Glen Arbor as we are getting to be afraid for our Lives on account of the Fires.   you say in your Letter that there are two Boats going down to G.A. for Wood and then they are coming up to Chicago if you can try to come up on them   that is if you are not otherwise engaged come up and go home with us as I have a Little Pet Dog and I would like you to come up here and take care of   it is so large that you can put it in your pocket   but that is not all that I want you to come for   I want you to come so you will be company for us   that is if you dont have any person that you have to take care of and keep company with. you say that would {not} let me go away again in a great hurry if I do come   I dont know about that   I may come Back again and learn to be a cigar Maker as I have had the offer of Learning the Tobacco Trade.   Saturday last  my Ma and Myself went up Town to get me a pair of Shoes she caught cold in one of her eyes and she can hardly see to do any kind of work. I agree with you that the Married Folks are having Gay Times also the young Unmarried Folks Oh! I almost forgot to mention that there was a very large fire this morning at four oclock   A large Hotel and a stable that was attached to it and 24 horses   the buildings were burned to the ground and everything that was in it but the Human Beings were burnt   the Horses were all burned to death and there was another one this morning nine oclock. Your watch keeps splendid time I had to get it cleaned and regulated   the Watch Maker said that it had not been cleaned for a great while.  I had forgotten to mention it when ever I would write untill this time    I meant to look what time it was and I saw it hanging up by the clock, the watchmaker showed me some silver chains and wanted me to buy one for the watch    they are splendid chains for Five dollars   if I had the money to spare just at that time I dont know but I would have got one that he showed me. I sent the ledgers and a Chicago paper   no more at present   write soon   our regards to all.  Yours sincerely
Maitie Boizard

Excuse all my poor writing and mistakes as I am in a great hurry  Ettie
two more fires since I wrote my letter   Ettie

**Long Distance Love 1855-1870**

From Marietta to Charlie

Chicago<br>March 2<sup>nd</sup> /68<br>Monday Afternoon

Dear Friend Charlie
I rec'd you wel. Letter dated the 20<sup>th</sup> of Last month   I was very happy to hear that you were all well and enjoying yourselves as this leaves us at present   you spoke of a man being shot over in Almira that is to bad   I am sorry also Mr Tobin is Dead   I pity his poor Family but misfortunes never come alone in this world. I presume that you all had a gay Time the 22<sup>nd</sup> of Last Month.  It seems more like Winter today than it has since we have been here.  it snowed all day yesterday and all night  I guess that the Winter is just commencing   you spoke of a Party over at Freemans  I hope that you all enjoyed yourselves  which you did I presume   you say that you wished I had been there   if I had been I should not have been in Attendance for I know that I should not have been welcomed and I never go where I am not welcome.   you say that this is **Leap year** and that the Young Ladies of Mich will engage their partners  well I shall leave that for Minnie  to do  as I dont know whether I shall be there or not.  if  I am I dont know what I shall   but I think that I shall be a Tobacconist or a Cigar Maker.  I wonder why Mrs Tucker does not write  I have written once to her and even to Willie and have not rec'd an answer from either.  I am glad that the House has not been disturbed and hope that nothing will be disturbed. It is snowing again just as hard as it can snow but I like to see it snow  I rec'd a letter from Sara Coggshell  they are all well at present or were when she wrote her letter   she is enjoying herself this winter   excuse all mistakes as I am in a hurry and have to write fast   I have rec'd Five very Pretty Valentines this year, but not one of them came from Glen Arbor. I know where they came from. I presume that the Valentines flew quite rapidly in Glen Arbor this year.  Well I have nothing more to add at present  My Parents send their Love to all enquiring Friends and to your Folks also  My kind regards to all   write at your leisure  Yours respectfully
Ettie


To Her Friend Chas. if permitted to call him so        please excuse all mistakes and poor writing. May B



From Marietta to Charlie

Chicago<br>March 14th/68<br>Saturday Eve.

Dear Friend Chas.
Your kind and welcome Letter dated the 27<sup>th</sup> of last month came to hand last Monday  I must beg pardon for not answering it sooner but we have had company from Milwaukee for over a week. "Mrs Tator" she went up North last night to Menasha & Fond Du Lac Wis.  I am very glad to hear that you are all well as this leaves us at present. I think instead of you apologizing for writing such poor Letters it ought to me for I never wrote so poorly in my life before.  you say that I know that you never Hug or Kiss the Girls   no I know that you never did  but I dont know what you do this winter as I am not present to know   I dont know about breaking any persons Heart if I should try to mend any of these young Gents Hearts for I am not sure it ever was mine to Break   if I was sure I could tell a little better.  you wished to know how my Pa's health was this winter  it has been quite well with the exception of colds and I rather guess that is prevailing through-out the Country. My Ma is not near so well she feels rather blue and wants to get home as she thinks her health would improve if she were there   but I wont say when we will be home as I dont know  I for my part am as well as usual   but that is not so well.  I rec'd that Silver ring  it was so large for

me that I could not wear it so my Ma wears it as it is just right for her.  I presume that Frank got the Valentine and note  it is rather strange that your Ma has not rec'd those collars that I sent  I am quite sorry.  I hear that it is reported around that George Getchel is married to Miss Charity Brotherton  I wish them good luck and happiness  I presume that you all had a Gay Time at the **Leap Year** party at Mr Caleb Millers  I attended a Sociable for the Progressive Lyceum last week and had a splendid time   I will send you the programme.  I am a member of the **Lyceum** they are going to have a Grand Ball on the Anniversary of the **Lyceum** which is the 31st of March.  I am not certain whether I shall attend or not  it is just as I feel on the occasion.  The weather is quite warm here it is just like Summer it is so pleasant.  well every person has gone to bed or retired I should say excepting myself and it is getting to be quite late.  How are your Parents this Winter  Spring or whatever it is   for I dont know   well I guess that I shall have to close  My  Folks send their kind regards  my respects to all    write at your leisure
Your Sincere & True Friend
May B


My Pa sent your Pa a Paper



From Charlie to Marietta

Glen Arbor<br>Mar 18th 1868<br>Wednesday Evening

My Dearest Ettie

I received your Letter dated March 2nd and was glad to hear from you.  You say it seems more like winter there than it has before.  I hope that winter is not agoing to last much longer up there for it is more like summer here than like winter  I saw four Robins today for the first this spring  that is a pretty shure sine *(sign)* of spring  the Folks are beginning to make some sugar.  it is not very plenty yet but I presume by the time you get this there will be gobs of it (as Gramps says) gramp often speaks of you and your mother   he often asks when you are coming home  I say  Oh about next summer.  he comes up to read the Ledgers every week and he says  Well Charly how is the gall *(gal)*  I say  Oh she is well and lovely  he says  that is the kind.  I talk of getting me a suit of Broad Cloth  and some things we are going to Be Married -shure- in the spring when you get home  I tell them of course we are agoing to Be Married.  So we are agoing to Be Married.  aint we my Dear Ettie.  You spoke about the girls Engaging partners  you said you would leave that for Min to do   now Dear E.  you know that  min freeman is my Worst Enemy and I never would go with her.  if it was to save her life.  My Dear Ettie I would like your company the fourth of July  I thought I would ask if we were engaged so no one could get you away from me any way.  My Dear Ettie you spoke of learning to make cigars.  Please dont think of staying at Chicago if you should learn the trade.  Be shure and come here in the spring  I suppose you will begin to think about starting for glen A. by the time you get this Letter.  Oh Ettie I had a splendid Dream about you last night.  I thought that we was married and was haveing a gay time  I dreamed that I was in Chicago three nights running   and was with you Every time  it must be that I am comeing up to Chicago dont you think so  I know that I would like to come  up and will try to come.  My Dear Ettie  I have bought me a gold Watch  I bought it today  it is quite a nice one. My Dear you spoke about getting some Valentines but not one of them came from Glen.  I feel ashamed for to ask you to Excuse me but there was not a Valentine to be got in the County  nor at Traverse so Chat. B says   I tryed to get one to send to you But never mind  I will make it all right  with some other presant  you wonder why Mrs Tucker dont write  she says she has wrote and expects an answer  my Dear Ettie this is all at presant    look on the first page  My folks send their love to all.  mother says that your house looks splendid  Please  Write soon

**Long Distance Love 1855-1870**

I remain your own Charley for ever

<u>my love to you my Dear</u>
<u>From your true one Chas. Fisher</u>
<u>To My Dear Little Wife Ettie</u>

Please Excuse all mistakes and Poor Writing.
Charles E. Fisher.


<u>From Marietta to Charlie</u>

Chicago<br>March 22nd/68<br>Monday Afternoon

My Dear Charlie
Your kind and welcome letter dated the 11<sup>th</sup> of this month came to hand this morning and you may be sure that I was quite happy to hear from you and that you were enjoying good health.  so you can not tell whether you will be up this Spring or not  I shall give you our address it is 195 S Canal Street Bet. *{between}*  West Jackson and W VanBuren upstairs so if you should come you would know exactly where to come.  but come if you can  for I should like to see you and I want you to come and see what a Fine City we are in.  your Pa has been here and he can tell you all about it.  you think that you would put your arms around me and kiss me if you were to see me  and you say that we would have a good talk  what kind of a talk is that  yes I know what it is in the spring especially in the country  My Dear Charlie you may tell your Ma that my Mother has had one of those spells with her Heart  it was the worst one she ever had  I thought that she would not live until morning  it was last Saturday night that she was so sick  My Pa was frightened more than I was  for he never saw her in one of those spells  she says if she lives to get up to Glen Arbor she would like you to save her a piece of Maple Sugar  if you please  for she feels as though she could relish a small piece.  you spoke of a pet Dogy *{doggy}* that I had  he was stolen from the house a short time ago  a nasty old yaw yaw (Dutch woman) stole it and carried it off and sold it before I knew it was gone.  but I dont know but that I shall get another one  his name was Pinky  he was cream color and his fur was curly  he was just as pretty and handsome as he could be.  There are not quite so many Fires as there were but still there are a few.  My Pa says that he will send us on the first or nearly the first Boat but if any one should ask you  tell them that you dont know  but remember that the story will not rest on your head  I am willing it should rest on mine  I have not been feeling very well for a few days back.  I have had to take care of a sick lady  she has been sick going on three weeks and I have had to take care of her  she has the *{?}* or Fever of the Lungs and my Mother not being very well  I have had to be doing the work in our rooms and then in hers  so you see that I have been between two fires and now I dont feel so very well myself  I shall do well if I can stand it.  Dear only knows when she will get well  I hope that you will excuse this poor writing as I have to write hurriedly  hoping to hear from you soon.
I remain your True L.W.E
To Charles E. Fisher


That Lady is in rather poor circumstance and not able to hire a nurse  and we could not see her suffer  they have been living in this house about three weeks and she has been sick most ever since they moved.

**Chicago and Glen Arbor 1864-1870**

From Charlie to Marietta

>Glen Arbor
>April 1st 1868
>Wensday Eve.

My Dearest Ettie
I received your most kind and welcome letter which I have been so long wating for. I am so glad that you overlooked those falsehoods. Oh My Dear if I could only see you to tell you how I felt. I cant express my feelings with a pen and ink   *(Not signed, but from Charlie)*


From Marietta to Charlie

>Chicago
>April 7th/68
>Monday Eve.

My Dearest Charlie
I rec'd your welcome Letter dated the 26th of March and you very be sure that I was very happy to hear that you were all well as this leaves us at present. I am so lonely here that I dont know what to do with myself but hope that it wont be long before I can see you. I wish I had been there when you sugared off but I dont think that I should eat any  You know yourself that I dont care much for 'Sugar" but then I could see you Sugar off. I am sorry to hear you speak as you do about coming up here but I do really hope that you will be able to come, for I want to see you very much. Tell your Grampa that I am very much obliged to him for that Kiss but I will tell you what you must do when ever you want to kiss any one. you must kiss the one that you Love the best  I will tell you who it is  if I only knew  but you know that I dont and of course cannot tell  I will have to be like E- Ayres  wait and see.  you say that you often dream that we are married and having Gay Times  what put a thot in to your Head pray tell  I rather think that your Heart must be diseased a Little Bit at Least with Love. If I was there I should sing the song to you of "Oh! My Heart goes Pit-Pat Pit-Pat "    I dont think that I shall Learn the Trade of Cigar Making as it would take me at least six months to get so that I could make them good  if I were intending to stay in Chicago I think that I should learn as it is clean and easy work.  My Dear here are a couple pieces of Poetry "viz" "Two Brides" and "Wooing and Winning" I would like you to tell me which Bride is the Best  which one would suit your taste the best the 1st or 2nd  I will tell you which one Suits me the best the last one. What do you think of the other Piece. Well I am Sleepy as it is getting quite late  I hope you will excuse this Poor writing  I know it is not very good  any of it - but it is the best I can do  My ma says that she wishes that she was at home for she misses her little home very much  although it is humble  I dont know which misses it the most Ma or Me.  well I can not think of any thing more just now  I guess that I shall have to close for I can hardly see what I am writing
My Folks send their Love to all   My Love to you My Dear C-.
Your Little Wife Ettie
From Ettie Boizard

To My dear Charlie Fisher

P.S. if you write again direct your Letter to Maitie E Boizard in care of my Pa at 167 Randolph Street for we may not be here then and if you direct it in care of my Pa he can send it to me for we may start the 20th of this month or the last.   Ettie

**Long Distance Love 1855-1870**

They are painting the Propellers and the **City of Boston** is most done  I guess that they will all be ready to start soon. My Mothers eyes still keep sore and they will as long as we live near this mill.  I rec'd a letter from Sarah Coggeshell.
Maitie B.   May B.


*{Eleanor & Marietta returned to Glen Arbor around May 2}*


From Eleanor & Marietta to Oliver (Written by Marietta)

Glen Arbor<br>June 13th/68<br>Saturday Night

My Dear Oliver,
We are well and hope these few lines will find you the same.  I dont know what to make of it for I don't receive any Letters   we have rec'd but one since we came home and that is six weeks tonight.  I will send this by Mrs. Clark, she is going to call at the Store.  Will you please send us some Flour as we are allmost out   we were out but we borrowed some from Mr. Tucker.  the weather has been quite favorable for the crops.  you had better not put the letters on the N.T. for there is a regular Lake Shore Mail  just put them in the Office and then we can get sooner  no more at present   write soon
Yours truly
E. M. Boizard

P.S. Ettie has not been so well for the last week   the last two nights I have been up untill 11 oClock


From Eleanor & Marietta to Oliver (Written by Marietta)

Glen Arbor<br>June 23rd/68

My Dear Father
We rec'd your welcome Letter a few days ago and we were very sorry to hear that you were so unwell.  but hope by the time these few lines reach you that you will be well.  I rec'd that Parcel.  I was pleased very much with the Shoes they were a very Good fit.  I wish that you would try and send us in a Barrel of Flour if you could   for we have had to borrow twenty six pounds from Mrs Tucker.  the Barrel that we did bring home was not near full and it was not packed any either.  we want Butter & Lard also   we use more Bread stuff than we would if Potatoes were Plentifull  there are none that a person can buy as there was such a Failure of the Potatoe crop last season.  I have not had a Spell with my Heart since we came home.  Goods and Provisions are just as high here as they were during the War and any how they dont have any thing in the store.  My Eyes are very weak yet   we will be here eight weeks next Saturday  I thought that you were not going to write any more   we have just rec'd two letters since we have been here, if we had not heard from you when we did we would have sold out and come up to Chicago again   tell Bertha and Mary Fink that I will write to them in my next or when I can get time  tell Lizzie Hass also when you see her.

150

**Chicago and Glen Arbor 1864-1870**

I shall have to draw this to a close as it is getting late it is now ten oClock
no more at present   write soon.
Yours Truly
E. M. Boizard
M. E. Boizard


From Eleanor and Marietta to Oliver (Written by Marietta)

Glen Arbor, Michigan
June 25th /68

My Dear Father
We rec'd a Letter and Box yesterday but I don't know how long they were at the Dock   Mr Tucker brought them up from Town   we were very glad to get the provisions as we were all out of everything but a Little Ham. we were glad to hear also that you are getting Better. you say that the weather has been quite warm in Chicago   it has been quite warm here also and then again it has been quite cool nights and mornings it is quite chilly now. you must not worry about Ettie for she is feeling much Better than she was   although it is true about spots in her cheeks when she first came back   she commenced to get poor and she did not feel well either and every afternoon there would be a purplish red spot come in her cheeks but now she is beginning to eat more and feel better   I did think that she was getting the consumption but I guess she is not   it was because she did not feel well. Charity Brotherton will be married day after tomorrow to Mr. George Getchels   Ettie to be Bridesmad for her. Oh! Gracious what a pest the Mosquitoes and Gnats are they pester the Life out of a Person.  if you should see Lizzie Haas tell her that Ettie rec'd that Parcel and she is very Much obliged to her   that she will write as soon as she can get time as she is quite Busy now   I wonder why she did not write a letter and send it when she sent the parcel. So Bertha is married   when you see her congratulate her for us both and tell her Ettie will write a letter to her before long   or after the Fourth we will not pay Mrs Tucker the Flour that we owe her out of this for it will take half of it.  Give our Love to Mary Fink and tell her that I shall write after the Fourth of July and then I will have some news to write. we don't intend to sell this place unless we are compelled to   as long as we can get anything to eat   the lot is all growing up to Berry Bushes and I am not able to cut them down no more at present write soon.
Your Truly   Eleanor M Boizard   Mary Etta Boizard

*{Possible visit here by Oliver as there is a 4 month period without any correspondence}*


From Oliver's Friend to Eleanor & Marietta

Chicago
October 29th 1868

Miss M. E. Boizard
By request of Mr Boizard, my old friend, I beg leave to inform you, that he has been sick for the last two weeks and not been able to perform his usual work, he has cough or very hard cold, and this in connection with a slight fever made him unable to leave his room for 4-5 days. He is getting better now however and will commence to work again next Monday, when he will also tend to your request about Provisions &c. You need not be anxious about him, because as I told you, he is all right now, and if there is anything that he wants he is in good hands here.
I am Madam, very Respectfully
Your Obed't Servant   Philip Miduen

**Long Distance Love 1855-1870**

From Charlie E. Fisher to Oliver

Glen Arbor<br>Nov. 3<sup>rd</sup> 1868

Mr Boizard   Dear Sir
As I have an opportunity to Send A Letter up to Chicago I thought I would Write you A few Lines letting you know that I am well   Also Mrs. Boizard and Ettie is all well. Mr. Boizard Mrs Boizard Has not Heard from you only what Mr Goffart told her, in over a month   she has written  rec'd no Answer. She Has Been Expecting a Box for some time she did not know But it had gone by on some other Boat   Mrs. Boizard says she is going to go out there if she don't hear from you in two weeks. I tell her that she must stay here this winter any way or else leave Ettie here this winter   I tell her we would take Good care of her. Well Mr. Boizard  I have not much time to write for the boat is most ready to start. I hope this will find you well. Please excuse mistakes and poor writing, Please Write soon.
From your Friend
Charles E. Fisher

Please send A letter Back on this Boat if convenient.


From Eleanor and Marietta to Oliver (Written by Marietta)

Glen Arbor, Michigan<br>Nov 3<sup>rd</sup> 1868

Dear Father
I shall hand this to the Capt as he is going off to Chicago, I would like you to let us know what we are to do   write and send a letter by him and let us know wether we will stay here this winter or come up to Chicago   as we can not stand the suspense much longer   If I don't soon hear  you may look for me. write as soon as you can and send it by the Capt no more at present
Yours & c.
E M Boizard
Ettie Boizard


From Eleanor and Marietta to Oliver (Written by Marietta)

Glen Arbor, Michigan<br>Nov 15<sup>th</sup> 1868

My Dear Father
We rec'd the letter that Philip wrote and I was just answering it when I heard that there was some Freight up at the other Dock for us and I thought that I would not answer it untill we got it home   we got it yesterday and we were glad to receive it as we were just out of everything   my shoes suited me very much but they are rather large   I wish that Ettie had a pair of such good Leather as hers have got so that they leak badly   if you get her a pair get Lizzie Haas to try them on   Ettie is going to send a letter to her in your letter and 50 cts to get an apron   hand the money to her if you can   you had better send her a pair and send her chain & pin whether they are mended or not, the apron is not for us   it is for one of the girls on the hill, we owe eighty lbs of Flour   I would like to have you send us some cornmeal if you can before the Boats quit running, we were getting ready to come out as we were out of provisions

**Chicago and Glen Arbor 1864-1870**

I was just going to sell the Furniture when the Freight came, we will have to buy some Potatoes, as we have only three bushels   there is three inches of snow and it very cold here all the time
no more at present write soon
Yours  & c.
E.M. Boizard
M.E. Boizard



From Eleanor and Marietta to Oliver (Written by Marietta)

Glen Arbor, Michigan<br>November 18 1868

My Dear Father
We rec'd your welcome letter yesterday Charlie brought it over, I had answered your other one and sent it by Boat I am sorry to hear about your Cough you must try to get something for it.   if you don't get anything else get Licorice root and chew it, I shall look for a Letter every two weeks if I don't get one than I shall think that you are sick, we shall try to get along the best that we can   I am quilting a quilt for Mrs Brotherton  I guess it will be about two dollars. Ettie has a dreadfull time with her face last week it was swollen so that she could hardly see out her eyes, she has got her feet wet so much lately she could not go out of the house hardly  Why don't Mrs Fink write me.  Old kittie and a kitten they all sleep together the Old Cat is larger than Pinky   he is playing with the kitten now   no more at present  write soon
yours truly
E.M Boizard
M E Boizard



From Emma Bridges Brown to Marietta

Gila City AT<br>Nov 22 1868

my dear Eta
i set down to write you a few lines after so long a silence but dear Eta i am sure when you hear why i did not write you will excuse me. the last time i wrote i was in **fort Macdowl**  right after i had to go to **camp reno** and i was allways moving after that all the time    my baby was born the 11 of aprill and died 29 of August and dear Eta i felt so unhapy i could not write to you    dear Eta you could not tell how bad i felt   it was a litel *{little}* girl she was so prety and i loved her so much  but then you cannot tell a mothers feelings and i hope with all my heart dear Eta you will never have to go through the same trial of losing a child   her name was Emma Alice she had dark blue eyes and Auburn hair. we are discharged now and keep a store here and are doing well   in 3 years we will have a great deal of money and then we will go in Califorina to setel *{settle}* down. for life i hope. i supose you are married by this time   i do wish you would send your picture   i want to see how you look. i have asked so often and you have never sent it. my mother is in **fort yuma** yet    i am 18 miles from them. tell your Ma when ever we are together she is allways talking about her and wishing she was with her. father is geting pretty old now  dear Eta i often wonder if we will ever meet again   i hope so. by the time you get this leter it be chrismas  i wish you all a happy chrismas and many of them   i wish i was some where i could send you some token of my love for you.  believe dear Eta i always regard you as a sister you know we allways opened our hearts to each other about our biter *{bitter}* troubels

## Long Distance Love 1855-1870

dear Eta i want you to answer this leter and send a great long one  for you know how long it has since i herd from you. i will answer every leter you write for i am living all alone and nothing to do and there is no danger of me moving for the next 3 years. i wish you would write every 2 weeks. if you posibly can. i have got tommy living with *{me}* he is geting quite a big boy   he don't forget you yet  i have writen a long leter  i am sure you will be tired before you get to the end   Eta if you think you could send me a mourning veil i wish you would   i canot get out here and i will pay you the price   i am in black for my baby   give my love to your ma and pa and kiss them for me and dear Eta except my love Edwin sends his regards   direct your leter to Mrs Edwin A Brown **Gila City Arizona Teteritory**  i remain your friend and sister
Emma

dear Eta   acept this pencil as a chrismas gift  Emma

never mind the veil


From Austin Newman to Oliver

Beaver Island<br>Nov 26th/68

Friend Boizard

As you will see by the date of this your humble Servant is on the Island known as **"New Ireland"** because of the great number of the Natives of that green Isle reside here   Whiskey is very plentifull so are Potatoes so are **Rows and ructions**. But that is enough of the "Greeks" (they speak their native Language it sounds beautifull)  The Propeller Potomaceing in here this morning  I thought I would drop or write you a few lines   I came over here with the Schooner "Burty Mac" she is 36 foot - keel  She is a large open Sail Boat which Charley and I have bought for pleasure as well as profit. She is a very little Boat  I came over with 25$ worth of freight and have been here 8 or 9 weeks and have made about 100$  would have made more but weather too stormy  I got tired working on the land and was wishing for some such business for a change and to get some cash for this Winter having been pretty well drained of the aforesaid commodity by payment of mortgage but as I said before the weather has not been very favorable.  Concerning the "loved Ones" at Home   I received a Letter from Ettie and returned an answer just before I left. The Young Lady did not say whether they were going to Chicago or not this Fall.  I had a pretty good time at G.A. last 4th and when navigation closes I would like and will I think, pay the Folks a visit.  I will try to be with them about Christmas and New Years.  I hope youre enjoying yourself and have good health.  I have been very busy the past Summer or season and so have you I suppose.  My health has not been bad   Well the Steamer is going   I will write again soon   Please answer this
Goodbye
Austin C. Newman


From Eleanor & Marietta to Oliver (Written by Marietta)

Glen Arbor<br>Jan 8th/1869

My Dear Father
Yours of the 20th and 26th of Dec. are now before me. we were glad to hear that you were well   we are well with the exception of cold but most - every person has that. we would not have known that it was Christmas here if we had

not attend a party Christmas Eve.  Charlie took Ettie and of course I went with them.  I am glad to hear that you have found your Brother's name *{could possibly be 'home'}* you spoke of writing to him and  sending Etties Picture   I should not send it until you hear from him as he might not receive your letter.  you wished to know the particulars   I have got my wood paid for so far  the hauling and cutting    I have earned 8 eight dollars by sewing for Brothertons.  and the Boys cut my wood   we live as saving as we possibly can.   you wished to know whether Austin was here spending the Holidays.  he did not come.    times are dull here as well as there.  Ettie rec'd a letter from Emma Bridges or Brown and she sent Ettie some Gold Pencils  I will send the letter in my next.  She and her Husband are keeping  Store at **Gila City**   they are out of the army now.  Mrs Bridges is at **Ft. Yuma**  eighteen Miles from Emma.  Ettie is going to send her Photograph to her.  She has lost her Little girl  she did not say what ailed it.  What is the price of Print and Muslin   a person can get eleven yds of Calico at Traverse City   no more at present    write soon. Yours Truly

E.M. Boizard

M.E. Boizard


Get me a mourning veil not a lace one.  get Mary to box it.




From Eleanor & Marietta to Oliver (Written by Marietta)

*The following letter is written on the bottom of Emma Brown's November 22nd 1868 letter.  Eleanor & Marietta sent Emma's letter out to Oliver in order for him to read it and they wrote a note on the end of it.  Based on the contents of the following note, it was written, January 20, 1869.*

I have a very bad cold and I cough a great deal.   provisions are very high   Sugar that is the color of Molasses they sell for 18cts a pound.  Day before yesterday was my birthday I was forty one   the veils that I send for are for Emma  she lost her little girl and she is in mourning, you spoke of Mary Fink getting married   I think she is rather young to get married she is not near as old as I am and I think that I am to young to get married yet.  we are getting along as well as we can   you spoke of me being a nice young Lady   Charlie told me to tell you I am   you imagined just right  I am getting poor   just as I did last spring   no more at present write soon

yours Truly E.M. Boizard

M.E. Boizard




From Eleanor & Marietta to Oliver (Written by Marietta)

Glen Arbor<br>Feb 4th 1869

My Dear Father

Yours of the 18th & 21st of last month are now before me   we were glad to hear from you and that you are well  as this leaves us at present   but Ettie has been troubled with the Ear and Toothache a great deal here lately   for the last three days and nights she as be so that she could not sleep a great deal.  but it is better now   we rec'd the four dollars also this week   last Mail we rec'd the paper and shoe Laces and we were glad to get them as were out of them   they have the short cotton ones down here at the Store they are very rotten  I went to put one in my Shoes and it broke in three places before I got my shoe tied.   The snow is very deep it is about three foot deep and last week the ground

**Long Distance Love 1855-1870**

was bare in a great many places   up at the other dock they are drawing wood on wagons   the weather had been very fine for about three weeks  but when it did commence to storm it stormed as hard as it could   you spoke of getting us a dress apiece and shoes  if you get my dress *{?}*  one get twelve yds of *{?}*  dark and an near plain as you can get if it is figured get the figures small and Etties dress  you *{ I can't read the writing as it is on a fold in the paper. There are about three words missing. }* it yourself    if you get her shoes get them high in the instep and as high the tops as you can   get twos  and you know my number 5 fives.  and you had ought to also get stuff for Shirts.  if you do get it  fine unbleached shirting yd wide and let me make them   where you buy them already made one costs as much as two would that I could make  and then they are not near as good  and I would rather make them  I would rather make your pants vests and all but your coats  Who did Mary Marry  what has become of Betty & Morris  well I guess this is all that I can think of at present   this is my last sheet of paper and I can not write any more. write soon and give our regards to all enquiring friends.
E. M. Boizard
M. E. Boizard

Feb 9<sup>th</sup>

The snow was so deep that I could not go to town to get an envelope and have not seen any person that I could send Ettie has been troubled with the tooth and ear ache for over a week  and she could not go on account of the deep snow.
E. M. Boizard


From Eleanor & Marietta to Oliver (Written by Marietta)

Glen Arbor
Feb. 18<sup>th</sup> 1869

My Dear Father
Yours of the 30<sup>th</sup> of Jan came to hand by this weeks Mail   also two dollars   we were glad to hear that you were well as this leaves us at present   The weather is rather changeable   one day the Sun shines the next it Snows and Blows and Thaws  the snow is quite deep   there was a time that it was all bare ground and those that were drawing wood had to quit. There was a Grand Concert down at Todds Hall and a good party after the concert there were two cutters and a Stage Load come through from Traverse City   all went off nicely.   now I'll change the subject and write more about home   the $2 that you sent this week we got $1 worth of meat & 50 cts Sugar  a quarter pound of tea at $2.00 a pound and you see that took it all.   I wish that you would Send me money to get a Barrel of Flour.  it is $12.00 a Barrel and when we get it by the small quantities it cost us about $14.00  we have bought seven doll's worth   I earned three dolls by quilting and took my pay in Flour and I paid $4.00 in money for some.  we have to pay two dolls $2.00 for Tea that is not fit to drink  I will be glad when Spring comes so that we can get some provisions in from outside   all the provisions that you sent in  in the fall are gone. I would give anything for a piece of beef  we have not seen any this winter.  did you write to your Brother Pete.  Charlie and Ettie went to the concert  he wanted me to go with them but I did not   I did not have anything decent to wear and beside I did not feel like going. This is about all that I think of at present    write soon   Give our regards to all enquiring Friends.
Yours as Ever
E. M. Boizard
Marietta Boizard

**Chicago and Glen Arbor 1864-1870**

From Eleanor & Marietta to Oliver (Written by Marietta)

Glen Arbor
Feb 25th 1869

My Dear Father

Yours of the 7th & 14th came in this weeks Mail.  we rec'd the veils and three dollars  Ettie rec'd a Letter from Mary Fink, it used to be.  the weather is very cold  colder then it has been this winter  and the snow is very deep.  you said that you were dreaming about the House  it was very near true what you dreamt  the plastering is all off and it is very cold  we can hardly keep warm with the cooking Stove you had ought to try as it is coming on Spring to get a Heating Stove  if it was nothing but a Box Stove  get a Second hand one and you will get it much cheaper than you would  get it next Fall  anyhow we will have to get one before Fall  for we can not do with just the cooking Stove.  Mr Decker was burned out about four weeks ago  they did not save any thing  one of the children  a boy of five years  was up stairs and he found some Matches and got to playing with them  and set the house on fire.  Mrs. Dorsey has a young daughter and the Family has got the whooping cough.  Flour is thirteen doll's per barrel and it is very poor  this has been a very hard winter on most every one. Rossman charges so high for what little he has in the store  he has not got any thing in the store only as he goes through with the stage and brings it from Traverse  he charges 20cts for lb of pork and it is all Fishy  this is all at present  Give our regards to all enquiring Friends  write soon.  Yours & c.
E. M. Boizard
M. E. Boizard


From Eleanor & Marietta to Oliver

Glen Arbor
March 12th /69

My Dear Oliver
Yours of the 24th of last month came in this weeks Mail and we were glad to hear from you  we rec'd the stationary and newspapers also two doll's.  you spoke of the winter just commencing in Chicago  it is about the same although for two days past it has been quite fair  the snow is very deep  the deepest it has been this winter  I am in hopes that it will soon go off so that the Boats will run  if not we will starve as there is nothing that we can get at the store  I will get wood cut with part of the money that you sent me   I have earned enough to get wood chopped until now  I wish that you would send us some provisions on the first boat and when you do send us some alcohol and camphor gum as we are out  Ettie used a great deal on her Face.  but I don't think she will be bothered with it any more for she had it pulled today  Mr Perry was down at Mr. Tuckers and he came over and pulled it  yesterday she was almost crazy with it and last night she did not sleep any with it   I presume when the snow does go off it will all go at once.  send us some Butter & Lard the first chance that you can get as there is none to be got  a dollars worth of meat when we can get it is not much larger then the dollar itself  it is not very often that we can get meat  there is none in the stores  only as Rossman brings it from Traverse in the stage  you spoke of getting us each a pair of Shoes  get them pegged as they wear the best here in the Land. Mrs. Dorsey had a Little girl baby and it died with the whooping cough.  the whole family had it  Charlie has bought the Spring and five acres of land for sixty doll's he is going to build a house on it next spring coming    if we don't get some new clothes we will have to {faint ?} and go naked.  how do you stand with the firm  no more at present  write soon  our regards to all enquiring friends  Yours Truly  E.M. Boizard
M. E. Boizard          P.S. Burdicks Grist  & Saw Mill was burned to the ground about two weeks ago.

**Long Distance Love 1855-1870**

From Eleanor & Marietta to Oliver

Glen Arbor<br>March 18th/69

My Dear Oliver
Yours of Feb 24th and March 5th came in this weeks mail  also a paper  the money $4.  we were glad to hear that you were well as this leaves us.  The weather has moderated somewhat  I hope that we are going to have a change in the weather now.  Ettie went down town today and got some tea and had to pay 18 shillings per lb  she wanted to get kerosene and meat but they did not have any.  and they don't have any Flour to sell  if they do sell any they wont sell more than 25 lbs and then it is not good  but the Flour at the Mill is cheaper and then it is good.  when you send in some provisions send three or four bars of Soap as soft soap hacks our skin so to wash with it  you spoke of us coming to Chicago another winter  we will have to get something to wear as we have nothing that is fit  our clothing all gave out at once.  Ettie and I have earned $18 this winter in quilting  and out of it all we have got each of us an apron for everything is so high.  you spoke of Big Charlie and Little Frank  it used to be that but if it is anything it is Big Frank and Little Charlie  for Frank is Larger now then Charlie.  Old Mr. Heeth is dead  he died with the heart disease last week.  he was Father in law to that Mr. Harrison that was killed that I told you about  that was killed by a Tree.  Well that is all at present  Give our regards to all inquiring Friends
write soon  Yours & c.
E.M. Boizard
M. E. Boizard


Mr. John O. Boizard   93 S. Canal Street   Chicago, Ill's



From Austin Newman to Oliver

Charlevoix<br>March 26

Dear Friend,
I received a letter from you a month or six weeks ago in answer to one I wrote from Beaver Island. I should have wrote to you before this but did not consider it a necessity very imperative and besides I had to let some time lapse so as to have some news. In regard to health we are all of us well and enjoying a pretty good share of that most inestimateable blessing and I hope you have also your full share in the level city. The winter has passed slowly away. I can't say as it has been very pleasant for me having so much to do preparing to have a home of my own and nothing much but the labor of my hands to get it with. I have plenty of land which in the course of two or three years will be valuable but I wan the means now. The present is the worst – everything to do but I am a pretty good fellow to work and if I keep my health and nothing happens to prevent shall be well along by next summer. One of the principle reasons of my great desire to have a home of my own is because then I think I could manage my affairs so that I would not be reduced to the straits that overtake me sometimes on account of living with my brothers. They manage their affairs so sometimes that is very unpleasant. Provisions are very scarce here now and that is the principle cause of complaint. This is a hard country to live in for the first few years with good management. Then what will it be with poor. I wish very much to be in a house of my own so as not to suffer by their miserable mismanagement and in my hurry to get a place ready I sometimes work harder than I ought to. I have beens o very busy that I haven't had time to go to G.A. this winter and besides the weather has been so irregular and besides having a boat I can go there in a day in the spring and stay a few days and view the old home once more.

To change the subject I am trying to get materials ready to build a house with next summer. I have got into the water 40 hemlock logs and I have upwards of 30 pine logs cut but they are not in yet. But will soon be I hope. Considerable work chopping them down and sawing them up then have to make roads; and to get a team to haul them out is the hardest of all. I have a thousand shingles made and have timber for more.

As for the great questions of the day. I think they are progressing very favorably- such as Grant's inaugural and Johnson's retirement – Sheridan's return to New Orleans – and other events too numerous to mention.

I am about ready for sugar making. Maybe I will send some to Chicago. If I have enough I will. I have 174 buckets which is more than the average sugar buckets around here. One reason of my not writing before is because of inconvenience yelling and screeching children below the stairs and freezing upstairs. I received a letter from G.A. a few days ago  They were all well and better some of them. I have plenty more to write but my paper is all used up. I don't know when I shall have the pleasure of seeing you.

Austin C. N.


From Eleanor & Marietta to Oliver (Written by Marietta)

Glen Arbor
April 2nd, 1869

My Dear Oliver

Yours of the 14th & 20th of last month came in this weeks mail  the money also  we were glad to hear that you were well as this leaves us at present  the weather has moderated here  the snow is going off very fast  last Saturday we could just see the top of a stump at the corner of the house and Monday we could see all the stumps in the clearing  some of our Neighbors are making sugar  I don't think that there will be very much made as the season will not be good for sugar  there have been two boats in this year  one from Chicago and I don't know whether the other is from Chicago or Mil. and I believe they expect three or four every day. we rec'd a Letter from Emma Brown this week they are all well and she says they would all like to hear from you  they are at **Gila City** and her Fathers at **Fort Yuma.** when you send in some thing send some factory for shirts so we can make them and don't go and buy shirts ready made for they are more expensive and then they are not half made.  anyhow I would rather make them. you Spoke of Charlie keeping **Bachelors Hall**  I asked Ettie about it  she says that he is  in about a year from her next birthday May 18th.  She says by that time you may expect a Son full grown about 21 years of age  as she will take pity on Charlie and help him to keep Bachelors Hall   She says that you must come home before his house is raised and help pick out the place that it will be built on and anyhow we want to see you.  how did it happen that the Family were Poisoned  was it done by Accident or did they take it themselves.  the next letter I write I will send you Emma's letter  send me in a paper of Lettuce and the long green cucumbers and also a paper of cabbage  the Large Drum Head  don't get the early York as it will not amount to anything here. This is all at present  write soon
Yours until Death
E. M. Boizard
M. E. Boizard

**Long Distance Love 1855-1870**

From J.E. Fisher to Oliver

Glen Arbor<br>April 3/69

Dear Sir

I take pleasure in introducing to you, the bearer of this note Mr. Henry Fisher. Mr Fisher lived for Several years at North Unity (Dutch Town) and carried on a Wood Dock there, but now lives in your City. he has been Spending the Winter here and now returns to Chicago I Send this to let you know that your Family and ourselves are all well– we have had a pleasant winter and good **Sleighing** for business in fact the Sleighing is good now, and we are beginning to grumble that we are having too much of a good thing, we wanted to See bare ground– Mr Fisher will return here in a few days if you wish to Send any communication by him he will bring it with pleasure Hopeing you are well and doing well I am
your truly
J.E. Fisher


From Eleanor and Marietta to Oliver (Written by Marietta)

Glen Arbor, Michigan<br>Apr 15<sup>th</sup> 1869

My Dear Oliver
Yours of March 28<sup>th</sup> came in this weeks Mail and the money also we were glad to hear that you are well as this Leaves us at present. you spoke of sending us in some provisions I will be glad of that We have earned about $21 this winter by quilting but we took our pay in Flour and such as that and also in stove wood I quilted for Brothertons and the Boys cut some stove wood for Me you spoke of Etties shoes she stands in need of them if she had them now as it is damp under foot. Mr Lloyd has finished the rails and we must try to pay him as soon as we can he made a thousand and I don't know how much he charges a hundred but it is some over a dollar if you can not send it all at once try and send about five dollars at a time as I presume that he needs it for he is talking of sending his children to an Asylum We could not do without the rails for a fence any longer for we never could raise anything on account of the cattle & pigs, and anyhow we have Lived just as Saving as we could this Winter but the two dollars that you send us a week if we had not been able to earn a little as everything is so high I will send Emma's Letter to you no more at present write soon
Yours & c.
E. M. Boizard
M.E. Boizard


From Eleanor & Marietta to Oliver (Written by Marietta)

Glen Arbor<br>May 8<sup>th</sup> 1869

Dear Oliver,
Yours of April 30<sup>th</sup> came to hand yesterday also the parcel of dry Goods Gardening Seeds and spool thread Ettie says she likes her dress very much but I don't like mine if it had been most any other color or even a calico I should have been better suited you hadnt ought to have got me a black dress for me. if I had been in mourning it would have done. the weather is very pleasant here and it begins to look like planting. I should have to buy

potatoes for such if I can get them. they are very hard to get as they were so scarce last season. What have become of Bertha and Mary.  I wish that you would get that butcher knife tempered and sharpened and send it some time when you are sending a box in   as we have not got any kind of a knife but a cane knife to cut meat with   when we have any to cut   we cant get any down here   our hens lay some, but we have only four   our trees look nice none are winter killed. I think they will bear this year if every thing is not killed with dry weather   I have been making soap   I have made a half barrel full   that will last all summer   Send me in some ether like that Mr Costan takes as I need to take it occasionally    if you can get hold of any book or papers send them to us as we don't have any thing to read.  have you written home yet.  I want you to try to come home this summer if you cant come in this first part come when it will be so warm.  Charlie has taken the Saw Mill to run all Summer   he is head Sawyer & Boss in it   he gets $40 or $45 per month   The Neighbors Send their kind regards to you.   remember us to all inquiring Friends write all the news
Yours & c.
E.M. Boizard
M.E. Boizard


From Eleanor & Marietta to Oliver (Written by Marietta)

Glen Arbor<br>May 14<sup>th</sup> 1869

My Dear Oliver,
Yours of the 8<sup>th</sup> is now before   we were glad to hear from you.  I hope ere this reaches you that you will be better   you had ought to be carefull of yourself.    you spoke of Ettie helping me   she does all that she can, but she is getting like she was last Spring   very thin and not feeling very well.  She weighs only 103 lbs and during the winter she weighed 109 lbs   Ettie & I earn all that we can but that is not very much now that we are through quilting   we intend to plant all that we can if the fence was only up I think that would help.   I shall try to get some meat if they have any at the store as I would like to know how it tastes.  I have sawed my own wood this three or four weeks.  I could get Charlie to saw it but he is working in the Mill  I wish that you would send me some glue as one of the bedsteads is coming all a part and I want to fix it.   we are having a great deal of rain now   do you still wear flannels   you had ought to wear it and not take it off    Ettie rec'd a letter from Emma B   she says that her Ma and Pa were three hundred miles from her and there is not another woman near her   white or black.   the next time that you send any provisions send some cornmeal   how much is flour per barrel.  write soon
Yours & c.
E.M. Boizard
M. E. Boizard


From Marietta to Charlie

Glen Arbor<br>June 5<sup>th</sup> 1869

My Dear Charlie
Will you come over early tomorrow  as Mr. Lloyd would like to see you   he was here yesterday and he left word that he would be here early in the fore-noon    if you do not come over early you scamp   I will give you a Scotch Blessing. No More at present   Your L  W___e          Ettie Draziob  {*Boizard spelled backwards*}

**Long Distance Love 1855-1870**

From Eleanor and Marietta to Oliver (Written by Marietta)

Glen Arbor, Michigan<br>June 29<sup>th</sup> 1869

My Dear Oliver
yours of June 25<sup>th</sup> is now before me and you may be sure that I was glad to hear from you as I was very anxious about you   I have not heard since the 15<sup>th</sup> of May from you.  in your last - you said that you would send us a Box of provision the next week but did not and didn't write either and of course we did not know what to make of it   we did not have anything in the house to eat and Charlie got us some Flour and other things for which we owe him   and Mrs. Tucker let us have some Butter on credit   Ettie is very mean sick and I worried myself nearly sick by not hearing from you   you had ought to have written or had some one write if you were not able to write yourself   as we were sorry to hear that you hurt yourself so badly   but hope as this reaches you that you will be well   I shall take part of this ten dolls to get something in the house to eat and the other part to pay some of my Debts.  Ettie rec's a Letter from Emma Brown   she says her Father has rec'd an **Ordnance** Appointment at **Camp Gaston Cal.**  Dr. Traplers or Tarply has charge of the company   she sends her regards to you.  you had ought to have a light to go through the house with at night.  buy yourself a candle if they don't give you one.  it has rained very much lately most every other day through June   I have tried to earn all that I could but of course I did not have much time as planting took up most of my time and another thing there is not very much that I could get to do,  this is all at present   write as soon as possible as we will be anxious to hear.
Yours & c.
E.M.Boizard
M.E. Boizard


From Eleanor and Marietta to Oliver (Written by Marietta)

Glen Arbor, Michigan<br>Aug't 6<sup>th</sup> 1869

My Dear Oliver
Yours of July 28<sup>th</sup> came to hand by this weeks mail and you may be sure that we were glad to hear from you   also to get the money $10.  as we were out of everything to eat   we hardly knew what to get for breakfast the next morning   Ettie is better now but she was sick quite a while   you speak of it being so unhealthy in Chicago   I wish that you would try to come home   if you don't stay but a week   if you don't soon come Folks will talk about you not coming.  anyhow I want you to come as I have something to tell you   Charlie says if you don't come he will come after you   he says it is so long since he has seen you that he has almost forgot how you look.  you would hardly know him he has changed so   Frank has changed also   Mr & Mrs Fisher are both well and send their regards to you   they often wish that they could see you.   the money that you sent I shall take some of it to pay some of my debts and the rest to get something to eat.  I do wish that you would get us a Barrel of Flour as I owe over 50 lbs and of course must pay for it.  send me a three quart pail also a two qt pan as all my tin ware is giving out   our pails leak and we have nothing to carry milk or anything   I wish you would send me Alcohol for camphor as I have none   they have some down here at Frank Todds but is more than half water.  Charlie will put up the Fence after he get through Harvesting <u>if we can board him.</u> yours as ever--
E.M. Boziard
M.E. Boizard
PS be sure to come home soon

**Chicago and Glen Arbor 1864-1870**

From Eleanor and Marietta to Oliver

Glen Arbor, Michigan
Aug't 23 1869

My Dear Oliver
We have not rec'd any letter from you in nearly two weeks and we are anxious somewhat.  we are well I rec'd a letter from Emma Brown she says that they are all well   they send their regards to you    she says they have not had any rain since January. I wish you would send us some Flour and provisions as we are very near out of Flour    there will be enough for just one more Baking   we got Flour with the last money we had   when this is done I don't know what we will do unless you send us some    I went Whortle-berrying the other day and got 15 qts   Blackberries will soon be ripe. The neighbors are Harvesting now and they are quite Busy.  some of the wheat is quite rusty this season. Mr Tuckers folk are out of Flour nearly and we owe them 50lbs and they would like to get it if we had it for them    when Charlie & Ettie were up at Frankfort they had their Photograph taken and he sends one to you   I presume you will think he is somewhat changed    the Picture is very good of them both they could not be much better. Ettie would have looked Better if she had a dark Dress – Charlie is here working   he is clearing to put up the Fence he is trying to get the Fence up    to put in some wheat this Fall for another Winters Flour and we certainly had ought to Board him while he is working for us. No More at present    Give our regards to all, write soon '
Yours & c.
M.E. Boizard
Ettie Boizard

send us some postage stamps if you can   Ettie


From Eleanor & Marietta to Oliver (Written by Marietta)

Glen Arbor
Sept 3rd 1869

My Dear Father
Yours of the 25th of Aug. came to hand in this weeks mail    we are sorry to hear that you are out of employment as we are out of everything to eat but potatoes   we cannot get any butter nor meat as we have no money    what was the cause of you not working for H & M any longer.   we have gathered whortleberries as long as they lasted but they are gone now, but we will have to get along the best that we can.   you were very foolish not to take up with the offer that McCarty made you    the man they hired is there yet and gets a thousand dolls a year.   our potatoes are splendid what we have dug of them    if it were not for them I guess we would starve.   I don't know what to do   I am near crazy.   if we had anything to live on we could tell you to come home and stay    if there was anything that you could do here    but we don't know of anything.   Charlie had to quit working as we could not Board him    he wanted to get the place ready to sow some wheat.   we don't know whether there will be many Blackberries or not as we have not gone berrying yet.   we have been as little  expense as we could possible be as we have not had any provisions from you since May and but very little money.   no more at present.   write soon
Yours  & c.
E.M. Boizard
M.E. Boizard

**Long Distance Love 1855-1870**

From Eleanor & Marietta to Oliver (Written by Marietta)

Glen Arbor
Sept 8th 1869

My Dear Oliver
yours of the third came to hand last evening   M.D. Todd handed it to some of Mr. Fishers Folks and Charlie brought it over last night   we are sorry to hear that you are still out of employment  but hope you will soon succeed in finding work.  if it were not for our Potatoes I don't know what we would do as that is all that we have   but they are splendid  we cannot boil them  we have to steam them for they are so meaty   Charlie says that we had ought to have twenty five or thirty bushels at the very least and that had ought to last us all winter and furnish seeds for to plant next season   that is if we can get anything else to use with them.  you spoke of Etties marriage to Charlie  they were intending to get married next May   but Charlie wants to get Married this Fall   but she has not got underclothing or anything that she could wear   she is not prepared in any way   she had some money that she earned her self   but we had to get the last flour that we had with it   she was intending to get some muslin to make underclothing with it.  she has not had any clothing of any kind in two years   as for calico dresses she has none. and I don't want her to get married and not have anything   if I can help it   but Charlie says he wont wait any longer than her next Birthday.  He was twenty the 29th of Aug't.   I have about eight or ten quarts of whortleberries dried but I don't know about Blackberries as my shoes are so badly worn that if I were to go berrying in them there would not be much left of them   anyhow the briars would get into my feet.  I wish that we had some tea or coffee. come home if you can when she is married as they both want you to.  No more at present. Yours & c.
E. M. Boizard
M.E. Boizard
P.S. we will let you know when it happens.


From Eleanor & Marietta to Oliver (Written by Marietta)

Glen Arbor
Sept 28th 69

My Dear Oliver
yours of Sept 20th came last week also the Barrel of Groceries which we were very glad to get as we were out of everything  but they were not packed very good   all the bags were broke open   Flour Tea Sugar and Coffee were all together.   Ettie was very much pleased with her cape  but if she had known what kind it was before you sent it she would have had you taken it to the Dyers and had it colored Scarlet   for we could not color it so nicely and dress it as good as they   although we could color it if we had the Dye.  if I could get it colored she could not buy it for less than four or five dollars   it is too good a cape for us to spoil.  I hope you will soon succeed in getting Employment   if we had our Winter Provisions you could come home and stay all Winter.  My Shoes I like very well  but they would have worn better had they been calfskin   that kind of leather don't wear as well   I was glad to get the Tea & Coffee for I had not had any for about three weeks. Charlie has got the Fence half way around the clearing and it looks real nice   More like a Farm   it is getting to be real wet and cold   and the house unless it is painted up will be very cold to live in this Winter and we have no lime and don't know of any in the place   I have just finished making a bed for Strawberries about five or six yds square   I am in hopes from this next Summer to have some fruit and that will help us a long some   no more at present   write soon.  Charlie sends his regards to you. Yours truly  E.M. Boizard
M.E. Boizard

Chicago and Glen Arbor 1864-1870

P.S. Did you pay for this can full of Butter or not  I guess that there was about three lbs of Butter. the can holds six pounds and was just half full.


From Eleanor & Marietta to Oliver (Written by Marietta)

Glen Arbor
Oct 12<sup>th</sup> 1869

My Dear Oliver
Yours of Oct 5<sup>th</sup> came in due season  we were glad to hear that you were well as these few lines leaves us  but we were sorry to hear that you were still out of employment  but we will have to do the best we can.  the weather is getting quite cold  it makes a person think of winter.  you spoke of Bertha having a Baby  is it a Girl or Boy.  I wish that it was so that you could come home  but we have not got provisions nor clothing for the winter  if Rossmans would buy wood it was my intention to have some cut  we would get two shillings per cord and that would be some for us.   I have but two calico dresses and one of them is of two kinds where I have mended it and Ettie has but one calico dress and that is all in rags  I have not had any underclothing since you were in Springfield and we are very near naked  our stockings  I ravel out some to fix others. I can not get work enough to buy a half gallon of Kerosene  times are very dull for both men and Women  along the last of this month we will have to dig the potatoes  I don't know what we will do for our Winters wood if Charlie don't cut it for us  Mr. King  that is Mrs Fishers brother in law has been here for the last year  he has been {?} all the time  he has a large Family to Keep he's been out twice to get employment but did not succeed.  you know just how we are situated  couldnt you work some place for your Board and not have your Boarding running up.  we rec'd a letter from Emma B this last week she says they are getting very tired of Arizona her Father & Mother are a Hundred Miles from them at a place called **Camp Gaston** she says that they wrote to her telling her what kind of a place they lived in  it is an Oak Grove and they have a cow and chickens and they have a Farm and are getting along finely.  they like it very much.  we see Mr & Mrs Dorsey yesterday they are well and send their regards  they are getting along nicely since they moved on their farm.  we rec'd the paper and was glad to get  we never sit down to a meal but we wish that you were here. I hope it will not be very long until you can come home and stay at home  when we get to raising more and then we will be independent. No More at present  write soon
Yours  as ever
E.M. Boizard
M.E. Boziard


P.S. Ettie says that she has such poor pens that she can not write good. E.M.B.



From Emma Brown to Marietta

**Gila City** A T *{Arizona Territory}*
Nov 8 1869

My Dear Ettie
yours of Oct 12 came to hand last night  i was Glad to hear that you was well and enjoying yourself.  we are all well and goying *{going}* along the same as usual  you bad girl you ought to be ashamed to say Glen arbor is lonely i am afraid if you was in Arizona you would go crazy for want of company.  you seem allways to have some

# Long Distance Love 1855-1870

pleasure on hand   it has been so long since i seen much pleasure  i don't know what it is   i tell Edwin  i wont know how to act if i ever go in a church again   i believe i would Stare my eyes out if i saw a theater   he says their not much danger.   i received a letter from my father last night  they are all well and send their love to you and your ma  they say times are dull there and plenty of rain to make it worse   while we at **Gila city** aint had no rain for over a year   what do you think of that.   there much difference in your age and Mr Fisher is their   Edwin will be 26 the first of next February   he is quite an old man you see.   we have very warm wether here now in the middle of the day.   in the mornings it is quite cold though   i think we will have a cold winter this year   i think we shall take your mothers advice about leaving Arizona if we can   i have not much news to write so you must not expect a long letter   their a great many soldiers camped here to day going up in to Arizona   there is a little Girl here on a visit to me   and i really believe i would rather be a lone   she bothers me to death allmost   she comes from **fort yuma** 20 miles from here   i have not received any letters from newport for a long time whatever is the reason   i received the flower seeds   and i thank you very much   i shall keep them until i go somewhere where i can grow them   but i don't think i shall plant them in this country   but i shall keep them till i go somewhere else.   i have written quite a long letter to you so i must stop for it is getting late and i have to write to my Father yet   Edwin send his love to your ma and your self.   give my love to your ma and pa and accept my warmest love   Dear Ettie   give our regards to Mr. Fisher   write soon and believe me to be your sincere Friend and well wisher   good bye
write soon
Emma Brown


From Oliver to Eleanor & Marietta

Chicago Ill's<br>Nov 18<sup>th</sup> 1869

My Dear Wife
I Send you by the Pro. **"Lawrence"** Box containing 10# Lard 10# Sugar, 10# Butter, 5# Coffee, 2# Tea, 6 yds of Domestic, 4 Hanks yarn   cost $12.50 all that I could possibly spare   I had to pay my Board, my washing & mending and bought a pair of Drawers and freight, which took all   I don't Know what to do, my job will run out about 2 weeks more and then I will be out of work   I will try to hold on to the job at the U.S. Circuit Court, till about the 1st Dec. and then if the Boats run till then and me out of a Job, I think I better try to come and See you all, and be present at Ettie's wedding, what do you think of it   do you think I could Sustain through the winter   Times are so dull in Chicago   I am afraid I shall be thrown on the Public for Subsistence.  I might do something up there at Glen Arbor  and you might help me through the winter. I dread this winter in Chicago for people are working for their Board.  I may be able to raise 20 dollars by the 1st Dec'r and then if the Boats don't stop running I may come to Glen arbor.   It is true I am not well fixed as I might be but I might be worse off –  I will see about your pork as soon as they commence Packing.   I may bring it up with me   If you can answer this   Send by Boat if possible in order that I can make Calculations.
Your Husband
"Oliver"

I rec'd Gus's Letter (or rather his) I could not get the Dresses yet Oliver

**Chicago and Glen Arbor 1864-1870**

From Oliver to Eleanor & Marietta

Chicago Ill
Dec 7 '69

My Dear Wife,
I send <u>Ettie</u> a Small Box containing Buttons and Silk trimmings.  I got <u>Bertha</u> to go and get them, but She only got the Buttons, so, I undertook to get the Trimmings myself.  I went to two or three places and I could not get the Exact pattern, So, I thought I would take the nearest I could find,  in fact I could not run about much, as my feet hurts me very much.  I have had for the last <u>two</u> weeks <u>Rheumatism</u> in both feet, about the <u>ankles</u>  so that I could Scarcely put my feet to the <u>Ground</u>.  I had to use a Stick to get along.  I Suppose the Court will End its <u>Term</u> this week, and I do not think, they will put us on the next term, as it is not <u>Customary</u>.  I am very much worried to think I lost the Boat   I See the "<u>**Allegheny**</u>" has returned from "<u>Traverse</u>"   we have been on one Case for 3 Days, it may last 3 Days longer.  If I possibly could get up this winter I would risk it, as I am in <u>dread</u> of this <u>winter</u>.  I think a great deal about Ettie's marriage.  it Seems to me, I can hear her in her <u>Childish talk.</u>  However all may go well with the Blessing of the "<u>Creator</u>"  I have nothing more to <u>add</u> at present, and as it is near 9 O'Clock (Court time) I must close.  Give my best wishes to Mr. <u>Fisher</u> and <u>Lady</u> not forgetting Mr & Mrs. Tucker also <u>Dorsey</u> and <u>Lady</u> for truly I <u>esteem</u> them <u>Highly</u> and receive a large Share for <u>yourself</u>  Kiss Ettie for me and tell <u>Charlie</u> to use her gently.  Bye the Bye, how is the little "<u>**Keesick**</u>"   you don't Say anything about him– Farewell and using the language of the <u>Orientals</u> "**May your Shadows never be less**"
Your  Husband
John O. Boizard


From Eleanor & Marietta to Oliver (Written by Marietta)

Glen Arbor
Jan. 2nd 1870

My Dear Oliver,
Yours of Dec. 21st came in the last mail   we were glad to hear that you were well as this leaves us at present  but were sorry that you could not get home this winter.  come in May if possible and then if we live we will have a dinner and invite in the Family, Dorseys, Tuckers, Kings & Fishers  you wanted to know why Charlie & Ettie did not get married on New Years.  they could not get ready in time and as my Birthday comes on the 19th they thought they would get married then.  they will have it put in the Traverse Herald and send you a copy  Ettie rec'd the trimmings and handkerchief and was very much pleased with them.
Now I must tell you how I spend our Holidays  Christmas we went over to Mr Fishers and took dinner  in the afternoon we went downtown to Mrs Fishers Brother in law, Mr King and spent the afternoon & evening  then came home.  New Years Eve we went to a party at Todds   had a very good time  Frank Todd did not sell a drop of Liquor and everything went off nicely and quietly.   I was very glad to get the money for it just Paid my Taxes as they were due.  if you see Lizzie Haas tell her I will write soon to her  also show her Charlies & my Photographs.  I am glad that you got some clothing for to keep yourself warm this winter.  we have had a great deal of Snow but it does not stay on long enough to get deep as the weather has not been very cold.  Charlie & Ettie will be married between 12 & 1 o'clock. Mr. Fisher will perform the ceremony as he is Justice of the Peace.  if you have the means get a dinner of Oysters on that day.  she says she would tell you to drink their Health but she says she don't want any of the Family to drink any kind of Liquors on that day.  Emma send Ettie Gold enough for a Heavy ring  that the gold was dug a hundred yds from their door.  see if Gus could make it   she wants it a hoop ring carved.   she don't

**Long Distance Love 1855-1870**

like to send it to Traverse to have strangers make it. This is all at present   write soon. The neighbors send their regards.   Charlie & Ettie their Love.
Yours as ever
E. M. Boizard
M. E. Boizard



From Oliver to Eleanor & Marietta (Written by Marietta)

Chicago Ill<br>Jan'y 12<sup>th</sup> 1870

My Dear Wife,
Your letter dated the Jan'y 2<sup>nd</sup> came to hand yesterday, and I am pleased to hear that you Spent your Holidays, Cheerfully.  I Spent Christmas with Gus at our Washerwoman's house   her Husband invited us and we furnished 2 cans of Oysters and She <u>Fried</u> some and <u>Stewed</u> Some and with other <u>nicknacks</u> we made out a good Dinner and Supper   but Still I was thinking about our <u>Log house</u>   I would have had a better appetite if I could have Eaten it at home with you and <u>Ettie</u>. I often wonder in my own mind, if Ever I can live home again, for it seems to me that my good fortune has declined for Ever –   At present I am doing nothing but may have Something to do after being brought down to the Extremity, Such is a <u>Poor Mans fate</u> in this <u>world</u>.   One Week from today, I Suppose the wedding will take place   I think this <u>Union</u> will be a Happy one, at least I hope so. In regard of that ring that Ettie wants made for Emma   I spoke to Gus about it but he don't work in that line, but he referred me to Mr. Zepp a <u>Jeweler</u> whom, I Seen. he told me to make a good ring and Engrave or have it <u>chased</u> it would cost from $3.50 to $4.00 but it would be a good piece of work.   So should you wish to have it done you must Send the Size of it up, So he can make it to fit. I did not understand, whether <u>Emma</u> wants it for herself or whether She wants you to have it. Either way, you must Send the Money down as I have no money   Should you Send it down, I think you might put in a newspaper with your marriage announced in it, otherwise Send it in a small <u>Box</u>. I have been Expecting to get on the Jury again, but there is a change among the Judges, hence the delay. It has been raining for the last 2 days and it is very disagreeable. it gives a person the Blues. I Enclosed 3 Handkerchiefs in <u>two newspapers</u> for your New Years gift, did you get them or not. Tell Charlie to write immediately after the 19<sup>th</sup> Jan'y. I will close   give my best regards to all my friends and accept my fervent wishes. "Oliver"

Mr. Graef & Morris Powers sends their respects. I will see Lizzie Haas shortly. J.O.B.



From Eleanor and Marietta to Oliver (Written by Marietta)

Glen Arbor, Michigan<br>January 26 1870

My Dear Father
Yours of Jan 12<sup>th</sup> came to hand last Wednesday Morning and we were glad to hear from you that you were well.  we wished for you to be at home and on that day as we were married.  the ceremony was performed by Mr Fisher at half past two oclock in the presence of Mr & Mrs Tucker, also Willie   Miss Allie Baldwin a Friend of mine was the Bridesmaid   Frank Fisher was Groomsman   Mrs Fisher was also present.  we had a splendid day the Sun shone all Day and everything went off nicely.  mother has gone off up to the upper Dock on Business we will write when she

come home. I thought I would write now and then again when Mother is at home. I should have written before this but we have been invited out ever Since we were Married. We will give a dinner in May when you come home, then it will be warm weather and we can invite our Friends. I have saved you some Wedding Cake. I wish it was so that I could send it to you but I will keep it good untill you come home  The weather is quite good now Mr & Mrs Dorsey were over a short time ago they were all well and send their regards to you. We rec'd the three Handkerchiefs and think they are quite pretty. Sunday we went **sleighing**  That ring that I spoke of Emma made me a present of the gold for a ring and I thought that Gus could make it. You must be sure and come home in May if possible, well I shall have to close as Charlie will write some.  write soon.
Your Affectionate Daughter
Ettie Fisher

P.S. I will not send the Gold at present as Charlie cannot get the money   for it is rather scarce here and mother has none.  No more at present yours as ever   Ettie Fisher


Written on the bottom of Ettie's letter

Glen Arbor Mich
Jan 26<sup>th</sup> 1870

Mr Boizard
I am Happy to Address you as Father, we was Married just one Week ago today   it was A splendid Day we all wished that you might have been here. we look for you in the Spring  Ettie wrote you all the particulars about the Wedding.  it will be Published in the Grand Traverse Herald I will send you a copy.  There is no more news at present excuse this short letter I will write more next time
Yours Truly   Chas. A Fisher

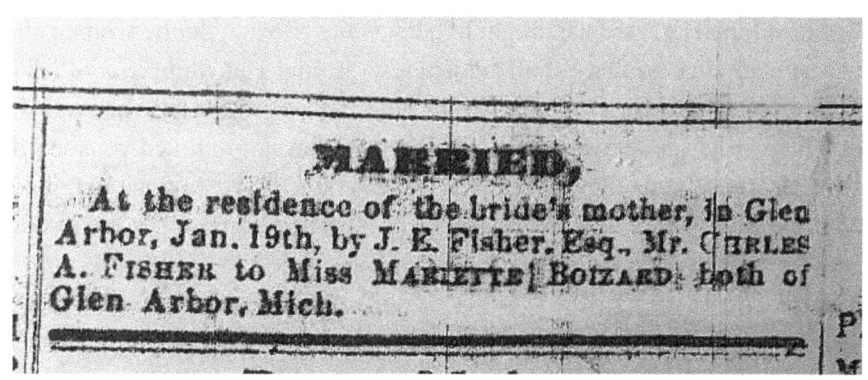

**Long Distance Love 1855-1870**

From Marietta to Oliver

Glen Arbor<br>Feb 14th 1870

My Dear Father
Yours of Feb 3rd came in Last weeks Mail, we were glad to hear that you were well as this leaves us at present.  The weather is quite cold now but for a while back it has been quite warm and pleasant   but it changes a good deal   I presume that ere long the people will think of making preparations for Sugar Making.  we are sorry to hear that you are still out of employment.   Mother says she was in hope that you did have as she would like to pay Mr. Lloyd what she owes him as he needs it.  She says she can not get hold of money enough for postage.  She is well with the exception of her Ear,   it is just the same.   I hope you will be able to be at home another winter.   you Spoke of the Air of Glen Arbor promoting Health Vigor and Fat Babies.   I guess it is pretty much so   but I guess that I shall not bother with them for a while.   Charlie says it is rather poor property to invest in at the Commencement of Life especially for poor Folks.   I hear of one every Little while.  There was a Little Girl born today    A Family by the house of Lowery were the happy Parents   they have five children now the oldest is about twelve years of age.   Charlie says he will write to you soon.   No more at present   write soon.   Mr Fishers Folks send their regards to you.
Yours as ever
Ettie Fisher


From Eleanor & Marietta to Oliver (Written by Marietta)

Glen Arbor<br>Feb 29 1870

My Dear Oliver
Yours of the 16th came in this last weeks mail.  we were Glad to hear that you were well as this leaves us at present but my Ear is not any better.   I hope that you will go back to Heath & Milligans in the spring   also that you can work there all Summer and be at home next Winter.   we are having fine weather now.   you asked if we all lived in the House, yes we do.  I am going over to Mr. Dorseys tomorrow to visit Mrs. Dorsey.   You must look very much like a Clergy man with your Stove Pipe Hat   you had ought to get a white cravat.   do the women all give you the wink since you got to look so spruce.   I guess that I shall get jealous.   is your Hat white. *{there is a change of ink right here. . indicating the rest of the letter was written at a later time.}*   the weather has changed   it is now snowing  but {?} then it not.   Mother has gone over to Mrs. Dorseys and has not returned yet and I don't know when she will   I just rec'd a letter from Emma they are all well and intend to leave Arizona before long.  There is not any news of importance.  Charlie says he will write before long. No More at present.   write soon.
Yours as ever
Eleanor M. Boizard
Ettie Fisher

John O Boizard
No's 48 & 50 Lasalle St.  Chicago, Ill's   Care of A. Graef

**Chicago and Glen Arbor 1864-1870**

From Eleanor & Marietta to Oliver (Written by Marietta)

Glen Arbor<br>April 14<sup>th</sup> 1870

My Dear Husband,

Yours of April 2$^{nd}$ came in this weeks mail   we were glad to hear that you had employment again. I rec'd the money $10. part of which I will pay Mr. Lloyd as soon as I can see him   I will give him half of it.   when you are sending anything home, send what old clothing you have,   we must try to work it so that you will be able to be in Glen Arbor this winter as you have not been at home in so long a time.   I want you to come home this winter. we have a half Barrel of Vinegar made.   about your old clothing   I can mend what will need mending and the rest I can put in the carpet rags.   If you possibly can send me a Shovel like the one I had.   but I don't care about it being so large.   when we went to Chicago we let Mr Tucker have our other one.   there is none in the place.   Don't forget my Lima Beans.   My Ear don't get any better   I am afraid that I am losing the hearing out of my other.   The snow is all gone here but I expect there is some back in the woods   it begins to look like planting time.   No More this time.   Charlie & Ettie send their love to you, the neighbors send their regards to you.   write soon.

Yours as ever,

E.M. Boizard

M. E. Fisher


From Oliver to Charlie

Heath & Milligan<br>White Lead, Zinc and Colors<br>170 & 172 Randolph Street<br>Chicago, Apr 18 1870

Mr Dear Charlie

Your letter dated the 7$^{th}$ and post Marked the 13$^{th}$ came to hand this morning and as the "**Oswegatchee**" Starts out this Evening, it affords me Chance of Sending a Small Box containing 2 Dresses of Calico, one for your Wife and that other for your Mother in law also 20 yds of Domestic   tell Ellen she must not make any Shirts for me, as I want her to use that Stuff for herself and Ettie. I can wear Flannell shirts with paper collars.   As regards the Pigeons, catch as many as you can and Keep them alive as they will bring from $2. to 2.50 per doz. as they are now Scarce   Hurry them up as fast as you can and Mr. Milligan will see them disposed of.   As regards packing them in Ice. I don't think that they will pay so well as if they were alive   besides I think it would cost more trouble and perhaps wont pay you so well.   If you can catch a large number, can't you coop them and Keep them and I can let you {know} when they will bring a better price.   however don't lose no time now, if you can Send a few Hundred on the first Boat from Ogdensburgh do so, don't wait too long.   I Send $10 to pay Mr. Lloyd did it arrive safe.   Kiss Ettie for me, also Mrs. B   I Sent Ettie ½ Doz Small Glass dishes to Eat her berries out of, also Pair of shears to cut carpet rags.   I think to send shortly some old Clothes for Carpet Rags.

Yours Sincerely

John O Boizard

Reply as soon as Possible

**Long Distance Love 1855-1870**

From Eleanor and Marietta to Oliver (Written by Marietta)

Glen Arbor, Michigan<br>May 2<sup>nd</sup> 1870

My Dear Oliver

We rec'd the Box containing the prints and Factory also the Dishes and Shears we were pleased with all. I wish you would send me a half dozen just like them if you possibly can   Ettie says she is very much pleased with them   also very much obliged for them. tell us the price of the calico and Factory when you write   I am pleased with them. I wish you had sent me some spool thread as I have none. If you send me some white and Black. Ettie send one dollar for you to send a Box of Pills **Dr. Cheesmans Female Pills** don't send any other kinds   send them as soon as you get this letter   you can send a Box or Parcels and put them inside of it. I wish you would send more Tea & coffee as there is none to be had at Rossmans    at the N T Dock it is not worth Buying it tastes like hay. The weather is very warm here. I wish you would send the Tea & coffee as soon as possible as we are out of Both.  also send that Butcher Knife when you send in any thing as we often need it. I have been working out in the lot and am very tired   Charlie is not home he is working in the mill. but I expect he will be home before long to stay through Planting.  if you should send lard or Butter don't send it in those tin cans as we have so many   send jars as we need them   Charlie has a young cow that will soon give Milk and we will need jars about for the milk this is all at present write soon
Yours as ever
E.M Boizard


From Harriet Fisher to Oliver

*There is no date on this letter; because Harriet Fisher refers to Charlie as Oliver's son, and a reference is made to Mr Fisher farming the letter presumably was written between spring & fall 1870*

Mr Boizard
Ettie has kindly allowed me to put a note to you in her letter. Will you in your next letter give me the price per lb of **Paris white**. I have a recipe for making **Kalsomine**, soak one fourth of a lb of glue over night in tepid water, the next day put it into a tin vessel, with a quart of water, set the pail in a kettle of water over the fire, untill it boils, stir constantly untill the glue is dissolved, take from six to eight lbs **Paris white**, in another vessel, pour on hot water and stir until it has the appearance of lime milk. Add the sizing. Stir well, and apply to the wall while warm. Is the above recipe the way **Kalsomine** is made in your establishment, Mrs Rosman got hers of Milligan. one more question, can **Kalsomine** be put on to a papered wall successfully. now friend Boziard if you will answer my numerous questions I shall be greatly obliged. We are having very fine weather, Mr. Fisher & Frank are farming. I presume you would hardly know the boys, to see your son Charly with whiskers, weighing nearly 160 and Frank larger than his father, you must not stay away much longer, or you will not know us, we are growing old so fast. Mr Fisher's hair is quite grey and I have lost my teeth – well it is what we must expect, time makes great changes, Mr Fisher & Frank send kind regards, please accept the best wishes of your old neighbor and friend.
Harriett M. Fisher

**Chicago and Glen Arbor 1864-1870**

From Oliver to Charlie

Chicago, Ill's
July 11<sup>th</sup> 1870

Dear Charlie

Your coop of Pigeons arrived on Saturday, on the "**Toledo**." I got your letters about 2 o'clock. I then went down to look at them and found them all right with the Exception that the Freight was not paid on them, although you Stated in your letter that you would pay the Freight. However, as before, I presume you did pay the freight on them and so did I. If you paid the freight, you should rec'd a voucher for it. I enclose you the receipt and also the **drayage**. I took them from the Boat about 4 o'clock on Saturday. It was too late. Consequently, I kept them until this morning (Monday) and disposed of them as well as I could.

Some offered me $1.00. Some $1.25. However I persisted and got $1.50. I sold them to a Commission Merchant on South Water St. I quit H. & M. I can't get along there any more. He told me to hold on to them till he saw his Pigeon man at the Stock Yards. He said they had some 11,000 more in Coops there to shoot them soon and I got tired of waiting. Consequently I sold them I had to pay besides the freight 70cts. for **Drayages** as I hauled them to Gus' shop and gave them water and feed all day Sunday, and then I was obliged to haul them back to South Water St. I send you by the "**Toledo**" the package of Dry Goods & c. with Bill & c. You were quite lucky with the Birds as I found but one dead one. I think now, as they are coming in such large numbers for shooting purposes they wont bring so much at present. If you find that they are plenty and you have the time to get them, pack them in Ice as before and I will try to sell them for you at the Hotels. I hope Ettie will like her Sheeting also her **Zephyrs** and Thread. Give my respects to your Father & Mother, also Frank. Kiss Ettie and mother for me and receive my regards. J.O.B.

I will send a letter to my wife about how I have been situated. The Zephyrs cost 87 ½


From Eleanor & Marietta to Oliver(Written by Marietta)

Glen Arbor
July 18<sup>th</sup> 1870

My Dear Oliver

Yours of the 11<sup>th</sup> came to hand last week   we were glad to hear that you were well, as this leaves us at present   I am very busy now as Berries are ripe and of course I gather all that I can. yesterday Ettie cooked over eleven quarts which I done up in cans and Bottles for winter use. I am living alone now for Charlie & Ettie are living down in a house just the other side of the Mill. they come and stay from Saturday until Monday morning with me. You say you will get me a pair of shoes as soon as you could   I should not ask you if I could get work to do. The ones that I have I cant but just keep them on   I am sorry to hear that you have quit H. & M. but am glad to hear that you have paid them the debt. I should try to keep out of their debt if possible.   we all think you had better come home and not stay there doing nothing.   this is all at present   write soon   the family all send love.
Yours as ever
E.M. Boizard

**Long Distance Love 1855-1870**

From Charlie to Oliver

Glen Arbor<br>July 18<sup>th</sup>

Dear Father
I rec'd your Letter and the parcel all right.  was well satisfied with the price you got for them.  there is not any pigeons here now but I expect they will be plenty after Harvest.  you say you have quit H. & M. Business is Dull.  we all think that you had better come Home.  now don't fail to come.  we will look for you.  if you have any freight I will pay the freight when you come.  I am now working for Mr. Grandy  he is building for a Grist Mill in addition to the old Saw Mill that Father used to own.  crops look well  corn and Potatoes especially.   I think I will have 125 Bu. potatoes.  50 or 75 Bu. corn.  200 Heads cabbage, cucumbers, Water Mellons, Tomatoes   Green Peas and string Beans plenty.  and there is any amount of berries.  Whortle Berries  Raspberries and Black Berries.  I have three live Red Foxes.  Would they be saleable there and much a price they are about ½ grown.  No more at present
Ettie will write soon
From your Son In Law
Chas. Fisher


From Eleanor to Oliver (Written by Marietta)

Glen Arbor, Michigan<br>Aug 30<sup>th</sup> 1870

My Dear Oliver
Your welcome Letter came to hand last week also the Shoes I am well pleased with them but they are rather low in the instep for me, we are sorry to hear of H & M's loss. Ettie rec'd a Letter from Emma Brown a short time ago they have sold their place for twelve hundred dollars in coins they think some of going to Texas to live.  I am picking Blackberries they are very nice this season we are having a great deal of Rain.  I believe I have never mentioned in any of my Letters that they are Building a Bridge over across Glen Lake, the narrows they are cutting a State road and the Bridge is in the Contract I believe the Bridge is nearly completed.  Charlie has been working on the State Road some.  when you come home, bring all your old clothing and if you can got hold of any Bottles small just bring them also as they will answer to put Berries in.  no more   write soon
Yours & c.
E.M.B.

**Chicago and Glen Arbor 1864-1870**

*Written on the back of the previous letter*

From Charles Fisher to Oliver

Glen Arbor
Aug 30th 1870

Dear Father Boizard
In regard to the freight on the last Pigeons I sent you. I payed the freight on them before they went on the Boat. I took the Receipt you sent me and showed it to the Agent. he then showed me a copy of the Bill he sent to R. Diefendorf Agt, of N.T. co. and it was Marked Paid. The Mistake is through R. Diefendorf. Now if you will go and see R. Diefendorf and ask him to look over that Bill and he will see that it was paid, and make him pay you Back what you paid him for freight. You spoke of coming home come as soon as possible because we are all looking for you no more at Present
From Your Son In Law
Chas. A Fisher


From Charles Fisher to Oliver

Glen Arbor Oct 8th 1870

Father Boizard
We rec'd your letter dated Sept. 22nd we were glad hear that you were well. We are all quite smart. I was presented with A young Son Oct. 6th 12 O'clock in Day He weighed 7 ½ lbs. A bouncer both Etta and the babie is quite Smart his name is John Edward Fisher. John is for you and Edward for Father and Fisher for Etta and I. Mother B says it makes her feel old to be called Grandma how is it with you. In regard to sending those potatoes I will first send some Sitron {citron} about 2 bbls and then if you can dispose of them and send me 12 of those Gunny Bags 2 Bu. Bags, I will amediately {immediately} send the Potatoes I am preparing the sitron {citron} now no more at present We All Send Love
Your Son In Law
Chas. Fisher
Glen Arbor Mich.

Will you let me know the market Price of cucumbers in the Brine Small nice cucumbers. C.A.F. G.A. M.
{Charles A Fisher Glen Arbor Michigan}


From Oliver to Charles Fisher

Chicago Ill
Nov 7 1870

Dear Charlie,
Your potatoes arrived last Friday the letter I got on Saturday but I had Sold the potatoes the letter was <u>delayed</u>. The Market is flooded with potatoes, they bring them in Car Loads you Can buy them from 65 to 80 cts per Bushel, fine large peach Blows, larger than yours, however I Sold yours to Heath as they had a quantity of Freight on the Champlain it did not cost me anything for **Drayage** he took them with his other freight I sold them for 80 cts, and was pleased to get that for them. I enquired the price of Flour, and they asked me $5.75 for ordinary family flour

and So I am at a stand what to do. I remit you $22 and if you want Flour at that price, I can Send it before Navigation Closes. The Bags I also Sold to Mr. Heath for 3 Dolls – he will pay me for them. I will retain then 3 Dolls as I am in want of a few articles of Drawers, stockings & c. The potatoes weight was 2000 pounds, by allowing 60 pounds bushel it would bring it about 33 Bushels, at 80 cts. $26.40 deduct f't 4.20 Bal - 22.20   I will get Etties nipple glasses I hope the young mother will get over her trouble I am sorry that I cant See you all this winter, as I think I can Still make a little this winter, by Staying with Graef and it may be occasionally I can Send my Wife a few dolls this winter   Ask my Wife if she will Send me a good Blanket, a dark one as I Sleep in the Shop, it Saves the cost of Lodging. I hope this letter will be Satisfactory to you and also my Wife – answer this letter by Boat pack up the Blanket, and give it to the Porter of the Boat accompanied with a letter. My best regards to all the family

My love to my wife and yours

Yours with respect

J.O. Boizard


I enquired about Pickles in Brine there is no sale this winter for them, they raised So many of them in Ill's that they Sold for 35cts per Bushel if you can keep them good until spring they will pay double from what they do now.

J.O.B.

**Chicago and Glen Arbor 1864-1870**

*No other correspondence has been found written between Oliver and his family. Based on Eleanor's obituary and various other papers, Oliver died in November 1870. It is possible that he was struck with some type of paralysis. We do have a letter that was written to Marietta from a Doctor approximately 18 years after Oliver's death. This letter appears to be in reply to a letter that Marietta had written to him inquiring about receiving some type of financial aid or pension from the Government due to the circumstances surrounding Oliver's death. It does not seem likely that they ever received the requested aid.*


To Marietta Fisher from Wm. Johnson M.D.

Newport KY<br>Sept. 25, '88

Mrs. E. Fisher

    Your letter has been received and in reply to it. I have to state that so long a time has intervened that the circumstance of your Father's sickness has passed out of my memory. The question arises how to prove that he contracted the disease in the performance of his duty. There is no records at this place now consequently I cannot refresh my memory the reports of sick and wounded at the time generally stated the disease treated for and if for Paralysis you might establish a claim. It would be almost impossible to get witnesses for in the first place the Doctor that treated your Father is dead, and I am afraid the records which is now in Washington might not show the disease in your Mothers favor, but in the event your Mother makes any application and she thinks I can be of any help I will do so. Sometimes in reporting diseases the cause is reported and not the results of same. Your lawyer may make a beginning the whole thing will depend how the case is recorded. I have forgotten dates, we know nothing of the Bridges family. My family joins me in sending kind regards to you all.
Respectfully Wm. Johnson M.D.

*While stationed in Newport Barracks, Emma Bridges stayed some nights at a Mrs. Johnson's house and there is one mention of a Mr. Johnson. Could this be the same person?*

# Epilogue

Oliver's last letter to his family sheds no light on his deteriorating health nor does it foreshadow his impending death, yet we are faced with a sudden and unwelcome end to their story. The abrupt ending leaves a longing in our hearts to know the rest of the story. I have asked my mom, "Are you sure you have given me **every** letter?" My search is not necessarily for letters from the middle of the story, I crave a letter that will bring closure to their story. I want the explanation and the circumstances around his death. The letter from the Doctor that was written eighteen years after Oliver died creates more questions than it answers.

Was Oliver sick in Newport? Is that why he took an early discharge? In a December 1869 letter Oliver mentioned that he had rheumatism in both feet and ankles with a lot of swelling and he had to use a stick to walk with. Was that problem related to the 'paralysis' mentioned in the Dr.'s letter? Why would his family have waited eighteen years to write to the Doctor?

As with any research project, the questions never seem to end. Each attempt to solve one part of the mystery exposes several other riddles that warrant investigation. With time, maybe some of these unsolved parts of Oliver and Eleanor's lives will be known, but in the meantime, we must focus on the wonderful treasury of knowledge that we do know.

Having read this book, it is my desire that you would be inspired to journal or write more letters to your loved ones. Ask yourself "Who is preserving **my** family's history for the generations to come?"

We have this unusual and special collection of letters detailing the lives of a married couple who experienced the joys of companionship and the loneliness of separation as they tried their best to make a life for themselves and their daughter in a rugged and unsettled land. May each of us, treasure a little more dearly the gift of community that the early settlers across this country sacrificed for and left for us to inherit.

Jodie Sewall

Addendum

# Time Line
Key
□±Glen Arbor events
* National events
×Boizard /Fisher family events

1831   xOliver Boizard's first enlistment November 17, 1831 6th Inf. Co. E
1835   x Oliver Boizard discharged November 17, 1835 6th Inf. Co. E
1838   x Oliver Boizard's 2nd enlistment March 2, 1838 6th Infantry Co. F
         xJohn Fisher's 1st enlistment April 17, 1838.  8th Infantry, Co. F
1840   *1835-1842 The first of three campaigns against the Seminole Indians.
1841   xOliver Boizard discharged from the US Army,  March 2, 1841 6th Infantry Co. F
         ×John Fisher discharged from the US Army, April 17, 1841.  8th Infantry, Co. F.
         x Oliver Boizard 3rd enlistment April 3, 1841  6th Infantry, Co. F & D
1842
1843
1844   *Telegraph system invented by Samuel F.B. Morse.
         *James K. Polk elected President
1845   *Annexation of Texas
1846   *Mexican War (1846-1848)
1847
1848   ±John LaRue moves to Leelanau Peninsula, making him the first Caucasian resident.
1849   *California Gold Rush
1850   ×Eleanor Melvina McGill marries James MaGill
         *Railroad growth begins to mushroom from 1850-1860 and by the time the Civil War begins it is the most important means of transportation.
1851   ±□John Dorsey moves to the mainland – Leelanau Peninsula.
1852   ×Marietta Magill born - May 18, 1852
1853
1854   ×John E. Fisher & family settle in Glen Arbor
         x Oliver Boizard 4th enlistment November 17, 1854 4th Artillery Co. K
1855   ±□SS Saginaw lands in Glen Arbor with 14 settlers
         ×John Oliver & Eleanor Melvina Magill married July 16, 1855
1856   ×Oliver serving in 4th Artillery Company K - Fort Myers& Fort McRae during Seminole Indian Wars
1857     ""
1858   ×Possibly - Oliver & Eleanor made a trip to Glen Arbor sometime during this year. The original paperwork for the Quit Claim Deed filed in 1859 was composed in October 1858.
1859   ×John Fisher builds a saw mill on Crystal River. It was capable of sawing 5,000 feet per day.
         ×Oliver – Discharged, November 17, 1859  Private 4th Reg. U.S. Army Fort Ridgely, MN
         ×40 acres of property were purchased in Glen Arbor for $40.00 from George & Anna Thayer (Traverse City Clerk, Quit Claim Deed 561) The deed was received for record on August 6 in Traverse City.
         Oliver, Eleanor & Marietta move to Glen Arbor after Oliver receives a discharge from the Army on November 17.
         *John Brown's attack on Harpers Ferry
1860   ×Oliver, Eleanor & Marietta live in Glen Arbor from November 1859- September 1860. Oliver re-enlisted for his 5th enlistment with the U.S. Army on September 6, 1860.

**Long Distance Love 1855-1870**

       *Election of Abraham Lincoln

1861  *Civil War begins. April 15 President Lincoln issues his first proclamation asking for 75,000 men to serve for three months. In May he asks for 42,000 volunteers to serve for three years.
      ×Oliver joins the US Army again and is stationed at Newport Barracks, KY.

1862   *Homestead Act passed
      ×Stationed at Newport Barracks

1863  *Emancipation Proclamation
      ×Stationed at Newport Barracks

1864  ×Oliver received an early discharge on February 3, 1864. He then relocates to Chicago with his family. He is employed as a civilian by Col. Pomeroy, in the Quartermasters office.
    ×In May, Eleanor & Marietta, probably for health reasons, relocate to Glen Arbor. They rent a house from the Fishers until they are able to build a log house on a 10 acre piece of property they buy from John & Harriet Fisher. They move into their log house in August.

1865 *President Lincoln is assassinated in April.
    *Civil war ends.
    ×Oliver stays in Chicago is employed in mustering out the troops, until October, when he moves to Springfield, IL to work for the U.S. Mustering and Disbursing Office.

1866  ×Released from duties at the U.S. Mustering and Disbursing Office in June. Oliver returns to Chicago, works for Heath & Milligan.

1867  ×Eleanor & Marietta travel to Chicago in October to stay with Oliver for the winter.

1868  ×Eleanor & Marietta return to Glen Arbor in May.

1869  *First transcontinental railroad completed
    ×Oliver quits his job with Heath & Milligan in August.
     ×Marietta & Charlie get engaged.

    ×Oliver works for a short time for the US Circuit Court as a juror in the month of December. He misses the last boat out to Michigan.

1870 ×Marietta & Charlie Fisher are married on Eleanor's birthday, January 19, by Charlie's father, John E. Fisher.

    ×Oliver takes a job with Heath & Milligan again.

    xMarietta and Charlie have their first baby, John Edward Fisher on October 6, 1870.

    ×The last letter received from Oliver was dated November 7, in which Oliver asks for a warm blanket.

    ˣ Oliver died at age 59 in Chicago.

1871   ☐ ±The bridge is completed across the Narrows of Glen Lake.

Addendum

# Military Records
## John Oliver Boizard Military Records

| 1st Enlistment | 1831- 1835 | | | | | | | | |
|---|---|---|---|---|---|---|---|---|---|
| Name | Age | Eyes | Hair | Complexion | Feet | Inches | Birth State | City | Occupation |
| Boizard John O | 21 | dark | dark | Fair | 5 | 8 | Pennsylvania | Philadelphia | Silver plater |

| When | Where | By Whom | Period of Time | Regiment & Company | Discharged | Cause Discharge |
|---|---|---|---|---|---|---|
| November, 1831, 17th | Newport | Lt. Bateman | 5 years | 6 Inf. E | 17, Nov. 1835 | Expiration of service |

| Deserted | Apprehended | Enlistment | Remarks |
|---|---|---|---|
| 6th, Oct. 32 | 7th, Oct. 32 | 1st | at Camp Worth La (PO January25/54 N°46270) |

****3 years************************************************************

| 2nd Enlistment | 1838- 1841 | | | | | | | | |
|---|---|---|---|---|---|---|---|---|---|
| Name | Age | Eyes | Hair | Complexion | Feet | Inches | Birth State | City | Occupation |
| Boizard John O | 26 | Black | Black | Fair | 5 | 9 1/2 | PA | Philadelphia | Soldier |

| When | Where | By Whom | Period of Time | Regiment & Company | Discharged | Cause Discharge |
|---|---|---|---|---|---|---|
| March, 1838, 2 | St. Louis | Lt. Alexander | 3 yr | 6 Inf F | 2 March 41 | Expiration of service ( PO Janry. 25/54 N°46270 |

| Deserted | Apprehended | Enlistment | Remarks |
|---|---|---|---|
| | | 2nd | At Fort Annuttgeliea E Fla (a Private) |

*****6 months***********************************************************

**Long Distance Love 1855-1870**

| 3rd Enlistment | 1841-1846 | | | | | | | |
|---|---|---|---|---|---|---|---|---|
| Name | Age | Eyes | Hair | Complexion | Feet | Inches | Birth State | City | Occupation |
| Boizard John O | 30 | black | black | dark | 5 | 9 1/2 | PA | Philadelphia | Soldier |

| When | Where | By Whom | Period of Time | Regiment & Company | Discharged | Cause Discharge |
|---|---|---|---|---|---|---|
| 1841 Sept 3rd | New York | Capt. Moore | 5 years | 6 Inf F, D | 3 Sept. 46 | Expiration of service |

| Deserted | Apprehended | Enlistment | Remarks |
|---|---|---|---|
| | | 3rd | San Antonio, TX ( a Corporal) |

*****8 years *********************************************************************

| 4th Enlistment | 1854-1859 | | | | | | | |
|---|---|---|---|---|---|---|---|---|
| Name | Age | Eyes | Hair | Complexion | Feet | Inches | Birth State | City | Occupation |
| Boizard John O | 42 | black | dark | fair | 5 | 9 | Penna | Philadelphia | Soldier |

| When | Where | By Whom | Period of Time | Regiment & Company | Discharged | Cause Discharge |
|---|---|---|---|---|---|---|
| 17 Nov 1854 | Pittsburgh | Lt. Wood | 5 years | 4th Artillery K | 17, Nov. 59 | Expiration of Service |

| Deserted | Apprehended | Enlistment | Remarks |
|---|---|---|---|
| | | 4th | At Fort Ridgely Minnesota    a Private |

*****10 months*******************************************************************

**Addendum**

| 5th Enlistment | 1860--1864 | | | | | | | | |
|---|---|---|---|---|---|---|---|---|---|
| Name | Age | Eyes | Hair | Complexion | Feet | Inches | Birth State | City | Occupation |
| Boizard John O | 48 | Blk | Blk | fair | 5 | 9 | PA | Philadelphia | Soldier |

| When | Where | By Whom | Period of Time | Regiment & Company | Discharged | Cause Discharge |
|---|---|---|---|---|---|---|
| 6 Sept 1860 | Newport, KY | Lt. Wilkinson | 5 years | GSPP Newport Barracks, | 3 Feb/64 | Per S.O. 72 ayo at |

| Deserted | Apprehended | Enlistment | Remarks |
|---|---|---|---|
| | | 5th | a Corpl |

*Source: https://www.fold3.com/image/310835562*

## Miscellaneous correspondence in John Oliver Boizard's Military Records at the National Archive

### Letter regarding Oliver's request to be discharged because he enlisted as a minor

To Hon Lewis Cass  Secretary of War

Philadelphia
September 5, 1832

Governor Cass,

Sir, A minor by the name of Oliver Boizard was enlisted on the 17th of November last past in the United States Army in Company E. 6th Reg. infantry. The said company let me remind you is now stationed at Jefferson's Barracks ten or twelve miles from St. Louis Missouri. Said Minor was enlisted at Newport Kentucky. He was born here and all his friends & relations reside here. He was Twenty years and two months old when he enlisted & will be twenty one the twentieth of this month. No application could be made to you sir on this subject. If it were possible to reach the case by Habeas Corpus – for you will readily perceive the impracticality of producing the witness or residents here before a judge in Missouri and as to sending a commission from here to Missouri. His friends being poor are unable to pay the expenses – besides sir a friendless soldier could get very few to draw up a legal commission for him. We propose therefore if convenient with your views to prove directly to yourself the exact age of the said Oliver and if you are satisfied to ask you to forward an order for his discharge. Your early attention to this letter is requested by yours, most respectfully  H Hubbele

**Long Distance Love 1855-1870**

*{The above letter was folded and written on the outside of the letter is as follows:}*

Philadelphia, September 5th, 1832

John Oliver Boizard a private of Company E, 6th Infy – enlisted 17 Nov 31 "Aged 21 years"

Asks his discharge being a minor.

On the N.W. Frontier

No later M. Roll than 30th Sept. 1832

Trial 10 Sep '32

B Unregistered 1831
John Oliver Boizard

*Source: https://www.fold3.com*

\*\*\*\*\*\*\*\*\*\*\*\*\*\*\*\*\*\*\*\*\*\*\*\*\*\*\*\*\*\*\*\*\*\*\*\*\*\*\*\*\*\*\*\*\*\*\*\*\*\*\*\*\*\*\*\*\*\*\*\*\*\*\*\*

## 1855 letter regarding Oliver's request for extra pay due to Mexican War Soldiers

120B  March 15/55

Recruiting Rendezvous Pittsburg, Pennsylvania

March 8th 1855

John O Boizard

Private U.S. Army

Attach'd to Perm't Recruiting Party

Inquiring if he is entitled to three months extra pay allowed to soldiers serving in the Mexican War.

Respectfully forwarded  W.H. Wood
1st Lieut. 3rd Inf'try
Recruiting Officer

Recruiting Rendezvous
Pittsburgh, PA
March 8th 1855


Rec'd March 10th/55

Pvt. John O. Boizard loses the benefit of his "former services" by the length of time he was out of Army. viz from Sept 3, 1846- to Nov. 17, 1854.  No man is entitled to the $2 additional pay who was not in the Army at the date of the passage of the Act of August 4, 1854, or who did not reenter it within one month after its passage & the date of his discharge, so as to bring such re-entry within the category of a re-enlistment – see on this point, par. 3 of G.O no. 16 of Sept. 13, 1854

This letter to be returned.

By order: W. G. Freeman
Asst. Adjutant General


Rec'ty Office, Pittsburgh, PA
March 13th, 1855

It appears from the above endorsement that the contents of Privates Boizard's letter have been misapprehended . He does not ask if he is entitled to the $2 additional pay for 'former services.' He knows that he is not. He asks if he is entitled to the "three months extra pay" allowed to the soldiers who served in the war with Mexico. Respectfully submitted W. H. Wood, 1st Lieut. 3rd Inf'try

March 15, 1855

My endorsement of March 10th now forwarded on as a misapprehension of the question asked by Private Boizard. It would seem from the Dep't of War letters of Aug. 3, 1848 to the Paymasters Dept., that Pvt. B is entitled to the "three months extra pay;" but that is a matter for the decision of the Pay Dept, this letter is respectfully submit to that dept. with the request that Lt. W. H. Wood may be notified of the disposition _____ of this case. By Order: W.G. Freeman A.A.G.

*Source: https://www.fold3.com/image/294271300, Publication Number: M567*
*Publication Title: Letters Received by the Office of the Adjutant General Main Series 1822-1860*

## John Fisher Military Records

| 1st Enlistment | 1838-1841 | | | | | | | |
|---|---|---|---|---|---|---|---|---|
| Name | Age | Eyes | Hair | Complexion | Feet | Inches | Birth State | City | Occupation |
| Fisher, John | 21 | Hazel | Light | Fair | 5 | 7 | New York | Salem, Washington | Machinest |

| When | Where | By Whom | Period of Time | Regiment & Company | Discharged | Cause Discharge |
|---|---|---|---|---|---|---|
| 17 April 1838 | Schenectady | Lt. Wells | 3 years | 8th Inf. Co. F | 17 April/41 | Expiration of Service |

| Deserted | Apprehended | Enlistment | Remarks |
|---|---|---|---|
|  |  | 1st | Ft. Brooke Florida    a Private |

Long Distance Love 1855-1870

# William Bridges Military Records

| 1st Enlistment | 1833-1836 | | | | | | | |
|---|---|---|---|---|---|---|---|---|
| Name | Age | Eyes | Hair | Complexion | Feet | Inches | Birth State | City | Occupation |
| Bridges William | 11 | Hazel | Light | Fair | 4 | 5 1/2 | | Council Bluff | |

| When | Where | By Whom | Period of Time | Regiment & Company | Discharged | Cause Discharge |
|---|---|---|---|---|---|---|
| 7 Oct. 1833 | Ft. Leavenworth | Lt. Conrad | 3 | 6 Inf B | 16 Sept. 36 | Re-enlisted |

| Deserted | Apprehended | Enlistment | Remarks |
|---|---|---|---|
| | | | PO N°47066 10 May/54  See Volume N°5 |

\*\*\*\*\*\*\*\*\*\*\*\*\*\*\*\*\*\*\*\*\*\*\*\*\*\*\*\*\*\*\*\*\*\*\*\*\*\*\*\*\*\*\*\*\*\*\*\*\*\*\*\*\*\*\*\*\*\*\*\*\*\*\*\*\*\*\*\*\*\*\*\*\*

| 2nd Enlistment | 1836-1839 | | | | | | | |
|---|---|---|---|---|---|---|---|---|
| Name | Age | Eyes | Hair | Complexion | Feet | Inches | Birth State | City | Occupation |
| Bridges William | 13 | Blue | Light | Fair | 5 | 7 1/2 | Missouri | Council Bluff | Soldier |

| When | Where | By Whom | Period of Time | Regiment & Company | Discharged | Cause Discharge |
|---|---|---|---|---|---|---|
| 16, Sept 1836 | Jefferson Barracks | Lt. Ketchum | 3 years | 6 Inf B | 16 Sept 39 | Expiration of Service |

| Deserted | Apprehended | Enlistment | Remarks |
|---|---|---|---|
| | | 2nd | PO N°47066 10 May/54  At St. Andrews Bay (musician) |

\*\*\*\*\*7 Months\*\*\*\*\*\*\*\*\*\*\*\*\*\*\*\*\*\*\*\*\*\*\*\*\*\*\*\*\*\*\*\*\*\*\*\*\*\*\*\*\*\*\*\*\*\*\*\*\*\*\*\*\*\*\*

Addendum

| 3rd Enlistment | 1840-1845 | | | | | | | | |
|---|---|---|---|---|---|---|---|---|---|
| Name | Age | Eyes | Hair | Complexion | Feet | Inches | Birth State | City | Occupation |
| Bridges William | 17 | Blue | Light | Fair | 5 | 9 | MO | | Musician |

| When | Where | By Whom | Period of Time | Regiment & Company | Discharged | Cause Discharge |
|---|---|---|---|---|---|---|
| 3 April 1840 | Fort Hulbert | Lt. Caston | 5 years | 6 Inf B | 1st March/45 | Expiration of Service |

| Deserted | Apprehended | Enlistment | Remarks |
|---|---|---|---|
| | | | PO N°47006 10/May54 Ft. Towson, Arkansas 1st Sergeant re-enlisted |

\*\*\*\*\*\*\*\*\*\*\*\*\*\*\*\*\*\*\*\*\*\*\*\*\*\*\*\*\*\*\*\*\*\*\*\*\*\*\*\*\*\*\*\*\*\*\*\*\*\*\*\*\*\*\*\*\*\*\*\*\*\*\*\*\*\*\*\*\*\*\*

| 4th Enlistment | 1845-1850 | | | | | | | | |
|---|---|---|---|---|---|---|---|---|---|
| Name | Age | Eyes | Hair | Complexion | Feet | Inches | Birth State | City | Occupation |
| Bridges William | 22 | Blue | Light | Fair | 5 | 8 | MO | Council Bluffs | Soldier |

| When | Where | By Whom | Period of Time | Regiment & Company | Discharged | Cause Discharge |
|---|---|---|---|---|---|---|
| 1 April 1845 | Ft. Towson | Lt. Belgen | 5 years | 6 Inft'y B | 1 March 50 | Expiration of Service |

| Deserted | Apprehended | Enlistment | Remarks |
|---|---|---|---|
| | | 4th | PO N°47006 10/May54 Fort Leavenworth, MO a Sergeant |

\*\*\*\*\*\*5 years – but we are missing his 5th enlistment record so we assume he re-enlisted during the years of 1850-1855\*\*\*\*\*\*\*\*\*\*\*\*\*\*\*\*\*\*\*\*\*\*\*\*\*\*\*\*\*\*\*\*\*\*\*\*\*\*\*\*\*\*\*\*\*\*\*\*\*\*\*\*\*\*\*\*\*\*\*\*\*\*\*

## Long Distance Love 1855-1870

| 6th Enlistment | 1855-1860 | | | | | | | | |
|---|---|---|---|---|---|---|---|---|---|
| Name | Age | Eyes | Hair | Complexion | Feet | Inches | Birth State | City | Occupation |
| Bridges William | 32 | Blue | Light | Fair | 5 | 8 ½ | Missouri | Council Bluffs | Soldier |

| When | Where | By Whom | Period of Time | Regiment & Company | Discharged | Cause Discharge |
|---|---|---|---|---|---|---|
| 21 Sept 1855 | Newport KY | Major Heintzelman | 5 | 6th Inf F | 21 July 60 | Re-enlistment |

| Deserted | Apprehended | Enlistment | Remarks |
|---|---|---|---|
| | | 6th | At Newport Barracks, KY |

***************************************************************

| 7th Enlistment | 1860-1864 | | | | | | | | |
|---|---|---|---|---|---|---|---|---|---|
| Name | Age | Eyes | Hair | Complexion | Feet | Inches | Birth State | City | Occupation |
| Bridges William | 37 | Blue | Light | Fair | 5 | 8 ½ | Missouri | Council Bluffs | Soldier |

| When | Where | By Whom | Period of Time | Regiment & Company | Discharged | Cause Discharge |
|---|---|---|---|---|---|---|
| 21 July 1860 | Newport, KY | Lt. Wilkins | 5 | | 13 July/64 | Re-enlistment |

| Deserted | Apprehended | Enlistment | Remarks |
|---|---|---|---|
| | | 7th | Per party N°_____ as a private |

***************************************************************

Addendum

| 8th Enlistment | 1864-1867 | | | | | | | | |
|---|---|---|---|---|---|---|---|---|---|
| Name | Age | Eyes | Hair | Complexion | Feet | Inches | Birth State | City | Occupation |
| Bridges William | 41 | Blue | Light | Fair | 5 | 8 ½ | Missouri | Council Bluffs | Soldier |

| When | Where | By Whom | Period of Time | Regiment & Company | Discharged | Cause Discharge |
|---|---|---|---|---|---|---|
| 13 June 1864 | New York | Capt. Benedict | | 14th Inf A | 3 June 67 | By YO___ aya 5___ |

| Deserted | Apprehended | Enlistment | Remarks |
|---|---|---|---|
| | | 8th | at Camp McDowell as a Sergeant |

\*\*\*\*\*\*\*\*\*\*\*\*\*\*\*\*\*\*\*\*\*\*\*\*\*\*\*\*\*\*\*\*\*\*\*\*\*\*\*\*\*\*\*\*\*\*\*\*\*\*\*\*\*\*\*\*\*\*\*\*\*\*\*\*\*\*\*\*\*\*

There is a Register of Ordnance Sergeant's Appointments of the U.S. Army

William Bridges was appointed as an Ordnance Sergeant on June 6, 1869.

The register shows some enlistment information for William Bridges.

| Enlistment | Discharge | Reason |
|---|---|---|
| June 25, 1867 | June 25, 1870 | Expiration of Service at Camp Gaston, CA |
| June 25, 1870 | June 25, 1875 | Expiration of Service at Fort Walla Walla, W T |
| June 25, 1875 | June 24, 1880 | Expiration of Service at Fort Walla Walla, W T |
| June 25, 1880 | Died 21 November 1881 | Strangulated inguinal hernia (right) general peritonitis at Fort Walla Walla WT  6372 Act 81 |
| https://www.fold3.com | | |

**Long Distance Love 1855-1870**

| 11th Enlistment | 1875 - 1880 | | | | | | | | |
|---|---|---|---|---|---|---|---|---|---|
| Name | Age | Eyes | Hair | Complexion | Feet | Inches | Birth State | City | Occupation |
| Bridges William | 52 4/12 | Blue | Light | Fair | 5 | 8 ½ | Missouri | Council Bluffs | Soldier |

| When | Where | By Whom | Period of Time | Regiment & Company | Discharged | Cause Discharge |
|---|---|---|---|---|---|---|
| 25 June 1875 | Ft. Walla Walla WT | Lt Miller | 5 | Ordnance Sergeant | 24/June 1889 | Expiration of enlistment |

| Deserted | Apprehended | Enlistment | Remarks |
|---|---|---|---|
| | | 11th | Character: desirable |

\*\*\*\*\*\*\*\*\*\*\*\*\*\*\*\*\*\*\*\*\*\*\*\*\*\*\*\*\*\*\*\*\*\*\*\*\*\*\*\*\*\*\*\*\*\*\*\*\*\*\*\*\*\*\*\*\*\*\*\*\*\*\*\*\*\*\*\*

| 12th Enlistment | 1880 - 1881 | | | | | | | | |
|---|---|---|---|---|---|---|---|---|---|
| Name | Age | Eyes | Hair | Complexion | Feet | Inches | Birth State | City | Occupation |
| Bridges William | 57 1/2 | Blue | Light | Fair | 5 | 8 ½ | Missouri | Council Bluffs | Soldier |

| When | Where | By Whom | Period of Time | Regiment & Company | Discharged | Cause Discharge |
|---|---|---|---|---|---|---|
| 25 June 1880 | Ft. Walla Walla WT | Lt Vesham (?) | 5 | Ordnance Sergeant | Died 21 November/ 81 | Strangulated inguinal hernia (right) & c. |

| Deserted | Apprehended | Enlistment | Remarks |
|---|---|---|---|
| | | 12th | Died at Fort Walla Walla WT |

\*\*\*\*\*\*\*\*\*\*\*\*\*\*\*\*\*\*\*\*\*\*\*\*\*\*\*\*\*\*\*\*\*\*\*\*\*\*\*\*\*\*\*\*\*\*\*\*\*\*\*\*\*\*\*\*\*\*\*\*\*\*\*\*\*\*\*\*

United States Registers of Enlistments in the U.S. Army, 1798-1914," database with images, *FamilySearch* (https://familysearch.org/ark:/61903/1:1:QJDR-3NZ6 : 13 March 2018), William Bridges, 25 Jun 1880; citing p. 98, volume 078, Walla Walla, , Washington Territory, United States, NARA microfilm publication M233 (Washington D.C.: National Archives and Records Administration, n.d.), roll 41; FHL microfilm 350,347.

# Genealogy Charts

**BOIZARD**

- **Jacob,** b 1809. In 1850 and 1860 census he was living in Philadelphia

- **John Oliver**, b. September 20 1811
  d. November 1870
  m. July 16, 1855
  Eleanor Melvina MaGill
  b. January 19, 1828   d. March 29, 1911

  **Marietta**
  b. May 18, 1852 (father was James MaGill)
  d. 1835
  m. Jan 19, 1870
  Charles Andrew Fisher
  b. 1849   d. 1909

Mr. Boizard
b. in France

m

**Catherine**
b. Aug. 3, 1786

- **Elizabeth (Libby)**
  -b. 1811 (not sure about this date— she died in 1871 at the age of 60 — but depending on her birthday month—it could be 1810. There is an Elizabeth Boizard buried in the Old Chester PA cemetery, next to Catherine Boizard. This is possibly Oliver's sister.

- **Lewis Pierre (Pete)**
  b. 1815
  m. Caroline
  b. 1813

  Caroline (Cally) b. 1849
  Charles (Charley) b. 1850

  In the 1860 census they were living in Philadelphia

- **Catherine (Kate)**
  b. Dec. 2, 1830
  m.
  Christopher (C.C.) Dow
  In 1860 census—living in Philadelphia

  Phineas

- **Mary**
  m. a Doctor and traveled to California in a covered wagon in 1856. Last heard from in 1858

GENEALOGY CHARTS

**John Edward Fisher**
b. 1817   d. 1900

m. April 1843

**Harriet M. McCarty**
b. 1826   d. 1914

→

**-Charles Andrew**
b. August 29, 1849   d. May 1909
m. January 19, 1870
**Marietta Boizard**
b. May 18, 1852   d. 1935

**John Edward**  b. 1870   d. 1937
m.
Amanda Carlson

**Etta May**  b. 1872   d. 1958
m.
1. John Westcott
2. Dr. Charles Todd

**-Charles Fredrick**
b. 1874   d. 1915
m.
Lottie Lowrie

↓

**Francis (Frank)**
b. 1851   d. 1933

m.

Charlotte Atkinson
b. 1858   d. 1934

↓

**Eugene**

**Clinton**

**Maude**

**Pearl**

**Myrtle**

↓

# Obituaries

**GLEN ARBOR.**

The mail boat from South Manitou was over today.

At the town meeting today the following ticket was elected:

Supervisor—Mark Randall.
Town Clerk—N. B. Sheridan.
Treasurer—Charles Ehle.
Highway Commissioner—John Westcott.
Justice of the Peace—Lansing
Member Board of Review—Raderick Dunn.
Constables—Fred Fisher, William Bennett, Charles Riggs, Herbert N. Sheridan.

Mr. and Mrs. Edward Fisher went to Leland, last week to attend the funeral of Mrs. Margaret Neilson, who was Mrs. Fisher's grandmother.

Eugene Fisher and his grandmother who came here from Maple City Saturday to attend the funeral of Mrs. Bozzard, will return Tuesday.

Another pioneer gone. Grandma Bozzard, who has been sick and a great sufferer, passed away March 29th, at the home of her daughter, Mrs. Charles A. Fisher, by whom she was tenderly cared for during her long illness. The funeral was held at the house on Sunday, Rev. Gliddon officiated. The casket was covered with flowers, the gifts of loving friends. The selections by the choir were well rendered. Her remains were laid to rest in the Fisher cemetery. Elenor M. McGill was born January 29th, 1828, in Wheeling, W. Virginia. At the age of four her mother died and she went to live with a Quaker family in Winan Town, Penn., where she was kindly cared for until her marriage in 1850, in Pittsburg, Penn., to John O. Bozzard. Mr. Bozzard was an Indian war soldier, was also in the Mexican and Civil war, served United States 25 years. He died 40 years ago. They came here in 1858, and she has lived here ever since. Mrs. Fisher and family wish me to thank the choir for their kindness, also Mrs. Shea, Mrs. Earl, Mrs. Burgess and all the ladies that so kindly rendered assistence during her sickness. They have our sympathy in this their hour of sorrow.

April 4, 1911

The obituary states that Eleanor married John Oliver Boizard in 1850. Whether intentional or not, it clearly left out her marriage to James MaGill in 1850. She didn't marry John Oliver until 1854.

I cannot find a "Winan Town," Pennsylvania. However, I can find a Union Town in the same local proximity of other towns mentioned in the letters. Union Town had a fire in their town hall in the 1800's which means that her orphan case information was probably lost in that fire. There is also a reference in the early letters of Eleanor's father living in McClellandtown.

**Another Tribute to Charles A. Fisher.**
For The Herald.

Charles A. Fisher, who had been ailing for several months was obliged to take to his bed three weeks ago, although a great sufferer, his family was not aware that he was dangerously ill until the last, and his death, which occurred last Sunday morning, was a terrible shock to them all. His funeral on Tuesday was held at his home and conducted by the Maccabees, as he was a charter member of that order. His remains were placed beside his father's, on the old homestead, where he lived. Charles A. Fisher, who was the son of John E. and Harriet Fisher, was born August 29, 1849, in Fon DuLac, Wisconsin. His parents with their family moved to Sleeping Bear Bay, now called Glen Arbor, in August 1854, where he has since resided. January 19, 1879 he was united in marriage to Miss Mary Etta Bolgard, who survives him. They are the parents of two sons, John Edward and Charles Frederick, and one daughter, Mrs. May Prescott, and six grandchildren. He also leaves an aged mother and one brother F. E. Fisher, and a large circle of friends to mourn their loss, as was evidenced by the great number of people that came to pay respect and take a last look at their friend, and by the tears that coursed down the cheeks of many as they left the side of the casket. Mrs. Fisher and the family feel grateful to those that rendered assistance and for the beautiful floral gifts, and to the Chair, and to the Maccabees, and wished me to give them their sincere thanks.

Eugene Fisher, who has been a very great sufferer, with an awful felon on his right hand, the swelling going to his elbow, is getting better, since it has been lanced on his thumb, hand and arm.

H. M. FISHER.

---

Word was received here Sunday morning of the death of Charles Fisher, of Glen Arbor. While it was known he was ill, it was not supposed that there was any danger in his illness, and the sad news was a shock to his friends throughout the township and surrounding country. Mr. Fisher has been our supervisor for many years. Of a happy disposition, all were his friends who knew him. He was "Charlie" to young and old alike, and his sudden demise removes one of the oldest settlers from our township.
May 12—

died May 9, 1909

---

**Death of Charles E. Fisher.**
For the Herald.

May 9th, at the hour of 7 a. m. Charles E. Fisher, aged fifty-nine, passed the Great Divide. Tuesday at 10 a. m. several hundred of Leelanau's citizens witnessed his interment on the beautiful hill where an inland lake looks like a bit of Italy's blue water while in the other hand the tortuous ribbon of Crystal river winds and turns on its way to Lake Michigan. Here, beside his pioneer father, the man who has long served his town as supervisor, clerk, justice, was laid to rest by members of the Knights of Maccabees, to which lodge he belonged and in which he carried an insurance of two thousand dollars. Deepest sympathy is felt for the wife, daughter and two sons of the deceased. His aged mother, Mrs. Harriet Fisher, his brother Frank, lumberman, two daughters-in-laws, several grand children, three neices, two nephews and many connections by marriage formed a large gathering. Glen Arbor is indebted to Mr. Fisher for his active interest in securing the bridge across the narrows of Glen Lake. His public spirit, kindness of heart and sincerity won for him a host of friends. His demise is a distinct loss to the neighborhood and county.

---

## PIONEER IS DEAD.

May 9, 1909

Charles Fisher, one of the early and highly esteemed residents of Leelanau county, died last Sunday morning at his home in Glen Arbor. For several months Mr. Fisher has been failing in health, owing to kidney trouble. He came to this county when a child 5 years old, having lived here 55 years, he has always been noted for his disposition to take an atcive interest in the welfare of the county. We and the entire community extend our sympathy to the surviving wife and sons in the loss of an old friend and old settles whom all knew so well.

The funeral services were held last Tuesday.

---

It is sad that one we cherish
Should be taken from our home,
But the joys that do not perish
Live in memory alone.

All the years we've spent together,
All the happy golden hours
Shall be cherished in remembrance,
Fragrance sweet from memory's flowers.

Not now but in the coming years,
  may be in the better land,
We'll read the meaning of our tears,
And there sometime, we'll understand.

---

### DEATH CLAIMS PAID.

| Name of Deceased | No. of Tent | Name of Tent | Location | Date of Death | Cause of Death | Amount Paid | To Whom Payable | Amt. Benefit Certificate |
|---|---|---|---|---|---|---|---|---|
| K O T M M | | | Transfer to Disability Benefit Fund | | | | | |
| Louis Larsen | 1687 | Washington | Ballard | 5 1909 | Malignant tumor of bladder | | Widow | 3,000 00 |
| Chas A Fisher | | Sleeping Bear | Glen Arbor | 5 1909 | Hepatic abscess | | Widow | 2000 00 |
| Oscar A Emmel | 304 | Au Sable | Au Sable | 5 1909 | Typhoid fever | | Children | 2000 00 |
| Oscar A Emmel | 304 | Au Sable | Au Sable | | Paid funeral expenses | | | |
| Thomas V Heston | 115 | Lincoln | Saginaw | 5 1909 | Blood poison | | Brother & sisters | |
| Galusha Turner | | S Evart | Evart | | Paid Tent for funeral exp | | | |
| Wm J Brenner | | Concordia | Saginaw | | Cancer of stomach | | Widow | |
| Fred W Richel | 275 | Lansing | Lansing | | Val heart disease, etc | | Sons | 1000 00 |
| Lafayette Weldon | 275 | Lansing | Lansing | | Dropsy & enlarg't of liver | | Widow | |
| Alpheus Carter | 556 | Cassopolis | Cassopolis | | Multiple sclerosis | | Widow | |
| Mark T Chappel | 414 | Stevens | Detroit | | Arterio sclerosis | | Widow | |
| Wm H Simpson | 501 | Kennedy | Detroit | | Paretic dementia | | Widow | |
| Chas LaFure | 715 | Newport | Newport | | Accidental fall | | Widow | |
| Lyman Munroe | 54 | Harmony | Port Huron | 7 1909 | Cancer of face | | Widow | 1000 00 |

(Continued on page H.)

# Pages from Family Bible

The following images are scans taken from a Fisher family Bible that is on display at the Empire Museum in Empire, Michigan.

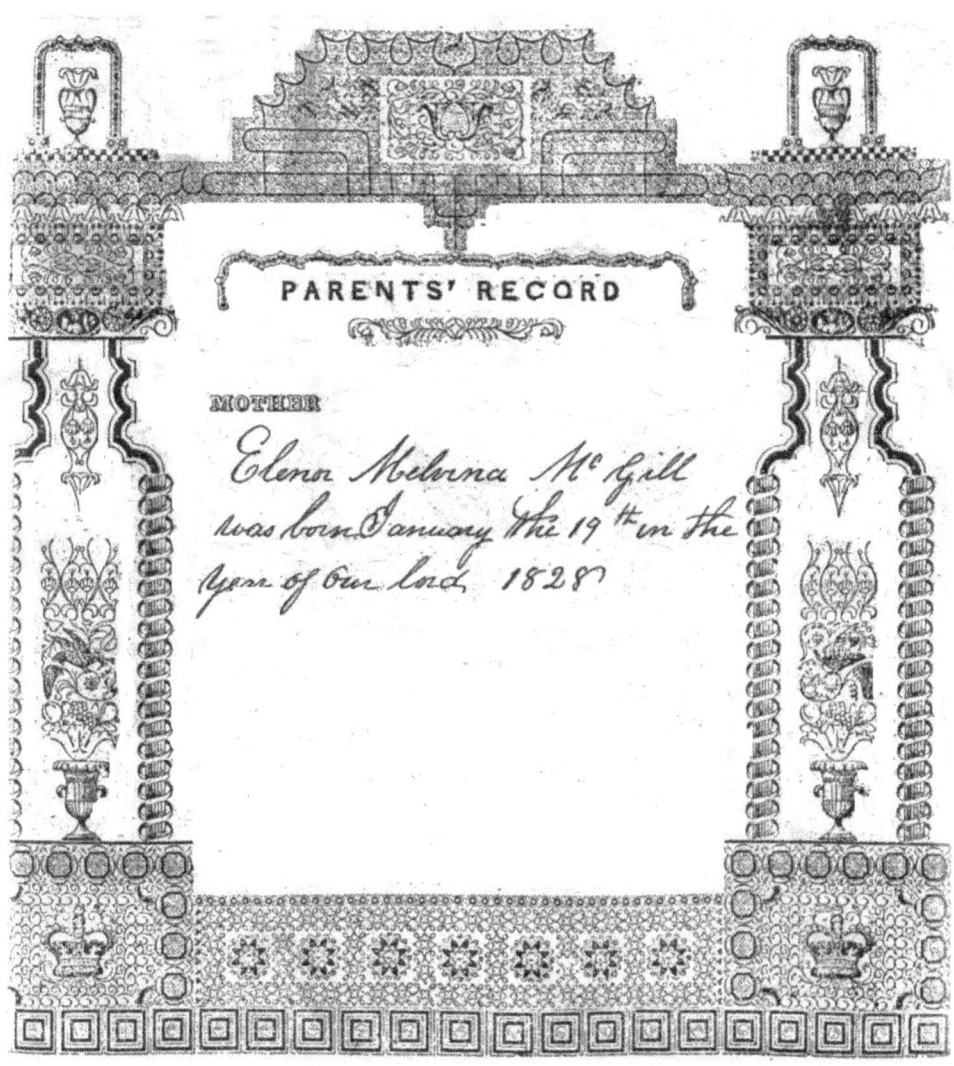

# Pages from Family Bible
## Marriages

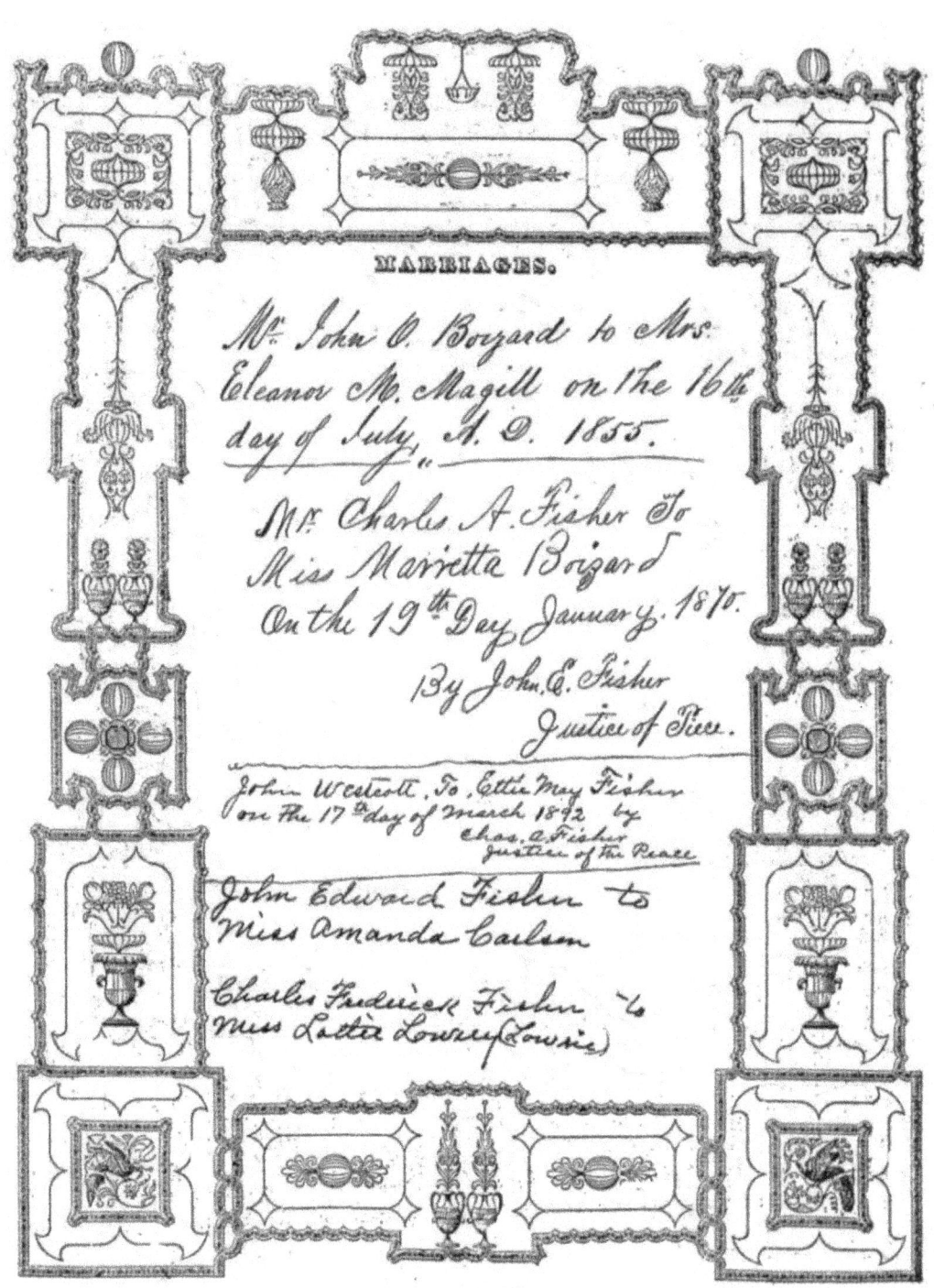

MARRIAGES.

Mr. John O. Boizard to Mrs. Eleanor M. Magill on the 16th day of July, A.D. 1855.

Mr. Charles A. Fisher To Miss Marretta Boizard On the 19th Day January 1870. By John E. Fisher Justice of Piece.

John Westcott, To, Ettie May Fisher on the 17th day of March 1892 by Chas. A. Fisher Justice of the Peace

John Edward Fisher to Miss Amanda Carlson

Charles Frederick Fisher to Miss Lotta Lowrey (Lowrie)

**Addendum**

**PAGES FROM FAMILY BIBLE**

**Births**

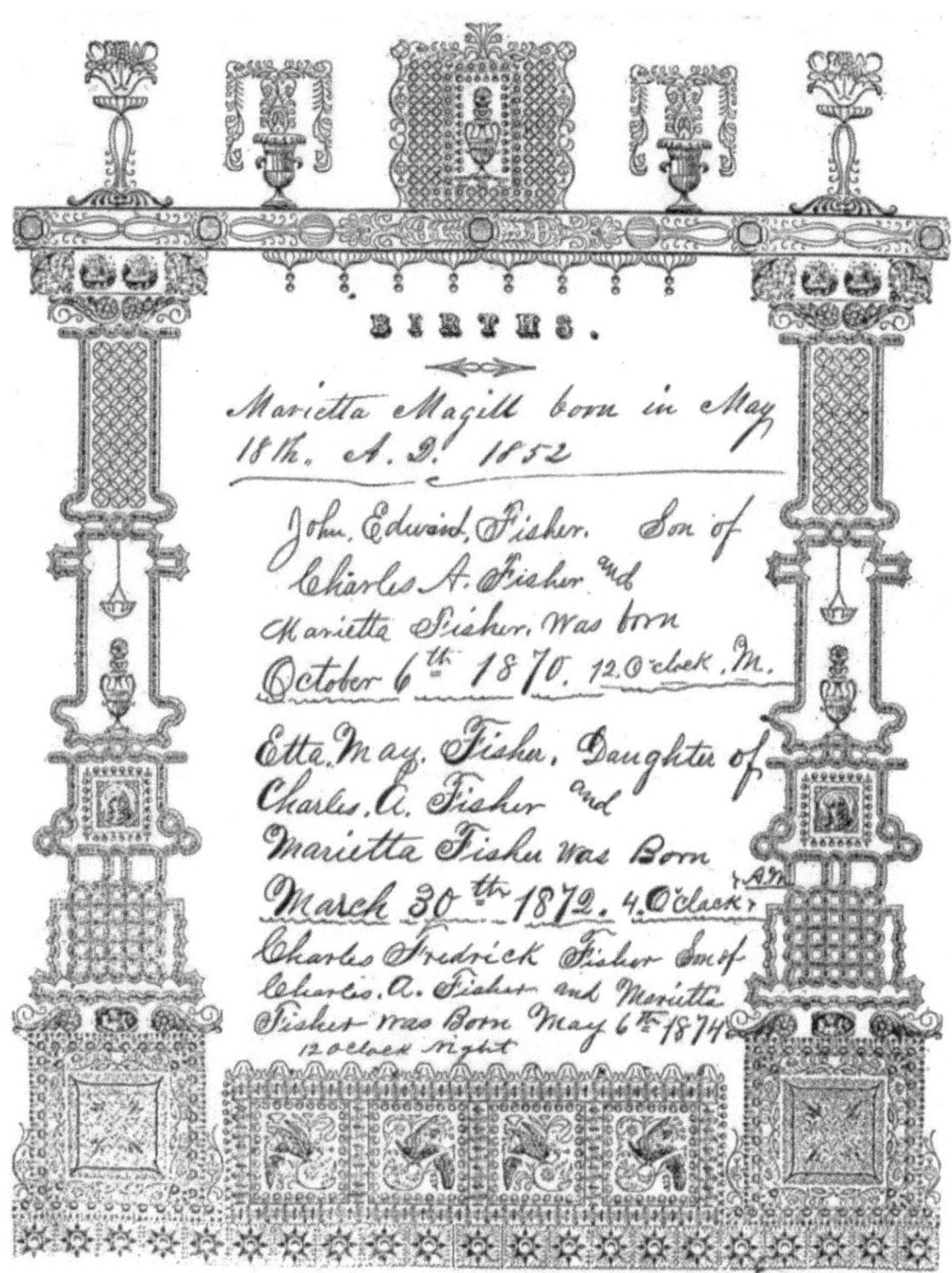

BIRTHS.

Marietta Magill born in May 18th. A.D. 1852

John Edward Fisher Son of Charles A. Fisher and Marietta Fisher was born October 6th 1870. 12 O'clock M.

Etta May Fisher Daughter of Charles A. Fisher and Marietta Fisher was Born March 30th 1872. 4 O'clock AM

Charles Fredrick Fisher Son of Charles A. Fisher and Marietta Fisher was Born May 6th 1874 12 o'clock night

**Long Distance Love 1855-1870**

## PAGES FROM FAMILY BIBLE
### Deaths

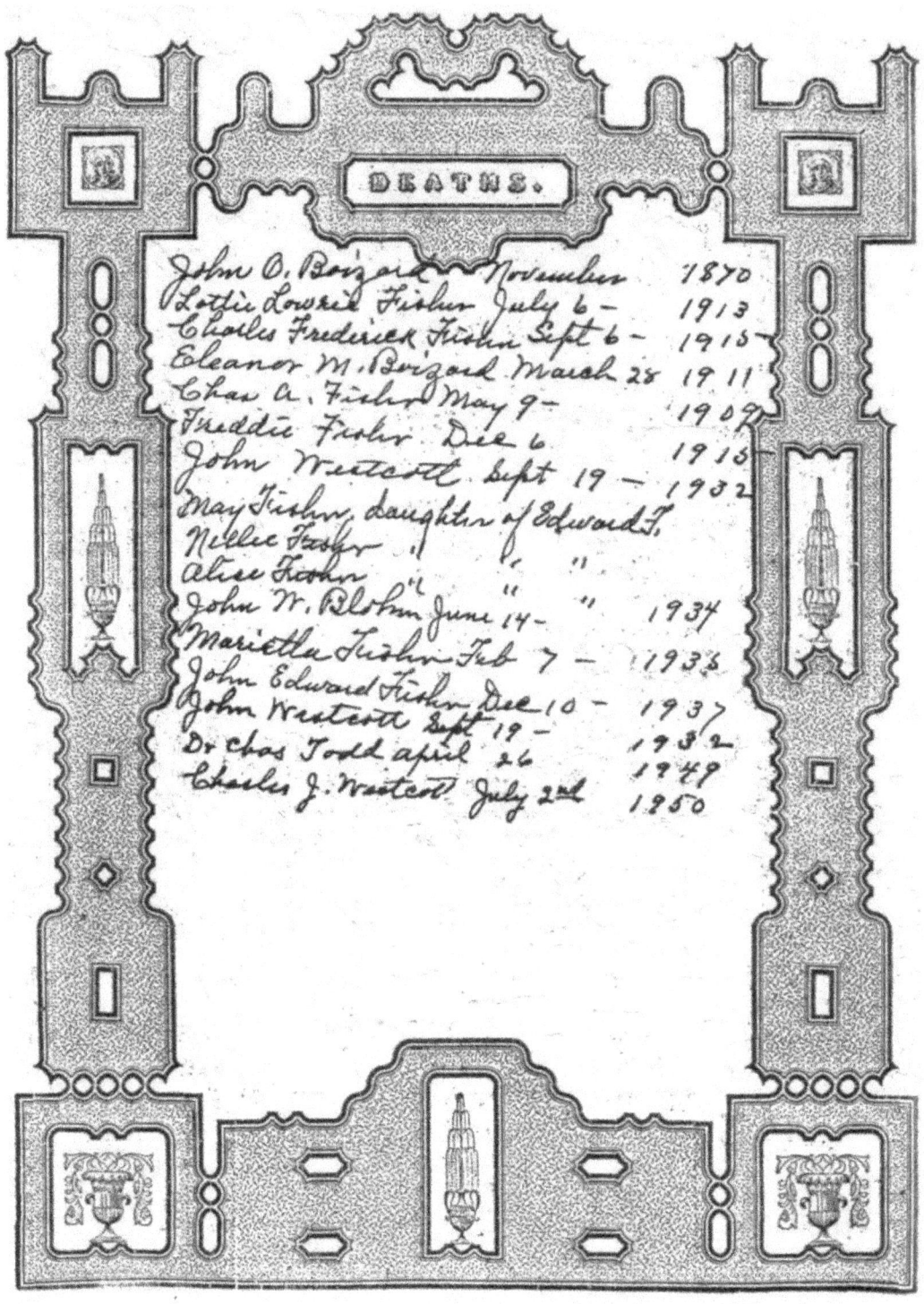

John O. Borgard November 1870
Lottie Lowrie Fisher July 6 – 1913
Charles Frederick Fisher Sept 6 – 1915
Eleanor M. Borgard March 28 1911
Chas A. Fisher May 9 – 1909
Freddie Fisher Dec 6 1913
John Westcott Sept 19 – 1932
May Fisher, daughter of Edward F.
Nellie Fisher "     "     "
Alice Fisher "     "     "
John W. Blohm June 14 – 1934
Marietta Fisher Feb 7 – 1935
John Edward Fisher Dec 10 – 1937
John Westcott Sept 19 – 1932
Dr Chas Todd April 26 1949
Charles J. Westcott July 2nd 1950

# PHOTOS & MEMORABILIA

Eleanor Boizard

John Oliver Boizard

Eleanor Boizard

1867

Eleanor Boizard

Grandmother Eleanor Boizard

Marietta Boizard—Age 16
1868

Charles and Marietta—possible marriage picture
January 19, 1870

Charles and Marietta Fisher

Charles and Marietta — in their later years.
Charles died in 1909 at the age of 60

John Edward Fisher
Born October 6, 1870
Son of Charles and
Marietta Fisher

Sarah McCarty King & Harriet McCarty Fisher

Sisters 1860

Harriet Fisher 1865

John and Harriet Fisher

Frank Fisher
Charlie's brother born in 1851

Frank and Charlotte Fisher
Married in 1874

Possibly Oliver's Army buddy
William Bridges

Emma Brown

She married Edwin Brown December 1866.

The photograph says they were killed by Indians on their way to California.

Edwin Brown — Emma's husband. He was a soldier and then they kept a store. They wanted to move from Arizona.

Edwin and Emma Brown's baby. In 1868 their four month old baby girl died.

The 1880 Federal Census shows Edwin and Emma living near Fort Worth, Texas. And at that time they had four children including a set of infant twins.

Mrs. Tator—School teacher in Glen Arbor

George Getchel and Charity Brotherton
They were married June 1868

Sarah Tucker — she died January 1865. Seven months later her mom, Elizabeth Fisher Tucker asked Oliver to have copies made of Sarah's picture so she could send some to her family members. This is likely the picture of Sarah that was sent out as a memorial. Elizabeth Tucker is John Fisher's married sister.

Etta May Fisher (Westcott, Todd) Granddaughter of Eleanor Boizard, daughter of Marietta & Charles Fisher. It was in Etta May's house that the letters were discovered in 1974. In this 1952 picture of her with her son Alvin, she is 80 years old. She died in 1958. The house set vacant until it was torn down in 1974.

Items found in the house that are on display in the Empire Museum, Empire, Michigan

Pencil box. The lid slides out and reveals a layer for the pencils and then it opens up again revealing a compartment for ink nibs, or erasers.

Cast iron dog

Sloan's liniment bottle

Iron car

**Unless noted the items on the following pages were found in Etta May's house before it was torn down.**

**Other items, are heirlooms that have been passed down through family.**

Amber colored beaded necklace. Could they be the beads that Marietta asked her dad to buy her to keep her neck from getting fat? He didn't sound like he wanted to buy them for her.

This is a tiny glass doll — about 2" tall.

This is an advertisement on the back of an oval mirror.

These are tiny tin plates. About 2" in diameter.

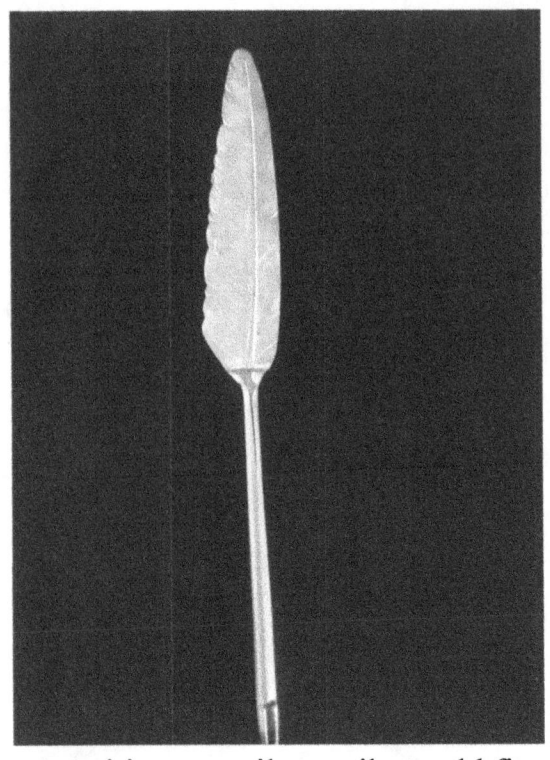

A writing utensil - a nib would fit in the bottom that could be dipped into the ink well.

Small portable razor. The blade unscrews from the handle and both pieces fit into the little gold case.

The little hand written note that was in the eye glass case says, "Mammas glasses."

This is a tiny baby ring

Another tiny baby ring

Men's wedding band

Necklace pendant. There is a face relief in the design

Nellie Westcott lock of hair. "She was a tiny baby." Nellie is Marietta's granddaughter, Eleanor's great granddaughter.

Other side of pendant

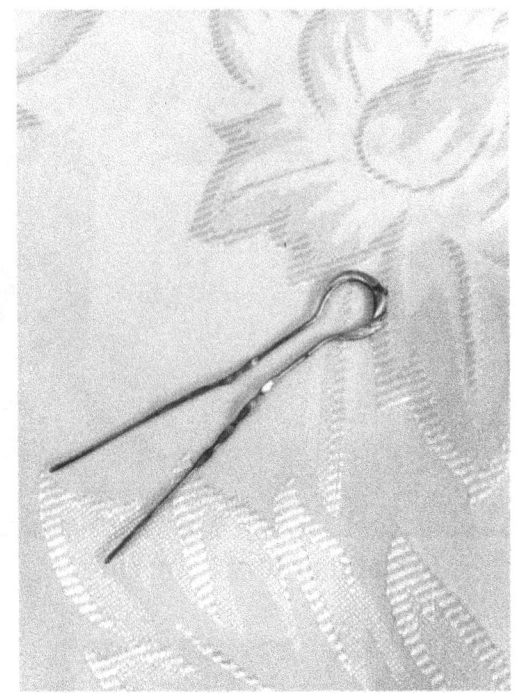

Hair pin

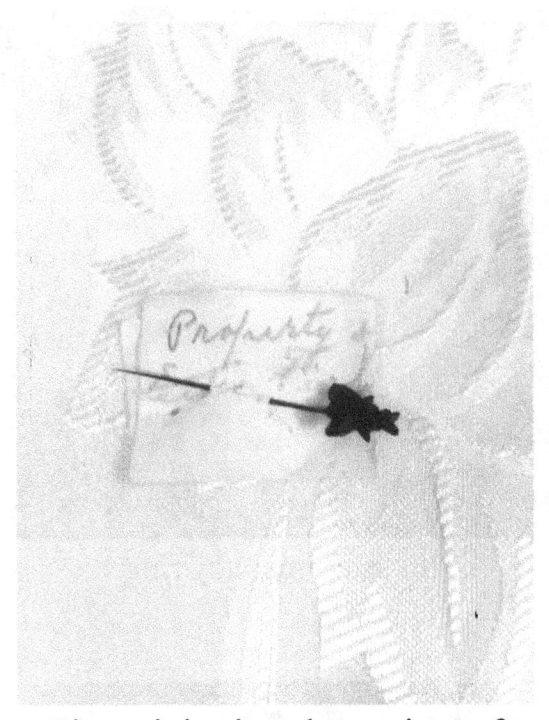

Pin — it is pinned to a piece of paper that says
"Property of Ettie Fisher"

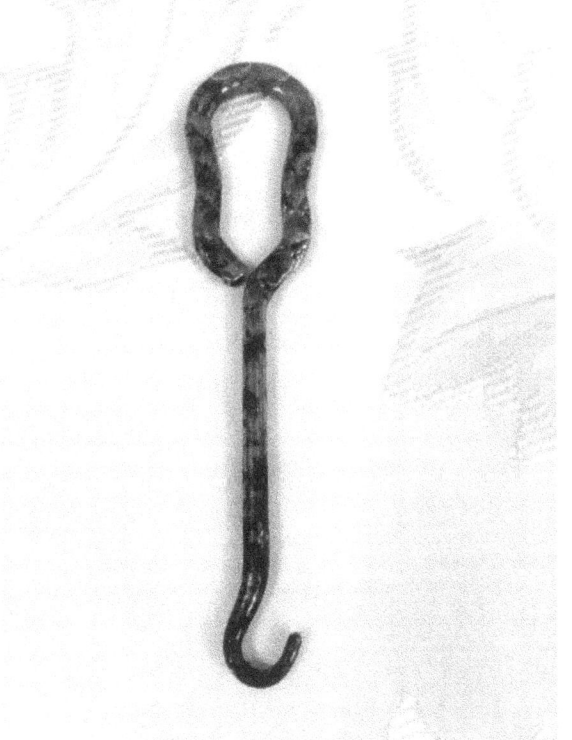

Boot Hook

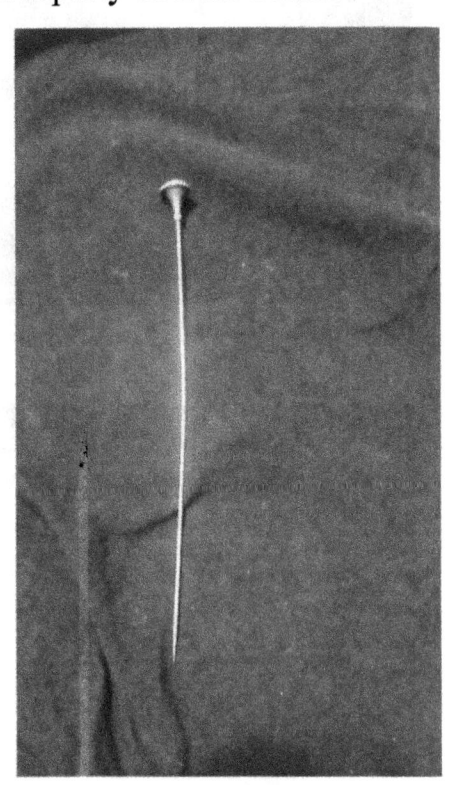

Hat pin

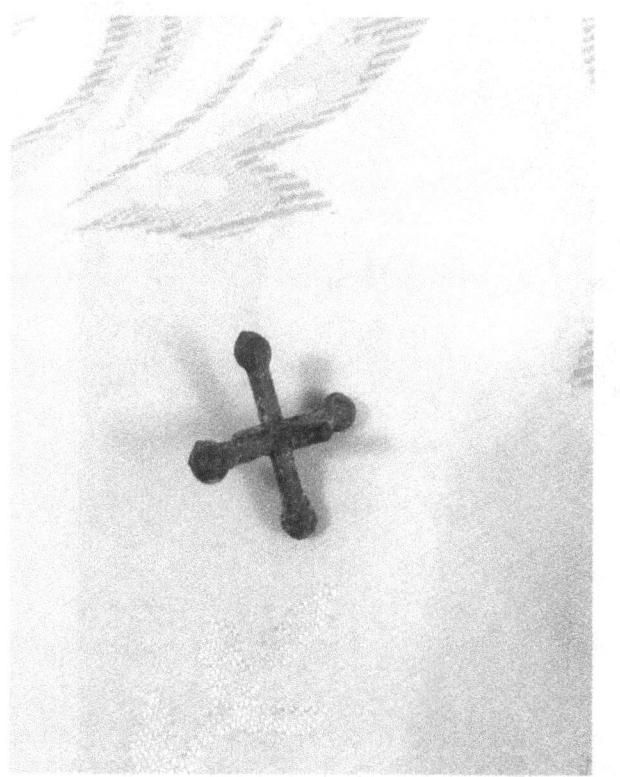

One lone jack

Thimbles and two metal thread spools

Heirlooms passed down through the generations.

The note that comes with these spoons says the following:

*"These three teaspoons are half of a set of spoons given to my mother for a wedding present from her father. She was married July 24th 1818. My mother's name was Lavina Darwin. Her father's name was Amos Darwin. The letters L & D for mother and her father are marked on the spoons. The large spoon belonged to my mother but one that she bought. I give it to you as you thought so much of grandmother. The value in both are as relics. From your mother, Harriet M. Fisher"*

Heirloom
Miscellaneous silver serving spoon

Pretty Rouge and lipstick compact

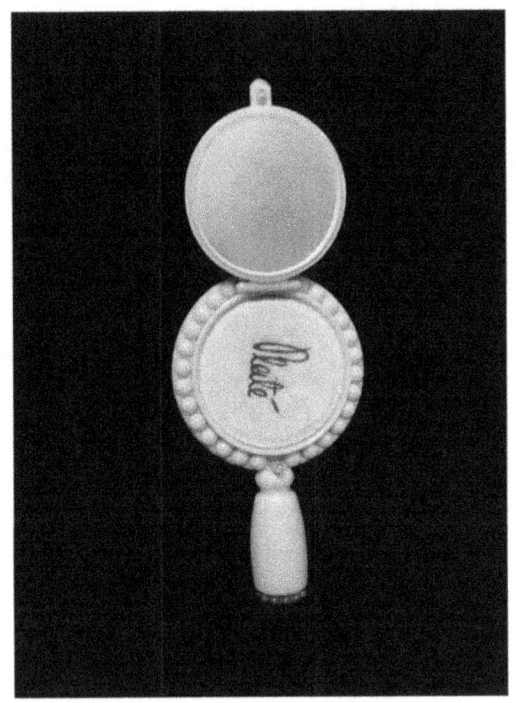

Compact open — mirror and
blush applicator

Various glass dolls found in the house.

Razor blades

Colorful collection of marbles

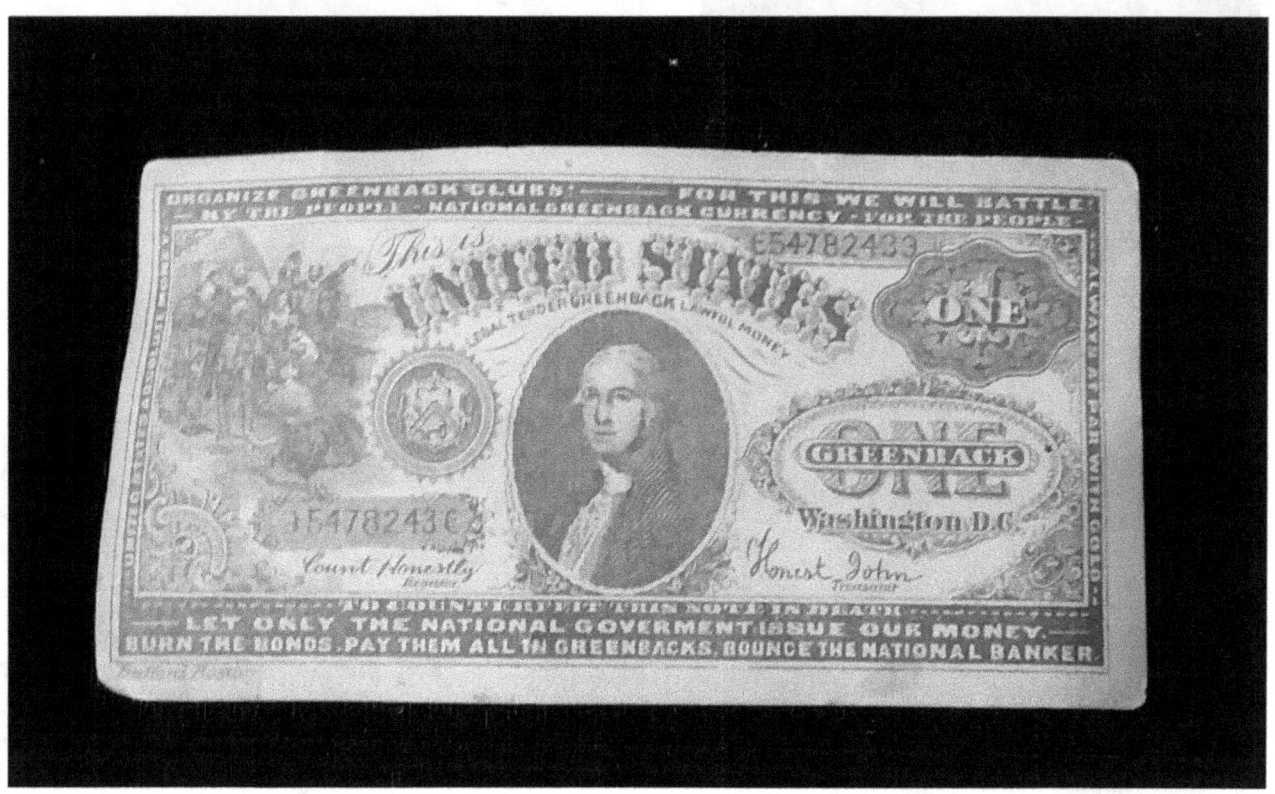
Greenback — I think it is a promotional piece

Small tin medicine containers

Iron figure that was part of a toy

Postcard in the letter collection. It has a hand written note that says "Grandma Todd"
The young girl in the picture is Etta May Fisher Westcott Todd.
It is the Post Office and Gas Station in Glen Arbor, Michigan.

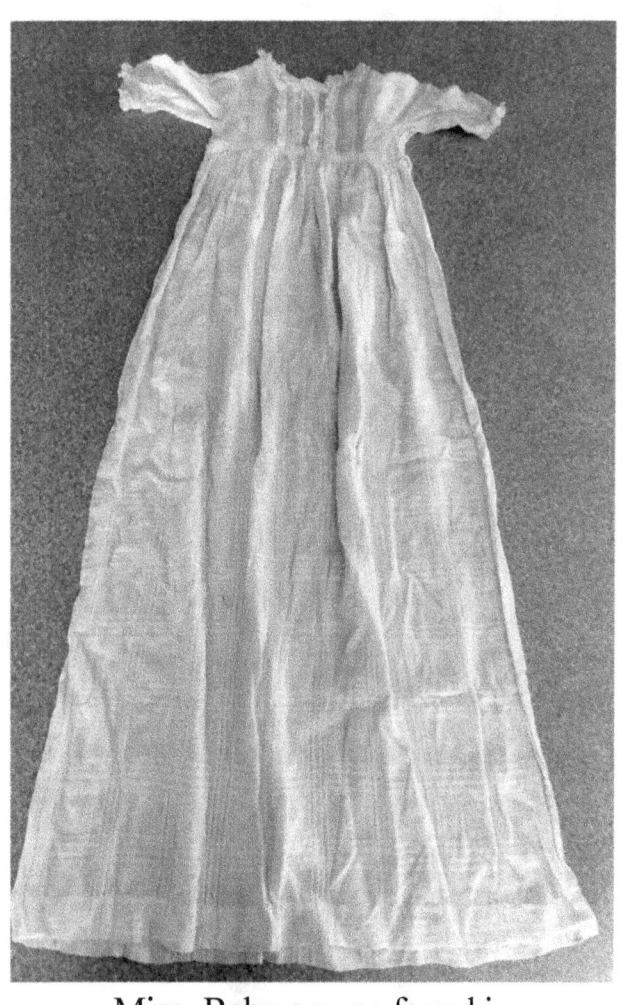

Misc. Baby gowns found in the Todd house

Christmas Card

Advertisement for Antikamnia Tablets. There is a calendar on the back side.

Sympathy Card

Valentines

This is Eleanor's Bible which belongs to Michele Baribeau Pattan. It was found at the Etta May Fisher Westcott Todd's house.

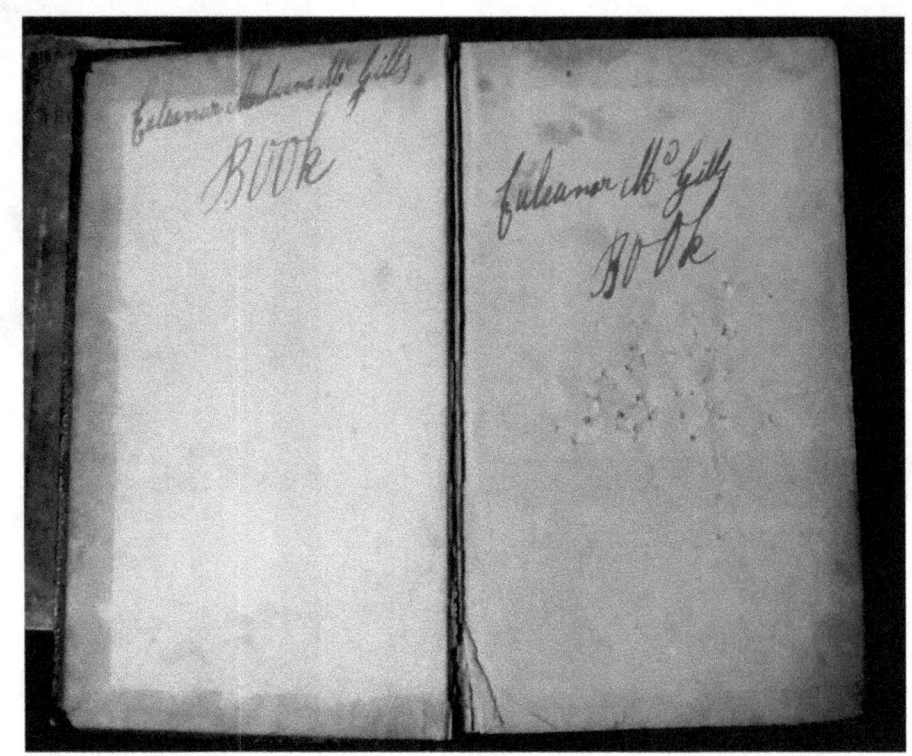

"Eleanor Melvina McGill's Book"

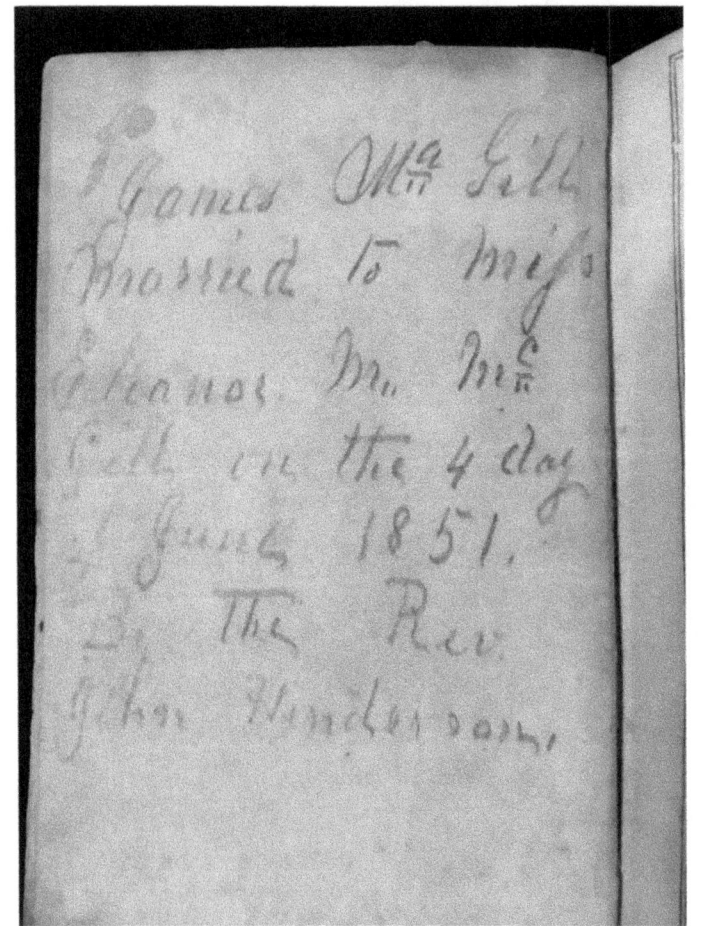

"James MaGill married to Miss Eleanor M. McGill on the 4 day of June 1851. By the Rev. John Henderson."

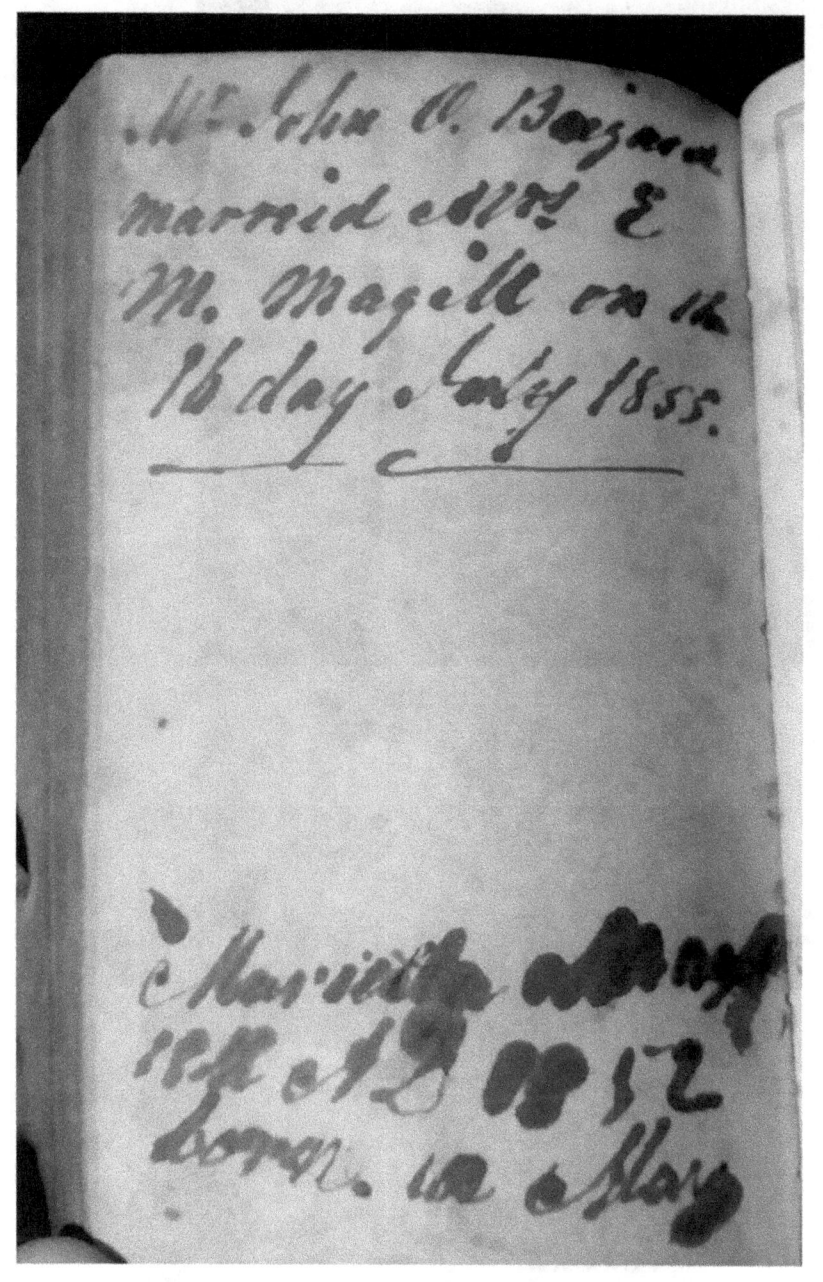

"Mr. John O. Boizard married Mrs. E. M. Magill on 16 day July 1855"

"Marietta Magill 18th A.D. 1852 Born in May"

Heirloom—This little jar has a note inside that says
"Given to Grandma Fisher is 1853"

Collection of handwoven baskets.

These items have been passed down through the generations and belong to Michele Baribeau Pattan. The note that accompanies them says they were a gift to Grandmother Fisher

Heirloom
The label on the bottom of this tea cup says:
"This was Grandma Fisher's wedding gift in 1818.
Given to Jessie *{Jessie Tobin Baribeau}*
from mom *{Nellie Westcott Tobin}* in 1970."

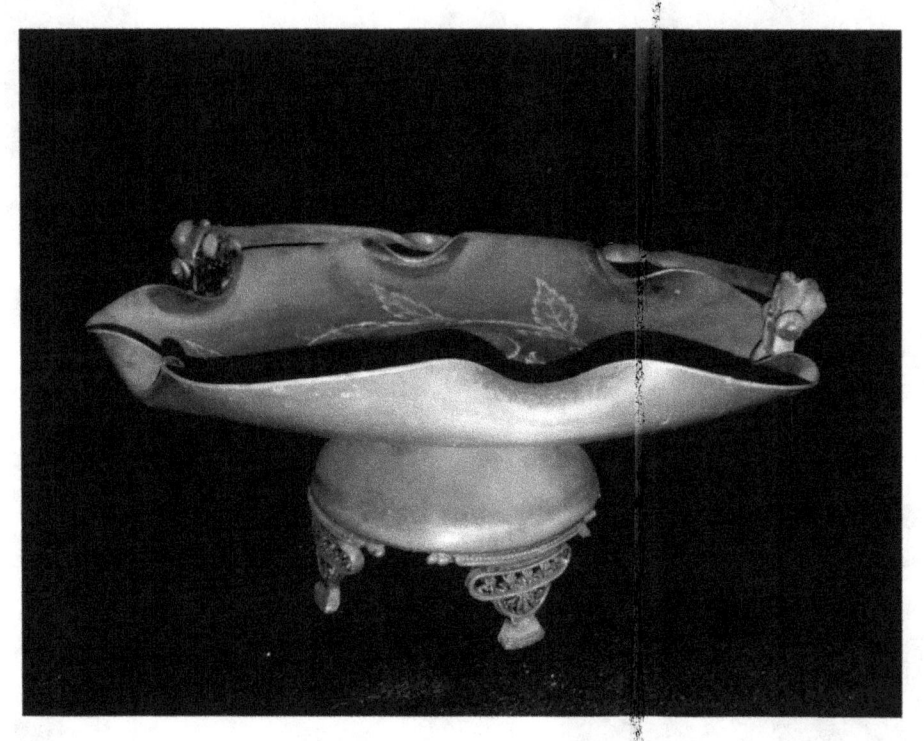

This is a silver plated fruit bowl. The silver plating has worn off.

## FORT DENAUD

The combined pressure of growing white settlement in Florida and federal policy of relocating Indian tribes west of the Mississippi sparked the outbreak of the 2nd Seminole War in 1835. Controlling the coasts and campaigning in the heart of Seminole lands were the objectives of Major General Thomas Jesup in 1837. Captain B. L. E. Bonneville established Fort Denaud in 1838 as one of a series of posts linking American operations south of Tampa to the east coast. It was constructed on the south bank of the Caloosahatchee River 27 miles from Fort Myers on land owned by Pierre Denaud, a French Indian trader. The fort consisted of tents with a blockhouse in their midst. It served as a supply depot for troops in the Lake Okeechobee area and was utilized intermittently until the war ended in 1842. Fort Denaud was reopened in 1855, soon after the outbreak of the 3rd Seminole War. Additions included company quarters, hospital, guardhouse, sutler's store and stables. A few months after a fire ravaged the post in June 1856, another site on the north bank of the river one mile west was chosen. fort, which was abandoned in May 1858, gave its name to the nearby community of Fort Denaud.

SPONSORED BY CALUSA VALLEY HISTORICAL SOCIETY

In the June 1, 1857 letter from Oliver to Eleanor, he mentions Fort Denaud. I drove past the area where it was located, near Lake Okeechobee, Florida, and took a few pictures of the historical marker and an old chimney that is standing as well as an old building on the site. I do not know if the building is from that era or not.

# Glossary

**& c.:** An abbrievation meaning "and such." Equivalent to our modern day *etc*.

**Anaconda folds:** This term was used to describe the strangle hold that the Union was exacting upon the southern states, through their use of a seaboard blockade which would prevent importing and exporting of their goods. The Anaconda plan also called for the Union to gain control of the Mississippi River in order to divide the South. The plan as it was proposed was designed to isolate the south and bring about a quicker surrender with minimum bloodshed. The Anaconda Plan was never officially accepted by the Government, but several of its key components were implemented. (http://encarta.msn.com/encyclopedia_761567354_5/Civil_War.html#p90) accessed 30 December 2008

**Arizona Territory**: From 1863 - 1912 this was an organized Territory of the United States that encompasses our current Arizona and New Mexico states. From 1861 - 1863, the Confederate States also claimed a portion of the land. This territory played an important role in the Civil War on the western frontier. (http://encarta.msn.com/encyclopedia_761570033_11/Arizona.html#p67 accessed 30 December 2008

**Ague:** Fever, sometimes accompanied by shivering and shaking. It was often indicative of the onset of malaria.

**Allegheny**: No information was found about this particular propeller.

**Bachelors Hall:** I have found many references to these words in writings around the mid 1800's, but nothing that gave me a specific definition or explanation of the phrase. In researching this phrase online, I even ran across a song written about keeping bachelors hall. The context of the words seems to point to young men when they would move out of their parents house and set up their own house. In some instances, a marriage was forthcoming.

**Bee**: This term is used to describe a large group of people that have joined their work force to accomplish a task together.

**Beechnuts**: The American Beech tree produces a small triangular shaped nut that falls to the ground in the fall. Many people have described them as being bitter. They are not highly valued as a food because of their small size and the difficulty in peeling the nut.

**Bigler, John**: The third Governor of California. He was in office from January 1852 - January 1856. At the time that he is mentioned in this book, April of 1856, he would no longer have been the actual Governor, which probably explains why he and his 'top ten' were staying in a boarding house. Bigler, remained active in politics and held many appointed offices before his death in 1871 at the age of 66. (http://www.californiagovernors.ca.gov/h/biography/governor_3.html) accessed 30 December 2008

**Bilious**: Nauseated, sick feeling to the stomach

**Bitter Aloes**: A laxative made from the leaves of aloe.

**Boils:** An inflamation of the skin, generally pus filled.

**Bonar:** Possibly a French word meaning 'gentle & mannerly.'

**Booth, J. Wilkes**: The infamous American actor who shot and killed President Abraham Lincoln on April 14, 1865. This assassination occurred just five days after the confederate south had surrendered. Booth himself was shot and killed on April 26. He was an outspoken sympathizer of the south. (http://encarta.msn.com/encyclopedia_761573391/John_Wilkes_Booth.html) accessed 30 December 2008

**Bounty:** A reward offered by the government to encourage men to enlist or re-enlist in the military.

**Brevet**: A temporary military promotion that does not include a pay raise.

**Brooklyn:** In 1866 this propeller was built in Cleveland by the yard of Ira Lafrinier for the Northern Transportation Company. http://www.hhpl.on.ca/GreatLakes/Extracts/Details.asp?ID=5429&n=2) 10 October 2007

**Brownsville:** There is a Brownsville, PA which is near McClellandtown (where Eleanor was raised) and there is an old military fort in that town, but I have not been able to determine if a company from the 4th Artillery occupied it during the years around 1855. There is also a Fort Brown in Texas. The 4th Artillery was stationed there for a time also during the Mexican war. (http://encarta.msn.com/encyclopedia_761578313/Brownsville.html) accessed 30 December 2008

**Camp Reno**: An outpost of Fort McDowell. It was occupied by the US Army, 1st Calvary from 1867-1870. Its purpose was to allow the Army to keep steady watch on the activity of the Apache Indians and to curtail the raiding that had been plaguing the farmers. (http://www.ghosttowns.com/states/az/campreno.html) accessed 10 October 2007

**Camp Gaston California:** This camp was located about 45 miles north of Fort Yuma and served as an outpost to the Fort. It was founded in 1859 and was intermittently occupied by soldiers through 1867. (http://www.militarymuseum.org/CpGaston.html) accessed 10 October 2007

**Camphor germ**: Camphor is a substance that comes from the wood and bark of the Camphor tree. It has a unique smell and is used medicinally as a topical substance to aid in healing infections and to stop itching. I could not find any reference to 'camphor germ,' although a lot of resources did state that camphor was good for killing germs.

**Carbuncle:** A painful inflamed area of infection in the skin. The infection is deep and the inflamed area may have several openings which ooze pus.

**Castile soap**: A hard white soap made with vegetable oil and sodium hydroxide.

**Chicago Marine List:** A record of ships at port, their destinations and schedules.

**Citron:** This may be referring to a small round watermelon. I couldn't find any word spelled 'sitron' as it is spelled in the letters.

**City of Boston:** This propeller was launched in 1863 for the Northern Transportation Company. It was built at Steven and Presley's yard. (http://www.hhpl.on.ca/GreatLakes/Extracts/Details.asp?ID=5557&n=16

**City of New York:** This propeller was built in Cleveland, Ohio and her home port was Chicago. She was launched in August of 1863 for the Northern Transportation Company. (http://www.hhpl.on.ca/GreatLakes/Extracts/Details.asp?ID=1207&n=2)

**Clarks Grammar:** A grammar textbook first published in 1847.

**Cleveland**: A propeller (boat) built for the Vermont Central Railway, by Moses and Quale at Cleveland, Ohio. (Julia Dickenson & Dorothy Bolton, *The Boizard Letters* (Empire, MI: Empire Area Heritage Group) pg. 145)

**Cosey:** Possibly – chatty; talkative; sociable

**Long Distance Love 1855-1870**

**Cotillion:** A formal dance or ball

**Cypher**: This term was used in reference to completing mathematic calculations.

**Day School Bell**: In the letters this clearly looks like the word 'bell,' however, it is unclear what that would refer to. If instead it were the word 'bill,' than it would probably refer to the school tax bill that was sent out twice a year.

**De oldest of de wimmins:** This quote is used three times by Oliver in reference to either Eleanor or Marietta. Its' meaning is not known, possibly a French Creole saying.

**Dickens, Charles**: Arrived for his second visit to America in November 1867, he stayed for five months. Initially his plan was to travel as far west as St. Louis, but due to poor health, he stayed on the East Coast. (http://charlesdickenspage.com/america.html) 30 December 2008

**Dr Hooflands German bitters**: A medicine formulated from vegetable products that guaranteed to cure problems ranging from 'disgust of food', 'liver ailments', 'nausea', 'constipation' etc. (http://www.whilbr.com/itemdetail.aspx?idEntry=898) 30 December 2008

**Dr. Cheesmans Female Pills**: A pill that was touted as being able to regulate a women's monthly cycle, as well as curing headaches, hysterics, disturbed sleep etc. (www.thomasgenweb.com/1859_scranton_republican.html) 10 October 2007

**Drayage:** a charge for hauling cargo

**Drilling:** A heavy linen fabric generally used for work clothes.

**Dropsey (on the Brain)**: edema - swelling

**Dutch Stews:** Possibly a combination of root vegetables (carrots, beets, potatoes, turnips etc.) simmered in a liquid.

**Empire**: A propeller merchant steamer, built in Cleveland, Ohio in 1861. Its home port was Detroit, Michigan. (Julia Dickenson & Dorothy Bolton, *The Boizard Letters* (Empire, MI: Empire Area Heritage Group) pg. 145)

**Epicurean**: A person who loves and seeks out pleasure in life.

**Erysipelas**: A severe skin infection, accompanied by vomiting, caused by the streptococcal bacterium. (http://encarta.msn.com/dictionary_/erysipelas.html) 30 December 2008

**Felon**: A pus filled inflamation around a finger or toenail.

**Fools cap**: A term for a large piece of writing paper that was approximately 13" x 17". (http://encarta.msn.com/dictionary_1861612760/foolscap.html) 30 December 2008

**Forage:** Food that comes from plant sources.

**Fort Denaud:** A Seminole Indian War fort, it was located about 20 miles north of Fort Myers. In 1857, its location was moved two miles from its original post. http://www.geocities.com/naforts/flsouth.html#seminole 10 October 2007

**Fort Grant**: Located in Arizona Territory, it was established as a Fort to scout out hostile Apache Indians. The soldiers were often sick with fever and ague. ( GrahamCountyArizona/apacheconflictii.msnw) 10 October 2007

**Fort Jupiter:** Orginally this was a settler's fort, but it was later used as a POW camp for the Seminole Indians. (http://www.geocities.com/naforts/flsouth.html#seminole ) 10 October 2007

**Fort Kearny:** This military post originally called Fort Clark was renamed in 1848 after General Stephen Kearny. It was a post established to protect emigrants as they traveled to Oregon. This was never a walled fortification, but it served as a supply depot and sentinel post. The fort was never under direct attack, but it served to outfit several companies of soldiers that were on Indian campaigns.
(http://www.esu3.org/nebraska/ftkearny/ftkear.html) 10 October 2007

**Fort Keis:** A Seminole Indian fort located ten miles south of Immokalee. It was used during the years of 1838-1857. (http://www.geocities.com/naforts/flsouth.html#seminole ) 10 October 2007

**Fort Lauderdale:** Located on the East coast of Florida. Used in the early part of the Seminole Indian War. It was abandoned in later years. Settlers did not arrive until around 1890.
(http://www.geocities.com/naforts/flsouth.html#seminole ) 10 October 2007

**Fort MacDowl:** 1865-1891 – This fort was established in 1865 in Maricopa County, on the west bank of the Rio Verde. It was initially called Camp Verde but was renamed Fort MacDowl. It was created to combat hostile Apache Indians. In 1890 it became an Indian Reservation. (http://jeff.scott.tripod.com/ftmcdowell.html ) 10 October 2007

**Fort McRae:** This fort was occupied during the years of 1838 and 1857 during the Seminole Indian Wars in Florida. It is on the eastern shore of Lake Okeechobee, it was a stockaded depot.
(http://www.geocities.com/naforts/flsouth.html#seminole ) 10 October 2007

**Fort Myers:** Fort Myers was Seminole Indian Fort that was occupied during the years of 1850 - 1858 & 1863 - 1865. It was a large stockade with four barracks, eight Officers' quarters, administration building, hospital, laundry, blacksmith, bake house, sutler, storehouses, and wharf. I visited the city of Fort Myers and the local musuem in January of 2008. There are no remains of the fort left to see, as the city of Fort Myers has been built over top of the actual site. Occasionally as street repair work is done, artifacts are discovered and placed in the musuem. (http://www.geocities.com/naforts/flsouth.html#seminole ) 10 October 2007

**Fort Ridgeley:** In 1853 the military began building Fort Ridgely. Its purpose was to be a police post to keep peace for all the settlers moving into the land. In August of 1862, after nine years of tension, the U.S.- Dakota war began. The Dakota Indians attacked the fort directly on August 20 and August 22. The fort that had been training soldiers for the Civil War suddenly found itself under a direct assault. Army reinforcements were sent in to end the conflict.
(http://www.mnhs.org/places/sites/fr/) 10 October 2007

**Fort Yuma:** First established in 1850 as a post along the Colorado river, its purpose was to provide protection, from the Yuma Indians, to emigrants that were traveling west along the southern route. The soldiers also maintained a ferry and they helped transport emigrants over the river. The fort saw sporadic use throughout the years, in 1864 it was used by the Quartermasters Corp. to establish a supply depot. In 1883 due to the extension of the railroads, the supply depot was not needed and the fort was abandoned. (http://www.militarymuseum.org/FtYuma.html) accessed 30 December 2008

**Fort Randall**: Constructed in 1856 in the Dakota Plains along the Missouri River. The fort was important in its day, strategically located as the Army's central supply depot.
(https://www.nwo.usace.army.mil/html/Lake_Proj/fortrandall/military.html) 10 October 2007

**Garrison:** A fortified military post that stationed soldiers.

**Long Distance Love 1855-1870**

**Gellots 303**: A metal tipped utensil dipped in ink and used for writing. The designation '303' refers to the style of the tip. The '303' is a stiff point that can be used to make fine lines.

**Gila City:** In 1857 gold was discovered upstream from Yuma on the Arizona side of the Colorado River. This began a gold rush to Arizona and Gila City was the boom town. The town had saloons, stores, a jail and church but by 1864, Gila City had become a ghost town. (http://www.ghosttowns.com/states/az/gilacity.html) accessed 30 December 2008

**Governor's Island:** From 1783 - 1966 Governor's Island was an Army post. After the Revolutionary War, two forts were built on the Island, Fort Clinton and Fort Jay. During the Civil War, Fort Clinton was used as a Confederate soldier prison and Fort Jay was used as a prison for Confederate officers. (http://encarta.msn.com/encyclopedia_761574939/Governors_Island.html) accessed 30 December 2008

**Granite State:** A wooden steamer that was built in 1852 for the Vermont Central Railway, by Moses and Quale at Cleveland, Ohio.
(Julia Dickenson & Dorothy Bolton, *The Boizard Letters* (Empire, MI: Empire Area Heritage Group) pg. 145)

**Grist mill:** A building that was used to grind grains into flour that could be used for cooking.

**Hickory Shirts**: A work shirt made of a heavy material.

**History of the United States:** Probably the textbook entitled *History of the United States, from Their First Settlement as Colonies, to the Close of the War with Great Britain, in 1815.* It was published in Cincinnati, Ohio by Morgan & Sanxay in 1837.

**Jackson:** Probably Jackson, Michigan. The soldier's had just been drafted. They may have had to report to Jackson Michigan to muster in and receive their orders.

**Jaconet:** A light weight cotton cloth used for clothing.

**Jessee:** old word possibly meaning a severe scolding or beating

**Kalsomine**: An inexpensive water based paint for walls and ceilings. It contained zinc oxide, water, glue and sometimes a tint.

**Keesick**: I could not find anything about this word. In context, Oliver seems to be referring to a child.

**Lager:** A beer brewed by a slow fermentation process.

**Lawn**: A lightweight, sheer cotton or linen fabric.

**Lawrence**: This propeller is part of the Northern Transportation Co. fleet of boats. It was built in 1868 in Cleveland, OH. The propeller cost $50,000 to build.
(http://www.hhpl.on.ca/GreatLakes/Extracts/Details.asp?ID=2618&n=5) 10 October 2007

**Leap Year**: One common leap year tradition relating to courtship and marriage is that women can propose on February 29.

**Lye:** A strong soap consisting of sodium hydroxide.

**Lyceum:** A hall or auditorium that was used for lectures or philosophical discussions. The Progressive Lyceum of the Spiritualist movement was analogous to the orthodox Sunday School program.

**Maine**: A propeller that was built in 1852 in Black River Ohio. Its' home port was Chicago. It was part of the Northern Transporation Company. (Julia Dickenson & Dorothy Bolton, *The Boizard Letters* (Empire, MI: Empire Area Heritage Group) pg. 145)

**Maricopa Wells:** The post was established in 1865 and was used intermittently until 1867. Maricopa became a station for the stage in 1868. . (http://www.geocities.com/naforts/az2.html#maricopa ) 10 October 2007

**McClellandtown :** A small town in western Pennsylvania. It is believed that this is the town that Eleanor McGill was raised in by the Quaker family that took her in after the death of her mother.

**McNallys Geography:** A textbook by Francis McNally called "An Improved 'System of Geography."

**Melodeon**: A small parlor size organ.

**Merrimack**: In 1861 when the Confederate Army took over the Norfolk Navy Yard they discovered the burned out shell of the *USS Merrimack*. This hull was revamped and covered with iron. A steel ramming bow was also added. The *Merrimack* was then re-commissioned as the *CSS Virginia*. She is most famous for her engagement with the Union's ironclad ship the *Monitor*. Neither ship delivered a mortal blow to the other, the battle ended in a draw. (http://www.history.navy.mil/photos/sh-us-cs/csa-sh/csash-sz/virginia.htm) 10 October 2007

**Miller, Leo**: A spiritualist leader who taught that when a body died, the soul came back and communicated with children.

**Minstrels:** a troupe of performers. Sometimes they were known to sing Negro songs, they often had their faces painted black. http://www.thefreedictionary.com/Minstrels) 30 December 2008

**Newport Barracks, KY**: Even though Kentucky was a slave state and many of its residents were divided about the war, Kentucky remained in the Union. During the Civil War, the sick and dying were brought to the hospital at the Barracks. Confederate prisoners were also held here. The Barracks experienced many floods throughout its existence and in 1895 it was abandoned for military purposes and turned over to the city of Newport. (http://www.nkyviews.com/campbell/newport_barracks.htm) 30 December 2008

**New Salem:** A small town in western Pennsylvania, south of Pittsburgh.

**North Port:** A small town north of Glen Arbor. It was the first county seat, and John Fisher traveled there to register the Boizard's deed as well as for other official business.

**Ordnance Appointment:** The ordnance department in the Army would oversee the procuring, safe keeping and distribution of the weapons, ammunition, tools etc.

**Oswegatchie**: A merchant steam vessel built in 1867 in Ogdensburg, NY. Her home port was Port Huron, Michigan. (Julia Dickenson & Dorothy Bolton, The Boizard Letters (Empire, MI: Empire Area Heritage Group) pg. 145)

**Paper cambric**: Cambric was a densely woven fabric with a smooth finish. It was widely used from clothing to shoes. It was available in many different weights and grades. Paper cambric was not washable.

**Paris white:** Crushed chalk that is used as a pigment in paint to make putty or filler.

# Long Distance Love 1855-1870

**Peterson's Lady Magazine**: A magazine that discussed ladies fashions in great detail. The November 1863 issue discusses the latest styles for: gloves, dressing coats, petticoats, hair, morning caps, morning wear, chemisettes, collars, cuffs bonnets etc. Other issues discuss recipes, review books and offer timely advice.

**Pinky:** In the early mentions of 'Pinky' I believe they are referring to a cat. After 1867, 'Pinky' is the name given to a small dog. The first dog was stolen, but Marietta talked about getting another one.

**Pomatum**: A perfumed oil or ointment for the hair.

**Preempted:** The right given to settlers to purchase public land.

**Quadrille:** A dance of French origins in which four couples dance a series of five sections. (http://encarta.msn.com/dictionary_/quadrille.html) 30 December 2008

**Quartermasters Department**: The Quartermasters Department in the Army was responsible for providing the soldiers with supplies, food, equipment, clothing, artillery. Sometimes civilian help was employed to help accomplish these tasks. (http://encarta.msn.com/dictionary_/quartermaster.html) 30 December 2008

**Quinine Pills:** A medicinal substance used to fight malaria that is extracted from the chinchona bark.

**Reverand John Henderson:** John Henderson Vance was licensed as a Methodist minister in 1850. He was from Beaver County, Pennsylvania. In his early days of ministry he was a circuit riding preacher. (https://www.findagrave.com/memorial/65324151/john-henderson-vance) 27 March 2018

**Row:** brawl

**Ructions:** a noisy fight, disturbance, uproar

**Rural New Yorker:** A newspaper that was published weekly in Rochester, NY from 1850 - 1878 called Moore's Rural New Yorker.

**Sanders New Series Spelling Book**: This was the title of a spelling book written by Charles W. Sanders.

**Secessia:** A name used in reference to the southern states that had decided to secede from the Union. (http://www.sonofthesouth.net/leefoundation/civil-war/1862/may/lincoln-slavery.htm) 30 December 2008

**Sect'y Seward**: Seward was the Secretary of State during Lincoln's presidential administration. An assassination attempt was made on Secretary Seward's life at the same time Lincoln was shot. Seward was stabbed, but he survived. (http://www.archive.org/stream/assassinationdea00gard/assassinationdea00gard_djvu.txt) 30 December 2008

**Senna oil:** This oil was used to relieve the symptoms of constipation. When combined with other substances such as pumpkin seeds, it was effective in the removal of parasites.

**Skeleton hoops:** lightweight, circular hoops that helped give a skirt, a round, full appearance.

**Sleighing:** The act of riding in a sleigh along the snow covered ground. In this time period, the sleigh would have been like a wagon, with skis instead of wheels and it would have been drawn by a team of horses.

**Sloughs:** lowlands or depressions that are filled with mud or mire, could also refer to bogs, or marshes.

# Addendum

**Slush**: May be referring to slop or mud along the streets, or possibly to the greasy nature of the food that he was eating.

**Soldier's Rest**: This refers to buildings that were built for the purpose of housing and feeding army regiments that were passing through. There is an article about a place called Soldier's Rest in Chicago. That building was fairly large with four rooms in it. There was a kitchen/dining room and the other three rooms were sleeping quarters. The dining room held twenty tables and each table could sit twenty men. It was decorated with streamers and stars and stripes. I have also seen an online picture of a kitchen in 'Soldier's Rest' Virginia. I am assuming that there was a building of this type in Michigan that Dorsey and Parker stayed at before they headed to Jackson to be mustered in, or receive their orders. (http://www.51illinois.org/page4.html)

**Spirit of hartshorn:** A solution of ammonia in water.

**St. Louis Arsenal**: This was a major supply depot for the states fighting the Civil war on the Western front. Oliver was working in Springfield at an arsenal in 1866, they cleared out all of their extra supplies and shipped them to the St. Louis Arsenal. (http://www.civilwarstlouis.com/arsenal/appendixC.htm) 30 December 2008

**Subsistence Department**: This department was responsible to secure contracts with suppliers to provide the needs of the army.

**Sutler:** A civilian storekeeper who had permission to operate a general store either on or nearby a military post. (http://www.thefreedictionary.com/sutler) 30 December 2008

**Toledo:** Actually called "The City of Toledo" this steamer received all new upper cabins and a fresh coat of paint in 1866. (http://www.hhpl.on.ca/GreatLakes/Extracts/Details.asp?ID=5422&n=3) 10 October 2007

**Typhoid Fever**: An illness caused by the bacterium Salmonella Typhi. It is common worldwide. It is ingested through contaminated food or water. Left untreated it can last for three - four weeks. It causes symptoms like: fever, headache, chills, and constipation. In severe cases death can occur. (http://encarta.msn.com/encyclopedia_761563010/Typhoid_Fever.html) 30 December 2008

**Woods Museum:** Colonel Woods Museum, Randolf Street (between Clark and Dearborn) in Chicago, Illinois.

**Young America**: The propeller was built in 1853 in Buffalo, NY. She was originally part of the Cape Vincent Line, later she belonged to the Northern Transportation Company. During the winter of 1859-1860, the Young America had many improvements made in order to accommodate first class passengers and to improve the comfort and convenience of its passengers. The Young America was rebuilt from the waters edge up in 1864. (http://www.hhpl.on.ca/GreatLakes/Extracts/Details.asp?ID=7418&n=8) 10 October 2007

**Zephyrs:** A light weight fabric.

**Long Distance Love 1855-1870**

**Index**

Ague..........................................29, 230
Allegheny.....................72, 167, 230
Almira.................................146
Anaconda folds ....................49, 230
Arizona Territory ...... 165, 230, 232
Ayres, Charlotte ................136, 149
Bachelors Hall...................159, 230
Bates ..............................14, 17, 18
Bee......................................116, 230
Beechnuts.............................93, 230
Bigler, John ..................10, 16, 230
Billious.................................70, 230
Bitter Aloes .........................59, 230
Boil 44, 84, 85, 114, 118, 120, 130, 230
Boizard, Catherine ................10, 13
Boizard, Elizabeth.......................10
Boizard, Jacob............................10
Boizard, Lewis Pierre............10, 15
Boizard, Mary ...........................10
Bonar.....................................34, 230
Booth, J. Wilkes............81, 85, 230
Bounty.........................75, 123, 231
Bowman, Mrs..............................17
Brevet....................................93, 231
Bridges 11, 51, 54, 55, 56, 59, 61, 73, 76, 115, 116, 120, 127, 177
Bridges, Emma 8, 11, 13, 54, 56, 73, 74, 75, 77, 80, 121, 131, 153, 154, 155, 159, 161, 162, 163, 165, 166, 167, 168, 170, 174, 177
Brooklyn ... 109, 112, 114, 133, 231
Brotherton 85, 86, 87, 88, 94, 100, 104, 129, 147, 151, 153
Brownsville .............14, 17, 18, 231
Burdick .........................27, 28, 124
Burty Mac .................................154
Camp Gaston.............162, 165, 231
Camp Reno ................121, 153, 231
Camphor germ ....................59, 231
Canada ..................................38, 45
Carbuncle.............................85, 231
Castile soap.........................91, 231
Charleston....................32, 34, 76, 79
Chicago 12, 54, 57, 58, 61, 62, 63, 64, 65, 66, 69, 70, 71, 73, 74, 75, 76, 78, 79, 80, 81, 85, 86, 87, 88, 90, 92, 94, 96, 102, 106, 107, 108, 109, 110, 115, 123, 127, 130, 132, 133, 134, 135, 136, 137, 138, 139, 140, 141, 142, 143, 144, 145, 146, 147, 148, 149, 150, 151, 152, 154, 157, 158, 159, 160, 162, 166, 167, 168, 170, 171, 173, 175, 180, 231, 235, 237
Chicago Marine List .........108, 231
Citron...................................175, 231
City of Boston.............92, 150, 231
City of New York ........57, 71, 231
Clarks Grammar..................63, 231
Cleveland 64, 65, 108, 231, 232, 234
Collins........................................90
Company K .............14, 35, 36, 179

Cooke.....................79, 128, 135
Cosey ..................28, 31, 231
Cotillion ...................29, 232
Cypher ......................99, 232
Day School Bell............ 69, 70, 232
De olddest of de wimmins 67, 85, 232
Dean.....................20, 22, 25, 37
Deickman......................22, 26
Dickens .......................143, 232
Dodge ........................137, 138
Dorsey 11, 12, 45, 57, 58, 63, 64, 65, 66, 71, 72, 77, 79, 80, 87, 89, 90, 91, 93, 94, 97, 110, 113, 116, 118, 136, 157, 165, 167, 169, 170, 179, 237
Dow ........ 12, 16, 26, 34, 36, 37, 38
Dr Hooflands ......................70, 232
Dr. Cheesmans Female Pills 172, 232
Drayage..................... 173, 175, 232
Drilling ................. 85, 88, 91, 232
Dropsey............................37, 232
Dutch Stews......................66, 232
Empire 7, 42, 70, 71, 72, 86, 195, 231, 232, 234, 235
Epicurean..........................28, 232
Erysipelas .........................118, 232
Felon..................................52, 232
Fermet.................................50, 53
Fink........... 150, 151, 153, 155, 157
Fisher 11, 12, 13, 43, 44, 45, 47, 48, 49, 51, 54, 57, 58, 59, 61, 62, 63, 64, 65, 66, 67, 68, 70, 71, 72, 73, 74, 75, 76, 77, 78, 79, 80, 81, 84, 85, 86, 91, 95, 97, 102, 103, 104, 106, 107, 108, 113, 115, 118, 123, 124, 126, 132, 133, 138, 148, 149, 152, 160, 162, 166, 167, 168, 169, 170, 171, 172, 174, 175, 177, 179, 180, 195, 235
Fools cap..................... 72, 142, 232
Fort Center................ 17, 22, 29, 33
Fort Denaud ................. 31, 229 232
Fort Grant ........................ 121, 232
Fort Jupiter.................... 18, 22, 233
Fort Kearny............. 38, 39, 40, 233
Fort Keis .......................... 21, 233
Fort Lauderdale .................. 18, 233
Fort McRae 14, 17, 18, 20, 21, 22, 24, 25, 26, 27, 29, 30, 31, 32, 33, 34, 233
Fort Myers 14, 18, 20, 21, 22, 23, 24, 25, 27, 28, 29, 31, 32, 34, 179, 232, 233
Fort Randall ........................ 39, 233
Fort Ridgely 35, 39, 40, 41, 179, 233
Fort Yuma.................. 159, 231, 233
Freemans..................................146
Gellots 303........................... 71, 234
Gila City 153, 154, 155, 159, 165, 234
Goffart 44, 51, 57, 58, 59, 60, 62, 65, 66, 67, 68, 76, 86, 88, 152
Graef ....................... 168, 170, 176
Grandz .....................................112
Granite State ........... 61, 62, 85, 234
Grant, General 67, 76, 102, 104, 232

238

Grist mill ................... 124, 174, 234
Haas, Lizzie ...... 151, 152, 167, 168
Heath. 115, 170, 171, 175, 176, 180
Henderson, John................. 14, 236
Hickory Shirt....................... 27, 234
History of the United States 87, 234
Hudson, Lieut........ 9, 15, 17, 18, 33
Jackson................ 72, 148, 234, 237
Jaconet ............................... 87, 234
James Magill .............. 9, 14, 179
Jessee ................................. 17, 234
Johnson ................... 55, 56, 85, 177
Kalsomine ........................ 172, 234
Kearny................... 38, 39, 40, 233
Keesick ............................ 167, 234
King ...... 12, 66, 103, 137, 165, 167
Lager................................... 52, 234
LaRue........................................ 179
Lawn ................................ 105, 234
Lawrence.......................... 166, 234
Leap Year......................... 147, 234
Lincoln, Abraham 79, 81, 84, 85, 94, 180, 230, 236
Lindsley ..................... 89, 90, 94
Lyceum ........................... 147, 234
Lye ........................................... 234
MaGill 9, 10, 14, 112, 115, 118, 125, 126
Maine .......... 67, 69, 70, 81, 85, 235
Maricopa Wells......... 121, 233, 235
McCarty 12, 45, 47, 62, 63, 66, 69, 70, 91, 92, 114, 115, 127, 129, 134, 163
McClellandtown.... 14, 15, 231, 235
McNallys........................... 63, 235
Mead ......................................... 47
Melodeon ................. 113, 114, 235
Merrimack....................... 105, 235
Miller, Leo 29, 62, 93, 94, 106, 113, 235
Milwaukee 84, 85, 92, 112, 115, 128, 134, 135, 136, 138, 146
Minstrels .......................... 136, 235
New Ireland............................. 154
New Salem ....................... 15, 235
Newman, Austin 13, 54, 57, 77, 116, 123, 127, 128, 129, 135, 136, 137, 140, 141, 142, 143, 144, 154
Newport Barracks 11, 13, 43, 46, 54, 177, 180, 235
Ordnance ..................... 73, 94, 235
Oswegatchie...................... 133, 235
Paper cambric .................... 87, 235
Paris white ....................... 172, 235

Parker................ 71, 72, 89, 90, 237
Pattan, Michele ..................... 5, 6
Patterson ............ 21, 23, 24, 25, 28
Pemberton................................. 39
Pfeiffer.............. 57, 61, 65, 81, 112
Pigeons ..................... 171, 173, 175
Pine Lake ......................... 135, 141
Pinky ............... 38, 148, 153, 236
Pittsburgh............... 14, 34, 41, 235
Pomatum .............. 58, 60, 62, 236
Pomeroy 10, 54, 85, 93, 96, 98, 105, 110, 180
Potomac ............................. 154
Preempted ..................... 45, 236
Quadrille ..................... 135, 236
Quartermasters Department 10, 18, 43
Quinine ..................... 26, 236
Ray....................... 12, 63, 119, 132
Roche................................. 27, 32
Rosman ................... 127, 138, 172
Row ............................. 30, 236
Rural New Yorker ............ 100, 236
Sacramento ........................... 10, 16
Sandess New Series Spelling Book 40, 236
Secessia............................. 49, 236
Senna ................................ 70, 236
Seward, Secretary ............... 81, 236
Skeleton hoop ..................... 86, 236
Sleighing.................. 141, 160, 236
Sloughs ............................... 38, 236
Slush ................................. 66, 237
Spirit of hartshorn ............... 59, 237
St. Louis Arsenal ............. 110, 237
Subsistence Department ..... 17, 237
Sutler .............. 32, 52, 77, 233, 237
Todd 5, 6, 7, 84, 88, 103, 125, 131, 164, 167
Tourison.......................... 13, 37, 38
Tucker 12, 69, 70, 71, 72, 73, 74, 75, 76, 77, 79, 80, 84, 85, 86, 87, 88, 89, 90, 93, 99, 100, 102, 108, 113, 114, 116, 120, 123, 132, 135, 136, 138, 139, 140, 146, 147, 150, 151, 162, 167, 168, 171
Typhoid................. 65, 70, 90, 237
Utah ................................ 34, 36
Vicksburg ............................ 49, 50
Woods Museum................. 137, 237
Young America 66, 69, 86, 87, 128, 143, 237
Zephyrs................................ 173, 237
Zepp.......................................... 168

# Long Distance Love 1855-1870

www.ingramcontent.com/pod-product-compliance
Lightning Source LLC
Chambersburg PA
CBHW080537170426
43195CB00016B/2591